S0-BJH-055

WITHDRAWN
NDSU

THE PAST THAT POETS MAKE

THE PAST THAT POETS MAKE,

Harold Toliver

Harvard University Press
Cambridge, Massachusetts
and
London, England
1981

Copyright © 1981 by the President and Fellows of Harvard College

All rights reserved

Printed in the United States of America

Library of Congress Cataloging in Publication Data

Toliver, Harold E
  The past that poets make.
  Includes bibliographical references and index.
  1. Poetry—History and criticism.   2. Literature and history.   I. Title.
PN1080.T6   821'.009'358   80-18825
ISBN 0-674-65676-8

PN
1080
T6

Acknowledgments

I have indicated in the notes the several directions from which help in posing and answering the questions of this essay has come to me and may come to the reader. I have drawn mainly upon those authors who have dealt with fictions theoretically and with their transmission of the past but also upon some who are not primarily interested in literature, such as George Kubler and Paul Schrecker. I am indebted in another way to the Simon Guggenheim Memorial Foundation for generosity a second time and to the University of California for a sabbatical.

I am grateful to Alfred A. Knopf, Inc., and Faber and Faber Ltd. for permission to reprint excerpts from Opus Posthumous and The Collected Poems of Wallace Stevens by Wallace Stevens; to Charles Scribner's Sons, Jonathan Cape Ltd., and the executors of the Ernest Hemingway estate for permission to reprint portions of The Sun Also Rises, A Farewell to Arms, and "In Another Country" by Ernest Hemingway; and to New Directions for permission to reprint excerpts from Collected Earlier Poems and Paterson (Book 3) by William Carlos Williams, copyright 1938 and 1949 by William Carlos Williams.

The poetry of Richard Wilbur and the excerpts from Four Quartets by T. S. Eliot are reprinted by permission of Harcourt Brace Jovanovich, Inc.; copyright © 1947, 1949, 1950, 1956, 1958, 1975, 1978 by Richard Wilbur; copyright 1943 by T. S. Eliot; copyright 1971 by Esme Valerie Eliot.

I wish also to thank Macmillan Publishing Co., Inc., and A. P. Watt Ltd. for permission to reprint excerpts from the works of William Butler Yeats, including Explorations (includes material from On the Boiler), copyright © by Mrs. W. B. Yeats, 1962; Essays and Introductions (includes material from The Celtic Element in Literature), copyright © by Mrs. W. B. Yeats, 1961; Autobiography, copyright 1916, 1935 by Macmillan Publishing Co., Inc., renewed 1944, 1963 by Bertha Georgie Yeats; and the following pieces from Collected Poems: "Easter 1916," copyright 1924 by Macmillan Publishing Co., Inc., renewed 1952 by Bertha Georgie Yeats; "The Hosting of the Sidhe," copyright 1906 by Macmillan Publishing Co., Inc., renewed 1934 by William Butler Yeats; "I See Phantoms" and "Nineteen Hundred and Nineteen," copyright 1928 by Macmillan Publishing Co., Inc., renewed 1956 by Georgie Yeats; "Fragment," copyright 1933 by Macmillan Publishing Co., Inc., renewed 1961 by Bertha Georgie Yeats; and "The Statues" and "The Circus Animals' Desertion," copyright 1940 by Georgie Yeats, renewed 1968 by Bertha Georgia Yeats, Michael Butler Yeats, and Anne Yeats.

Laguna Beach, California
January 1981

Contents

Introduction

W HAT SORT OF RETROSPECTIVE vision do literary fictions possess with their "dark backward and abysm of time"? Whatever else it may do, an answer to that question must compound paradoxes. As opposed to other arts, fictions are capable of a detailed citation of particulars from the past and thus may resemble histories; at the same time, they are capable of exploring ideas and abstractions in the manner of philosophy. Yet fictions also put both ideas and particulars under the guise of symbolic play in a way that neither historical nor philosophical discourse ordinarily does (except in inventing examples). Also, fictive systems can station events at precise distances from the reader and from each other in a highly articulated past; yet their networks of allusion and echo also bring selected moments of the past into an immediately experienced present, as each new text modernizes what it absorbs.

Again: any culture that retains its literary past displays some of the principles of accretion and aging that a remembering self follows—as it grows, in Proust's words (at the end of *The Past Recaptured*), to a "dizzying summit" by an accumulated, organic change. But a new text, especially an important one, also discards the past and rebels against it—as an act of youth against age. Moreover the sort of recollection that Proust mentions when a smell or sound retrieves something from the temporal distance has the experienced unity of a continuous self. In contrast, the literary past is consciously and communally sequestered: as a matter for public education, journals, and critical books, it is discussable and therefore complex in the manner of things surrendered to the many. One interpreter in a society of interpreters reacts to others; together they create a literary history. Even new texts are shaped partly by what critics, in their very formidable mass, have encouraged us to think about tradition. As T. S. Eliot tells us, new works stem not solely from writers of genius but also from "secondary writers" who "provide collectively . . . an important part of the environment of the great writer."[1] And unfortunately, just as any word loses some of its robustness in the hands of a dictionary maker, the institutions of literary study tend to bureaucratize whatever they touch (especially now that they borrow a good deal of vocabulary from the social sciences). Nearly all older texts must detour through such things as afternoon colloquia and morning classes if they are to reach the public—which consists largely of enrolled students.

The past of literary fictions belongs to anyone who takes part in its discussion; and it must belong, at least piecemeal, to any practicing poet when he reuses the language of his predecessors. It is Eliot's consistent position that it should belong to a major poet in something more than a piecemeal fashion, since the writing of a classic depends upon a maturity of language and presupposes a good deal of cultural accumulation. "A mature literature . . . has a history behind it: a history, that is not merely a chronicle, an accumulation of manuscripts and writings . . . but an ordered though unconscious progress of a language to realise its own potentialities within its own limitations."[2] Maturity of mind, language, and manners—together with comprehensiveness—is the chief requirement of a classic. Even though the text that displays such maturity may be restive under the burden of its predecessors, it is necessarily retrospective.

The pastness of literary fictions, then, is neither simple nor avoidable. Of the total past that falls within our possession, it is perhaps the most mixed and variable part. Regional novels such as James Michener's *Centennial, Hawaii,* and *The Source* convey a very full impression of ways of life, but they are also unreliable and transform what they absorb from records. The value of fictions lies less in their realistic detail than in their confessional, lyric, elegiac, comic, or tragic intensity. Richard Wilbur's ferns "which laid their fragile cheeks against the stone / A million years" are not exactly the geologist's or botanist's ferns, and more than the style of presentation is different. Yeats's poems construct a different past out of his cones and gyres than his or other prose versions of cyclical history do.

It is also true that the making that poets perform can be intangible compared with the past of actual documented chronicles. As anyone who makes cabinets or automobiles could point out, it is a phantom making, inasmuch as nothing real comes of it, only words and images. Poetic presence and recollection are undercut by the ghostliness of the verbal world, as not only Plato and Shelley but a good many poets have realized. (Eventually, in addition to Shelley, I select Shakespeare, Milton, Marvell, Keats, and Pope as a final board of advisers, all of whom find suspect the fictionalist's attempt to conjure reality.) Whereas a few poets (such as Herbert and Milton) fall back on a sustaining sense of the privileged Word and its reduplication of types, for others the discrepancy between the primary world and the poet's secondary recreation of it suggests a serious evaporation of specific content.

But here again the paradoxes must be compounded. Proust makes a critical point, for instance, when he remarks that revisitation and exact recall are not necessarily the best ways to seize the essence of something. "How many times in the course of my life had I been disappointed in reality," Proust recalls, "because, at the time I was observing it, my imagination, the only organ with which I could enjoy beauty, was not able to function, by virtue of the inexorable law which decrees that only that which is absent can be imagined."[3] Although it may lose the texture and substance of physical reality, language may also conjure a sense of reality that only the inner self can verify. The past that poems reflect is not totally decomposed in them, merely recomposed, as they share with internal recollection the quality of vivid dreams. In brief, acts of fictive making may reduce the ontological density of an actual world and still enable the imagination to seize upon it and rework it under new arrangements, classifications, relations. Or as John Crowe Ransom suggests from another direction, the contingencies of a real world break in upon poetry and keep it from becoming captive to mere ideas; and at the same time, poetry frees the mind to play with unusual and extraordinary images. Sidney wished to call that aspect of the poet's lies a decided improvement, as a reconstituting of that real time, the Golden Age: "Nature never set forth the earth in so rich a tapestry as divers poets have done; neither with pleasant rivers, fruitful trees, sweet-smelling flowers, nor whatsoever else may make the too much loved earth more lovely. Her world is brazen, the poets only deliver a golden."[4] Whether or not the reconstituted world of fictions is better than reality, it is arguably different and valuable.

That it is in fact frequently past oriented might seem relatively undebatable. It is true, after all, that even before the work of recollection that Wordsworth assigned to the lyric and to the autobiographical narrative, one of poetry's age-old functions was precisely to canonize a past. Several modes—among them pastoral, the historical novel, romance, epic, tragedy, and elegy—are highly retrospective. Such figures as Wordsworth, Yeats, and T. S. Eliot interpret the past systematically and deliberately. It is also true that in looking forward, poets are sometimes really setting out to build in sonnets enduring (as well as pretty) rooms, so that the future becomes an anticipated past. Nonetheless, no one who lives amid the hum and buzz of the literary exchange these days can speak lightly about how a poem works without putting certain premises under scrutiny; and many recent critics would permit us to speak not of an actual past that poetry constructs but only of a past that both poets and critics constantly *unmake*—in an ongoing discourse that has no center.

Whatever their disagreements in other areas, formalists, neo-Marxists, and structuralists all dispute the concept of classics and the revival of historical landmarks. From another direction, certain sociologists, too, would deny criticism the capacity to restore past tests on the grounds that only contemporaries truly understand one another. Going even further, poststructuralists would so disperse all discourse among never-completed commentaries that the restoration of "a" text is illusory. Together with Harold Bloom's notion of the strong poet's willful misreading of predecessors, these views of the text constitute a serious challenge to tradition and cultural replication, a challenge that Michel Foucault's *The Archaeology of Knowledge*, for instance, has put very forcefully.

Antihistoricists of all kinds, taken together, are a formidable group, and it would be an act of hubris to tilt with them en masse. Without suggesting that I see an easy way out of the dilemmas they pose, I do imagine some relevance in Prospero's version of a similar problem with the performance of the magician-historian-poet, which appears to speak for Shakespeare and the play. As the pageant of the word magician vanishes, it suggests to Prospero a comparable dissolution of the world, and such an evaporation is already implicit in the phantomlike unreality of words and staged actions. All the histories of things and all their present shapes disappear together. But when the reader suspends disbelief and plunges into the magician's illusions, the connection between his pageants and the world's body holds long enough to have an effect. Prospero puts together a connected story that directs the play's restoration of order and gives us a sense of renewed social forms. Before the poet breaks his wand and blends into an ordinary cosmopolitan, he tricks us into believing in the bounty of Ceres and his own powers to right the several wrongs that have made society abrupt and discontinuous. The likeness of his phantoms to real shapes also urges us to explore the readability that a text sustains through time and determine the impact of temporal distance on the sense of a real society that it generates.

Such a text is not merely a window upon something historical outside itself but its own repeatable installment of the past. Ultimately, it exists not in its place or ours but in an interchange or set of complex negotiations between the present and the past. When the materials of a text are themselves historical, and when the cultures of the author, his subject, and the reader all unfold by different national logics and customs, the negotiations can be complicated. (Thus James Clavell's *Shōgun* may eventually be read, let's say, by Africans of the twenty-first century, deciphering the author's American setting in the 1970s as it gives him a certain slant on an Elizabethan Englishman's introduction to late-sixteenth-century Japan!) One thing perplexes another in fiction as sources are perplexed in the poet's use of them and further wrapped up in the educated reader's resounding. Linguistic structures, common types and archetypes, the echoing of precursors, psychological patterns, and unpredictable associations all contribute their wrinkles to the original document. But it stubbornly insists upon itself. *The Tempest* must be substantially before us if it is to talk convincingly of evaporations and disappearances.

It is my impression that none of our critical methods is quite capable of handling the hermeneutic problems of this cross-cultural exchange and the historical flow that takes place under the aegis of fictions. In any case, my hope is not to resolve these paradoxes of the text's presence or to establish central traditions and lines of influence but to pry open a door and glimpse some of the store of the topic. Although such a lack of thoroughness would be unjustifiable if there were only a few workers in the field, sooner or later every corner gets looked into. At the same time, no mere random excavation of literature's remains would do quite what is needed. The location herein roped off lies in a corner of the digs occupied roughly by the theory of fictions, their relation to social and historical institutions, and their function in both collecting and remaking ideas, events, traditions, other works of art, and transmitted influences.

Ultimately my concern—perhaps like everyone else's—is the shape the present assumes under the urgings of those messages that fictions deliver: What sort of reality is built up for us by *these* sorts of performances in their temporal copresence, then and now, and in their stringing out of an organized, time-deepened field of perception? What sort of balance can we strike between the immediacy that poems have and the detachment we gain from acknowledging their origins and their places in the accumulated library that surrounds them? Can the study of literary history maintain the special momentum and integrity that a succession of texts generates when one recognizes another, forms a network, and organizes its own historical field? The crucial matter in that recognition is the writer's selection of a genre and thus of pertinent predecessors and his broader decision to write in a fictive mode to begin with. I want to begin with the implications of that decision and the special sort of ongoing diachronic logic that a text joins at its inception.

I

MODELS OF HISTORICAL RETRIEVAL

CHAPTER 1

The Wayward Temporality of Literature

I think that two conceptions, that of reality as a congeries of being, that of reality as a single being, alternate in our emotion and in history, and must always remain something that human reason . . . cannot reconcile.

W. B. YEATS, *Explorations*

ALTHOUGH LITERARY TEXTS are documents as well as monuments, they are obviously more self-reliant than other documents—more detachable from the events that produce letters, memoranda, and rhetorical addresses whose usefulness is expended in functional communication. The class to which a literary text belongs, its genre, likewise pursues its course apart from the momentum of instrumental messages—not totally apart, but with an independence that cannot usually be attributed to nonfictional discourse. Following their similar conventions, the members of a genre evolve according to inner dynamics, so that in echoing and alluding to its kind, a text contributes to a subsystem possessed of its own rules of longevity, aging, alteration, and redundancy. It is largely this integrity of literary kinds that justifies our setting them apart from other subjects of the "sciences" of man as a separate matter of study.[1]

Yet no text or genre exists in a vacuum, and most genres overlap others, as the novel, for instance, includes some elements of history writing, the essay, epic, and even lyric. Given its extrinsic connections as well, literature leads a temporal life of some complexity. It presents us with a dilemma that inhabits this and other rooms in the house of disciplines: in order to account for chronological histories full of turns and deflections one must sacrifice recurrent forms, types, and systematic grammars. Diachronic and synchronic methods are, if not totally incompatible, at least highly unfriendly, and the fine arts are especially vulnerable to the tension between them. We hear the claim frequently that the arts should not be treated historically at all because of the universality of their themes and forms. Poets too are eager to forestall the effects of time on their products, which will, they hope, be read centuries hence. Since many works do in fact reenter the historical stream at intervals, the antihistoricist can maintain that they exist in many minds and that one should therefore define them by transferrable properties, by definition unattached to particular times and places. New critical explications, for instance, could not function were it not for some such assumption. What the text was, it still is; deciphering is essentially undating. As Northrop Frye remarks, "When the imagination is doing the reading, it operates in a counter-historical direction—it redeems time." Ideas, for instance, never become obsolete in literature as they do in the history of ideas; they exist "in the present tense as a total form of verbal imagination."[2]

While I do not deny the validity of these arguments in general, the case that can be made for historical knowledge in other forms of discourse works also for literature, and other arguments are conceivable. Most defenses of literature's historicity are quite properly based on the generation of texts within cultures and, of course, on their referential dimensions. Even imagination may be an ally of perception as "nascent logos," in Merleau-Ponty's phrase; it causes thought to stoop to the perception of particulars, and ideas to dawn upon consciousness in a time and place.[3] Because literary language is both abstract enough to encompass ideas and specific enough to collect details and proper names of the sort we find in chronicles, it possesses what Geoffrey Hartman has called an "ontic stubbornness" in the face of our "explanatory assaults" and contains a "reservoir of resonances." It is part of a "reserve of forms which claims to present for each generation the genius of a nation, class, or culture." In that same cultural reserve, we find not only ideas and specific events but "the official commonplaces; the symbols and passwords that bind a community together or identify members to each other."[4]

Clearly, the historical and the synchronic coexist in literary study, not in some loose détente but in interaction. One phase of that interaction can be seen in the distinction between the times a text refers to in the scattered and miscellaneous historical setting and the unfolding of its own enactment, which is one of the most organized arrangements of time that we encounter anywhere. Every moment of a fiction places something in an educative, cognitive sequence roughly equivalent to what Friedrich Kümmel describes as "vital duration."[5] A poem's duration has its own measurements; and living vicariously within its temporal scheme, the reader supposedly puts out of mind temporarily his own concurrent world and even the duration of reading. As Harry Levin writes: "Like other institutions, the church or the law, [literature] cherishes a unique phase of human experience and controls a special

body of precedents and devices; it tends to incorporate a self-perpetuating discipline, while responding to the main currents of each succeeding period." It translates those currents "into its own terms,"[6] as an
elegy removes bereavement from the context of an Edward King or
Arthur Hallam and treats it as a partly conventional, pretended course
of events.

As fictions pull in more or less recognizable parts of an outside
world, they not only close off their own frames of reference but cross
kinds and vocabularies from the greater world they recollect. As Marshall McLuhan points out with respect to Joyce's remark on his own
puns (that "some of them are trivial and some of them quadrivial"),
Joyce makes his puns "crossroads of meaning in his communication
network."[7] In its temporal dimensions, such a network is free to cross-
reference ancient and contemporary affairs or anything in between
without necessarily sorting them out analytically. Thus when aspects of
Homeric epic turn up in Milton or Joyce, they tend to collapse the distance between the past and present into a single cognitive field, similar
to the way in which a pun collects far-flung materials into a single in-
sight. What Joyce calls attention to is imaginative writing as a special
time-mixing, sort-crossing game and composed system.

Nonetheless, the capacity of literary texts to serve as gathering points
not only of near and far associations but also of social phenomena from
at large—their capacity to blueprint, mirror, and compress their settings—prevents us from straying too far from approaches that recon-
struct their social-historical surroundings. I want to dwell on some of
those approaches sufficiently to suggest both their usefulness and their
disadvantages.

In back of the modern upsurge of anthropological, Marxist, and sociological criticisms lies a large body of commentary on the likeness of
literary to social structures, which often goes a step further and posits a
determinacy of literary products by their social contexts. Although the
roots of literary sociology go as deep as Greek and Hebraic traditions,
not until the nineteenth century, and particularly Herder and Taine,
was a sociology of literature sufficiently developed to risk a suggestion
of determinism and to become a discipline of its own. Its main thrust
has been to contest the aloofness of classics and associate them with the
same economic and linguistic paradigms that organize other human activities. Seating literary texts within a describable sequence of social
events, it interprets their production and reception as symbolic extensions of social consciousness. Like Taine's early efforts of a similar
kind,[8] twentieth-century literary sociology likes to impose on a variety
of forms a common social typology, making individual performances
indexes of social evolution in general. In the case of Vilfredo Pareto,

that general social change is multifaceted and acknowledges the survival of hidden structures and "residues" from the past.[9] Others more rigorously march literary history in particular and social history in general to a single cadence. The most influential of the approaches that do so is Marxism, which tends to coerce several levels and tiers of change into one.[10]

Not all Marxist critics do so equally, however. Lucien Goldmann and Georg Lukacs, for instance, make the economic base influential on literary products and, like Taine, presuppose a considerable likeness between social and literary forms; but the connection remains loose. In Goldmann's opinion, to begin to locate laws of mutation for literary kinds, we must look first to sociological theory, which "manages to discover more easily the necessary links in associating [great cultural works] with collective unities"—more easily, that is, than psychological study, whose phenomena are less accessible to scientific observation.[11] In agreement with Plekhanov about the evils of "subjectivism," Goldmann finds only collective psychology tangible. No individual can have an impact on others unless he thinks like them and forms some sort of social bond with them. The active nature of his thought renders it communicable.[12] The collective character of literary creations "derives from the fact that the *structures* of the universe of the work are homologous to the mental *structures* of certain social groups, or in an intelligible relationship with them" (*Velocities*, p. 93). For Goldmann, "The great writer is precisely the exceptional individual who succeeds in creating in a certain field . . . an imaginary, coherent—almost rigorously coherent— universe whose structure corresponds to that toward which the whole of the group is tending" (p. 94). Great works do not draw away from social intercourse but complete the linguistic circuit from the group through the writer and back to the group: "These works . . . represent . . . the expression of world visions, that is, slices of imaginary or conceptual reality structured in such a way that, without having to complete their essential structure, one can develop them into all-inclusive totalities or universes. This structuration, then, can be related only to groups whose consciousness tends toward an all-inclusive [global] vision of man" (p. 94).

This view of the writer's necessary participation in social norms unfortunately reduces literary progression to a single one-way flow— without backward casting, leapfrogging, recapitulation, replication, echoes, or reverberating temporal depths; and it tells us little about those strictly literary influences that work within a generic framework, as novelists influence other novelists, dramatists other dramatists. Nor does it acknowledge the linguistic pleasures of a form apart from or in collaboration with communication—pleasures locatable in the work as a self-proclaimed symbolic game. Texts and their social settings are obviously not analogous in all phases. Whereas texts are meant to be deciphered as contrived language systems under the laws of conventions and genres, societies merely happen—or are planned as living rather than communicative orders; they are not integral sign systems, although they employ signs in going about their business. As Louis Althusser points out, the concerted actions of a society (unlike literary plots) are composed of innumerable intersecting forces from an infinite series of parallelograms.[13] Meanwhile, literature may look upon both institutions and the unspoken motives of individuals, exploring as well as illustrating the dynamic relations between social norms and individual variants constantly being generated in the private will, the memory, and the imagination.

Despite the difficulty of our binding literary creations to collective visions, sociological models assume that by one means or another, communication follows the lead of social exchange and encounters the barriers of class misunderstanding. For this reason, they find it easier to bind literary to social history when they shift from the genesis of texts to their reception and situate literary products among their consumers. Thus Marxist theory often maintains that no message from one class can change the basic perceptions of another, locked as each class is into its place in the social order: changes of heart or conversions cannot take place under the sway of mere information or even eloquent persuasion unless a change in class identity accompanies it. Even the most insular and private creative act is incomplete unless it makes that entire communicative circuit—which it may not do if it is totally foreign to its audience.

The use of agents, forms of brokerage, publication, and copyright makes the poet's business even more explicitly public and involves him in the vocabulary of ownership and trade. Thus as Marx suggests, exchange defines its participants as well as its commodities; it orders the successive relationships among those participants and the historical process they mutually create: "The guardians of . . . commodities must enter into relation one with another as persons whose will resides in these objects, and must behave in such a way that neither appropriates the commodity of the other, nor parts with his own, except by means of an act performed with mutual consent."[14] In this respect, it would not matter whether one had a sonnet, a religion, or a painting to peddle; the situation of those ready to pounce upon a significant message defines all parties to the exchange. No purely private act of making becomes historical without that exchange; whatever a fiction is as a product in itself is secondary to the value it collects when it enters the social system. Thus Milton's pastorals may retrieve a selective tradition and thereby

create their own predecessors and their own system of relations between the present and the past; but they become truly historical only in
completed acts of communication.

Marxist critics such as Trotsky, Lukacs, and Lipshitz are equipped to
tell us something about the class associations involved in those acts—
something invisible to an ordinary psychology of influences, as Goldmann suggests. However, even before there arose the confusion of class
identities that characterizes modern technological societies, making the
poet out to be a kind of textile worker or handicraftsman was a questionable policy. Because literature may invent realms quite different
from specific societies and may deal with universals apart from what
economic ideologies say about them, the poet is freer to select alliances
than the statesman or the social theorist. Closeness in theme, image,
style, or form among poets does not necessarily mean chronological or
social proximity. Another way of saying this is that we do not leave
great works behind us in the way we discard an outmoded means of
manufacture or certain social forms; instead, literary texts reenter the
social consciousness at every reenactment. They gain entry through at
least some readers who are receptive to them on other than economic
grounds. All classes and all societies trade in certain general "commodities" such as the loss of innocence or the undertaking of quests.

Although economic elements bear upon a poet's attitudes and the
disposition of his work, too much intervenes between the generation of
a text and its reception to make social typology by itself a reliable index
of literary continuity. In imaginative literature, as opposed to other social discourse, the conveying media of messages are not dialogistic but
often remote and complex. The answer of one writer to another is not
made in person or straightforwardly but is delayed, fictive, and symbolic. Because such messages are frequently unsynchronized with other
messages that dominate the current exchange, they promote a certain
alienation in those who focus upon them. The call of Virgil, which may
not have been heard by many contemporaries compared with addresses
at the Forum, can still be heard with some force by certain people,
whereas Caesar's rhetoric, though closely attended for its content then,
is unheeded now except for its style.

This lengthened stay of poets alters not only the tempo of the exchange but also the concept of the communicative group. It is true that
the readiness of the times to receive a writer influences the size and
make-up of his enclave and that we receive every author into a set of
biases and into a knowledgeability over which he has little control. But
the spiritual and intellectual motives of a Virgil cult have nonetheless
gone awry from the viewpoint of a modern collective sensibility. Although Virgilians might gather together and hold forums, they issue no
commandments and do not use their collectivity to solve problems

(Eliot's view of a centralized Western culture notwithstanding); they meet in moments aside and then go about their other business. The reason is that whatever the predispositions of modern readers, they must go at least part way to meet the injunctions of the text. Strictly as readers of classics, they presumably cannot diverge as far from one another as do members of the societies around them in pursuing their occupations or responding to popular arts.

Those sociological studies that speak of a poet's belonging to his time or being ahead of his time make several questionable assumptions about the remote influence of major figures. Can we say positively that a reader of classics is really behind the times because he has strayed from a consensus? Or is he merely outside a particular mass that rules the communicative circuits at the moment? That some components of our reading are ancient means little in itself, since many of the elements of the language even of contemporary texts are similarly ancient—grammar, diction, common nouns and verbs, even structures of thought. Only the smallest fraction of any present statement is truly new. The error of the defense of pastness that Temple, Swift, Pope, and others made once upon a time was to assign the living past merely to a canonical set of Greek and Roman predecessors and ignore those other injunctions that civilizations, natural environments, and psychological patterns pass from generation to generation. These elements are obviously not so particularized as forms of rhetoric, architecture, sculpture, and poetics, which constitute the neoclassical reserve of forms; they do not enter the field of choices through which consciousness traces its way. But they operate no less powerfully against innovation and the projects of invention.

What we appear to be doing in setting something behind or ahead of the general cultural calendar is recognizing that dominant and subgroups march to different drums. Their tempos may be poorly integrated, as when feudal values clashed with bourgeois values throughout the sixteenth and seventeenth centuries; they may be relatively well integrated, as when Homer's *Odyssey* feeds into and enriches Joyce's *Ulysses* (albeit with many an ironic turn and much arbitrariness). That a poet seems ahead of his time, then, means that he has combined something from one influence—perhaps a very distant one—with something from another influence in a manner that not many of his contemporaries are prepared to appreciate. His style may never catch on (very few new styles do), in which case what he has delivered will always remain a kind of detour or minority report of the kind that Donne constituted for neoclassicism and for romanticism. The history of reputations is full of anomalies, such as the eighteenth-century assumption that the worthwhile Andrew Marvell was the loyal patriot who put down Bishop Parker rather than the lyric poet of "The Garden" or "To

His Coy Mistress." (It was not until a certain political distance opened up that readers were able to close the gap between them and the creator of "On a Drop of Dew.") Like Donne and Marvell, any out-of-phase writer may sooner or later reenter a new time by roundabout means, through a kind of cultural feedback loop.

Another complication is that a classic's current influence is undoubtedly less exacting for a contemporary writer echoing a predecessor than it is for a loyal enclave of scholars. The insights of Aeschylus are less binding to Milton in writing *Samson Agonistes* than they are to a member of a classics department teaching drama to graduates. In this respect, one text does answer another as a kind of delayed return message—as a triggered, imaginative remaking that is something quite different from replication or translation. Transformations of a poem such as Wyatt's conversion of Petrarch's "Una candida cerva" into "Whoso List to Hunt" are always timely in a special sense. A reused or translated predecessor is both a distant point of reference and a participant in contemporary circumstances. Milton's Samson among Philistines carries certain inevitable parallels to a blind, outcast exrevolutionary among unregenerate moderns. Neither a contemporary provocation nor a classic can pass through the imagination without suffering a voltage change.[15]

As this difference between scholarly readers and poets suggests, notions of timeliness and of homologous social and literary structures do not invariably establish the representatives of a given time. Who precisely are typical? Are country readers, city readers? Critics, aristocrats, proletarians, the young or the old?[16] Even if the people of a certain period do possess a common "global" vision (in Goldmann's term)—if there is such a thing as an Elizabethan mind, as scholars once professed to believe—we would still have the imposing task of determining how a multiplicity of works from various periods registered upon it. We do not receive much evidence of that presumed mass opinion from published reactions, since those who appear in print are a preselected group. Thus we have little notion of the housewife's response to *Paradise Lost* in the 1720s—or the tradesman's or the university student's; and without such reactions in detail, we have difficulty reconstructing period norms.

Given these qualifications, it is perhaps better to set aside altogether the notion that literature functions like other messages in a responsive, timely social dialogue. To begin with, that dialogue is varied, pluralistic, and unsynchronized in more than its literary components. Literature's part in it merely brings to the foreground prominent voices of ancestors who speak to us not strangely or distantly but with an intimacy that even the voice on the radio at our side may not possess. Anything that registers with the impact of a *King Lear* or an "Ode to Autumn" cannot be irrelevant or left by the wayside. It complicates diachronicity without totally defeating it; certainly it complicates the society of the mind in all its receivable messages beyond the disentangling of any sociological model we now possess.

Some of what I have said of sociological reductions of literary temporality is also true of certain kinds of structuralism, especially those that make use of Saussure to curb the historical study of language and its mutations.[17] Their concept of finished grammatical systems has proved to be widely accepted by other disciplines. Building upon underlying structures, for instance, Lévi-Strauss sets aside social evolution in the study of kinship relations and considers societies as more or less like grammars.[18] Thinking of Marx, too, as a kind of structuralist, Maurice Godelier finds *Capital* an attempt to uncover internal forms behind surface valuations of worth, or an exposing of deep structures in a profusion of surfaces. What is at stake in this transcendence of diachrony is not merely how much of a society is stable and how much is evolutionary but also, as Edward Said suggests concerning beginnings, whether "the significant or systematic differences that individuate the various activities and productions of mind really begin at the level of self" or are "located more basically (or transcendentally) at a general epistemic level, a transindividual level," a level that Noam Chomsky, Freud, and Foucault locate in different places. Insofar as grammatical, literary, or social variants are merely surfaces of reiterated structures, historicism is limited to individual differences and must treat even these as merely new exemplars of old forms. (As Lévi-Strauss points out, the conscious and documented levels of cultural experience are opposed to the unconscious data of anthropological study.)[19]

In its bias against historical consciousness, then, structuralism minimizes the changes by which systems settle into their habits and practices. (Of course, evolutionary change had been the main concern of eighteenth- and nineteenth-century sociology, philology, and natural history.)[20] This denial of deep change would probably not have been possible or at least not so effective had not Saussure divorced sign from signified and thereby seemed to justify the study of language as something detachable from objects and events. This step was decisive in eliminating philological mutations as the central focus of linguistics; but it was also a step about which Saussure had more reservations than many of his followers have had. While it is true that *langue*—the total system of signs—follows a history quite different from that of things cited in individual linguistic acts (*parole*), no language is a rigid set of forms and rules established once and for all.[21] Can we argue that there are enough unmodified structures in the itineraries that Western languages have taken—or enough similarities in mythology, literary forms, and social order—to maintain that all variants are governed by the same underlying structures? Grammars change as well as vocabularies, but more slowly, just as genres and social structures alter despite a tendency to become habitual under a consensus. They require concepts of linear development not apart from but in dynamic interaction with systematic laws.[22]

The difficulty is that more than one context can be set for nearly any statement we wish to explain. At least five come readily to mind: (1) the immediate string of statements that unfold within a given text and their totality under a given title; (2) the author's other works, reserve of experience, and legacy of forms; (3) the social-historical setting, including any responses one statement may be making to others; (4) the genre and traditions of the work; (5) all the possibilities of all the words and sentences in language as an implicit set of expectations. If the study of a text's historicity too often narrows to the third of these, structuralism usually focuses on the last. My limited point is that it has not been sufficiently concerned with change and succession either to help us construct the poet's special pastness or to deal with the contemporary impact a poem has.

It is also true that literary modes vary a good deal in their interactions with the social-historical context, so that the novel's rates of change are quite different from the essay's or the lyric's—which again puts us on guard against borrowing from nonliterary vocabularies for the analysis of generic recurrence and alteration. Genres, like cultures, have their histories; and insofar as these are true histories, they involve changes not merely of surface but of basic structure. How much can a kind change and remain the same kind? Are its patterns truly recurrent, or do they merely retain some features while changing others? These questions essentially ask whether or not any feature of a culture recurs as it is, changes randomly, is keyed to intelligible factors, fluctuates in patterns, breaks and shatters, or engages and disengages from a limited number of other phenomena in some determinable way.

If we are to make headway with such questions, we must assess what various forms of literature have in common and must concede something to the pluralism of kinds.[23] Despite their number, to what degree are kinds parts of a collaborative group? No aspect of a society—not even its imaginative fictions—goes totally its own way or generates its own history regardless of others. What devices of representation give them contact with other semi-independent institutions? Can history as a discipline master the blizzard of documents and informal messages by which the components of a culture take their small steps toward collective change? Advertising, artistic representations, small talk at cocktail parties, brochures, slide shows, a chance remark here and there—almost anything among the mass of communiqués that fly through the air—can serve a purpose and change, or retard the changes in, other things that have their own momentum, from individuals to institutions to various types and kinds. Every humanly devised signal can be said to carry forward an infinitesimal portion of an order—a motive or a task to be done, a principle to be understood, a piece of knowledge. Nothing short of an analysis of all the media and the impact of their messages on all self-perpetuating kinds and institutions would suggest the extent of the cross-referencing that a complex society illustrates daily. In a typical day, each of us brushes up against innumerable small collectives, each pursuing its own work and making its own history. The formal contacts among these pluralities may be peripheral, but informal ones are frequent and, in total, telling.

The moral is clearly that a theory of linear change and recurrence in any single area must respect the concurrent movement of adjacent departments and kinds, which is what makes some concept of the aggregate necessary. It is true that to the extent that the members of a social group recognize each other, they pursue a collective course and may have their histories written. Any identifiable department, category, genre, specialty, or idea sets up its differentiated codes and its own timetable of change. But at the same time, individuals who join such collectives are not exclusively ruled by them: never totally contained in a single public body or manifest action, they have within them the potential for swerving from or recombining with the several collectives the self constantly assimilates. It is perhaps the waywardness of literary temporality that most clearly demonstrates that potential.

I have mentioned that waywardness several times, and in speaking of enclaves and the historical-antihistorical nature of fictions, I have circled around a matter that should be addressed more directly: literature's simultaneous apartness from and yet participation in other aspects of social recurrence, change, and periodic renewal.

One way of putting it is to say that literature is to other social messages as a digression or parenthetical statement is to a given line of statements. It establishes terminals between systems that are otherwise unconnected but maintains its peripheral nature in doing so. Thus a parenthesis complicates a progression by layering two or more sequences together, but not as equals. What Swift neglects to say about such devices in *A Tale of a Tub*, Sterne supplies in *Tristram Shandy*; and not incidentally, both authors are also concerned with madness. The ability to entertain jumpy, unintegrated, nonintersecting lines of thought becomes mad whenever a parenthesis is not clearly marked and the main line of thought is lost among its intrusions. The line between a complex plot and incoherence can be very fine, and both Swift and Sterne recognize, in the waywardness of creative genius, the connection between madness and logic. Swift is especially aware of the way in which innovation, in riding some winged thought into irrelevance, flies out of an established order and never returns. Both recognize that one may gain a new respect for order from such imaginative flights, as though the breaking of a tightly woven logic enables one truly to appreciate the miracle of a rational order that holds its thread despite assaults from all sides. As Swift's modern projector attests in *A Tale:* "There is something individual in human minds, that easily kindles at the accidental approach and collision of certain circumstances, which, though of paltry and mean appearance, do often flame out into the greatest emergencies of life. For great turns are not always given by strong hands, but by lucky adaption, and at proper seasons."[24] Understanding dwells in the neighborhood of misunderstanding, and madness is akin to imagination, which is a very bad thing in Swift's view, kindled as it is by vapors and spirits in the scheming minds of would-be innovators.

Swift was not the first to see close ties between madness, rationality, digression, and imagination. Inflation near to madness has often been thought inseparable from poetry, as Plato suggests in the *Ion*. Pope tends to agree, at least as far as high-flown or bombastic poetry is concerned. His rules for flying and sinking in poetry play upon our scorn for the stylistic oddity of those poets who set out on a grand scale and depart from the arena where people speak plainly and transact their necessary business. On a lower level, many readers will tolerate a rhymed jingle but not a bard wound up to great height; they are quick to suspect a poetry that pretends to seriousness. From these common viewpoints, poetry seems to lie outside the workaday world. With respect to ordinary society, both madness and poets are sources of parentheses. Almost by definition, what a poet invents does not bear directly on any particular business at hand; and from this perspective, a serial chain of poems in a generic tradition becomes a series of joined discontinuities. Along that chain, poetic perceptions may pass from party to party without need for routing through the bureaucracy of obligatory social relations. Therefore in one sense, a change in perceptions through poems costs nothing; operating in the wayward moment or pause, the innovative mind is free to pursue its whims.

In contrast, the daily life of a society is repeated with few sudden changes. As George Kubler points out, "The replication that fills history . . . prolongs the stability of many past moments, allowing sense and pattern to emerge for us wherever we look." Thus "every stage follows its predecessors in a close-meshed order." However, recognition of change in "a corresponding mode of expression in the arts" may be "discontinuous, abrupt, and shocking," as in the changes that occurred across a spectrum of the arts in about 1910. At that point, "the fabric of society manifested no rupture . . . but the system of artistic invention was abruptly transformed, as if large numbers of men had suddenly become aware that the inherited repertory of forms no longer corresponded to the actual meaning of existence."[25] This is not to say that moments aside like those the fictive imagination offers may not provide the substance of tomorrow's blueprint: as Swift's projector realizes, "When a man's fancy gets astride of his reason, when imagination is at cuffs with the senses, and common understanding, as well as common sense, is kicked out of doors; the first proselyte he makes is himself" (p. 331). Other proselytes may follow; it depends on how moving one's madness is, "For cant and vision are to the ear and the eye, the same that tickling is to the touch" (p. 332). But the immediate usefulness of the imagination's projects is clearly limited and special. Most fictive digressions are enacted behind the mask of a playful, stylized other self.

Madness and carnival go together in this enterprise.[26] The difference is that in pure madness, the pretender is more or less alone in the game he chooses and helpless to be otherwise, whereas in a carnival, participants consciously deviate from norms and have the company of others who have also set aside their habitual selves. A carnival, as a communal daydream rather than a private one, enables its participants to play against each other. And such play, too, is analogous to the poet's deviancy, as public poetry readings and play goings illustrate: they require their listeners to subscribe to the waywardness of the parenthesis, to take seriously, for instance, the poet's exclamations and apostrophes, to believe it permissible to call out "O wild west wind, thou breath of autumn's being" as though the wind could hear. They allow a play with words that they would not tolerate in a serious speaker, as the poet twists words out of common usage in the gamesmanship of meters, rhymes, and puns.

Most of the conventions of poetry, in fact, are symptomatic of the carnival performance that readers and audiences are preconditioned to accept. The poet's trademarks are a sing-song voice, alliteration, periphrasis, prolixity, amplification, tropes and figures, apostrophes, and other devices that people without masks use sparingly or with a wink, to let us know that the fit is on them only momentarily. Normal speech may dabble in catachresis or antithesis and meddle with oxymorons and double meanings, but it is not likely to proceed as far as invocations of the Muses, addresses to absent gods, or profundity and pathos cast into conceits. Only the poet has free license to use such things professionally; he has been granted that license in the expectation that he will entertain us with it.

If we ask whether this alliance of poetry and carnival has always been the case, the answer should probably be no. In archaic societies in which social institutions are cemented by common myths, ceremonies, and rituals, the poet's rhythmic chants, we are told, help govern the social and economic life and even the hunt for food.[27] Once pragmatic institutions and occupational specialties are sorted out, however, the poet is necessarily set up differently; his utterances are removed from prosaic history, science, and the fields of work. Some semblance of the poet may return, in the popular singer over the radio, for instance; but what he sings runs through the head at another level from the commands the brain issues to the working fingers. Even within the tribe of poets, some may be quite specialized, as kinds of carnival are boxed and channeled through different outlets—classical and serious here, popular and trivial there.

In brief, most of what is intrinsic to poetry is extrinsic to habitual styles of social exchange from economic productivity (where real goods pass from hand to hand) to politics and bureaucratic jargon. Only a little of common speech is useful to poetry, and only a little poetry fits neatly into any of our other schemes—an advertising jingle here, a communal song there. It would seem to follow that a history of such wayward performances will swing in and out of other histories somewhat capriciously to most appearances. Attempts to lock literary history too tightly into the social concourse falter where they lack respect for the difficulties of that digressiveness. It is the bent of serious critical prose and scholarship, for instance, to be itself hostile to digression and waywardness. It grinds the history of ideas, economic and social history, biography, and poetry into a mingled meal. Its own unitary explanatory mode usually fails to be answerable to the plurality of kinds and hence to the mode of interaction each kind shares with others. We must therefore recognize the separate kind that fictions are before we can hope to see the collective course that poets manufacture among themselves. In certain connections, some of them are main line, some marginal, some more than usually digressive. What goes on in the evolution of inventions, modes of production, forms of government and social attitudes is only obliquely encapsulated, dreamed, and transformed in literature, even in relatively realistic modes such as the novel. *Robinson Crusoe* is as much an archetypal dream in response to the pilgrimages of Bunyan's Christian as it is a representation of eighteenth-century bourgeois reality, which did not need Defoe to be lived out and transferred to later generations and was probably not lived and transferred much differently because of him.

But this may seem to make sociological criticism and the embedding of literature in social history more errant than I mean them to seem. Despite the apparent irrelevance of the poet-pretender, we are reminded of Sterne's admonition to his reader to beware *especially* of digressions. All appearances to the contrary, they may actually carry forward some main line of business that we scarcely recognize until later. In fact, it may be the inattentiveness of madame the reader, not the oddity of the performer's devices, that makes what he says seem irrelevant:

> I fly off from what I am about, as far, and as often too, as any writer in *Great Britain;* yet I constantly take care to order affairs so that my main business does not stand still in my absence . . . By this contrivance the machinery of my work is of a species by itself; two contrary motions are introduced into it, and reconciled, which were thought to be at variance with each other. In a word, my work is digressive, and it is progressive too,—and at the same time.[28]

So progressive are some digressions that "they are the life, the soul of reading!" Likewise, the stylist behind the carnival mask does not necessarily forget his common self—the self that lies in waiting to speak rationally of practical prospects, the marketplace, or matters of life and death. He may combine that identity with an antiself, and these together may fashion a commentary on each other. One difficult trick of literary history and theory is to maintain not merely a balance between pragmatic and pretended lives that poets lead outside and inside their works but also a sense of their dynamic interplay. Indeed, one or the other way of proceeding—main line or digressive—by itself lacks the defining potential of the two as counterforces, progressing as contraries. This is unquestionably what makes the serial successions of literature so complex and what makes the past that poets make so disturbing to other pasts that we take as more authentic—that is, more educative, more rationally applicable to our current state of affairs.

For one thing, the poet complicates ordinary succession by imposing on it the pauses of interpretation and redirection. It is in a time-out that we hatch new strategies. Performances on the floor or in the field tend to be merely reactive or mechanistic in that chains of circumstance are relatively self-perpetuating and undeviating. Yet a newly conceived strategy generated in a time-out may be entirely responsive to the surrounding context. Even the radio by the workbench might accidentally instill in the unwary mind some catalyzing agent, some rhymed idea that lodges there and begins to organize a mutation until for some, the hours on the job may well become the parenthesis: the encompassing flow of life, the truly crystalizing continuity, may issue instead from the impulses and motives of the poet's odd language or the private dream. In archaic societies, the chant, the communal poem, and the ritual clearly have such a governing effect; in sophisticated societies, the subversive element must come from elsewhere. When George Kubler notices the sudden revolution of art forms around 1910, he does not imagine art disengaging from society at that point but precisely the opposite: it comes to sudden awarenesses that "the inherited repertory of forms" had missed up until then.

If we seek to minimize the digressive nature of moments aside rather than giving them their due, we are apt to forget that the mind is sometimes curtailed by pragmatic matters in which it finds little chance to expand the horizons of the possible. We require opportunities to play in and around our contexts. Also, digressive flights in literature may be goaded by poetry's very oddity of tropes, attitudes, and stylized conventions. These may be generative, just as in searching for a rhyme the poet is also presumably searching for a nexus of thought; searching for an image, he is ransacking the world of his experience and drawing portions of it into the poem. Thus one of the virtues of such devices as catachresis, rhyme, the bardic voice, or of the pastoral and tragic modes (to list them quite arbitrarily) is their liberation from the straightforward march of reason; they guarantee detours through the riches of association. Even the lowly pun may free the mind from the rigor of a single meaning and let it play with surprise. A second or third level in a word is equivalent to a mask put on or removed; we suddenly realize, on seeing the pun fly loose, that we have all along been at a carnival, though the occasion may have seemed straightforward.

In the poet's hand, such unexpected associations are controlled surprise; we are guaranteed by the poet's undisguised setting forth as a performer that the entire world will not prove to be deceptive, that the carnival will not spread everywhere until no identity is safe. True, it is the contention of playwrights like Pirandello and other twentieth-century skeptics that deception is universal and is built into language—that play-acting is the rule offstage as well as on. But we are reassured by the boundaries of the performance itself that we may resume our habits and accept the workaday world at near face value once we leave the playhouse, though it may have altered in our perception. The outset of a performance is marked by ceremonies and gestures, its internal movements by units and development, and its ending by final gestures and dispersal—which is to say that the parentheses bend left and bend right to imitate a circle of containment.

We accept the controls of such arbitrary marks in more than poems, of course. When we accept a social engagement or an appointment for a committee meeting, we take the first step in isolating a temporal span, unifying its moments around an agenda, and magnetizing a patterned set of responses. But literature is extraordinarily organized by comparison to most such agenda activities. Because *Paradise Lost* is so insistent on its own beginning, middle, and end—on its own structure as a narration—its entanglements in such things as Milton's biography and Puritanism are recast in its terms. Of course Milton quite literally took time out from everything else to proceed with the poem. He reengaged in the terms it provided some of his other preoccupations, rescheduling them under the sway of the inventions the mode encouraged and the overall coherence of an unfolding plot. To be sure, he did not forget the Puritan revolution in all this, but he reconceived it under the relatively free play of the imagination.

His twenty years of writing political tracts is a conspicuous example of one career interrupting a second (after the first had already diverted his original intent to enter the ministry). His return to plans for a great epic (about 1658) is a double retreat—from the political activities of the nation and from the left-handed writing of the essayist and polemicist. However, as it turns out, his prose when it resumes has something to do with the nature of the poetry. A number of threads run between the two bodies of writing and between the poems and the active life, so that the poems are timely with respect to certain civil and religious reforms. Thus those works that may seem most apart are the very ones a historian might consult for their reading of religious, moral, and political matters—provided that he has mastered the difficult art of getting from the fictive digression back to the "real" matters of history. Certainly *Paradise Lost, Paradise Regained,* and *Samson Agonistes,* so self-contained in one respect, continue Milton's running commentary on the nature of empire and worldly ambition. The contrasting kingdoms of Christ and Satan in *Paradise Regained* address political issues from a vantage point that denies the worth of secular empire at a moment when Milton himself had found secular kingdoms disappointing: if Christ finds nations and armies irrelevant to the founding of his kingdom, it is partly because Milton, the former advocate of Cromwell's ruling instrument, had discovered much the same thing. It is poetry's privilege not only to make that decisive break with history's business as usual but to approach the kingdom that will replace it and thus to reinterpret those interim moments that paradoxically become the world's great digression from its ultimate destiny—a destiny encapsulated in the poet's vision.

But I do not wish to labor a point that Sterne makes much better and that most readers of literature may concede anyway. The question for the potential literary historian is this: Can we account for this digressive and recreative nature of literature without being drawn too far out of the serious matters of historical study to reintegrate them? It would of course be nice to be able to repeat again with Sterne that one has "constructed the main work and the adventitious parts of it with such intersections, and have so complicated and involved the digressive and progressive moments, one wheel within another, that the whole machine, in general has been kept a'going" (Chapter XXII). Certainly one's ambition as a critic or historian is to fold digressions into some serious task of explanation so that one can make literary explanation responsible to the more insistent social facts. Unfortunately, whereas Sterne's metaphor implies the meshing of gears in a single machine, which is proper for a novel, we have no guarantee that the turning of historical wheels—either art history or social history—does in fact constitute one movement. Whatever it may be, history is not a novel with plots and subplots, themes and contrasts; nor does the way literature moves forward within it suggest that anyone could guess where it is going. The past is complex beyond full definition, and the future is unpredictable. Rather than one machine, then, we may have a score, each fueled, geared, and directed differently. In that case, the moments aside that fictions constitute may not form a network accessible to explanation; an excursion into one such moment might necessarily be a digression from all others.

My guess, however, is that we will never lack connections between literature and its several contexts, that in fact we are blessed by too many connections to reduce the literary network to learnable principles. Our difficulty is not that Homer's *Odyssey* has nothing to tell us about its civilization but that it tells us far too much to be assimilated. In any case, my immediate concern is not to suggest what our approach to the entire social conglomerate should be but to explore the on-again, off-again functioning of literature within it.

To that end, I want to close this parenthesis with an illustration. The most appropriate choices for literature's digressive aspect come from pastoral, which is frequently and self-consciously recreative and distant from ordinary society. Shepherd-singers drop most of their contacts with the surrounding urban and country life: they make no history, leave no documents, and usually maintain no contact with their kin, as normal characters in epic, drama, and fiction do. The literary shepherd is usually without father, sister, or uncle; he has no tribe, no politics, no chieftain, no occupational specialty beyond herding and singing. Although he makes exchanges of gifts and sometimes is aware of property differences and ownership problems, the economic matters that he notices are controlled by ceremony; they provide a framing contrast to his main performance, which draws him into the realm of artifice and away from such things as dispossession and hardship.

Theocritus' fifteenth idyll is a good example. In it, Theocritus dramatizes at first not a moment of singing aside but household and urban ties that prevent the easy access to recreation of two ordinary housewives who have the entanglements more usual to modern prose fiction—servants, husbands, children. A city press besets them on the road to the festival of Adonis, which constitutes their vacation and their access to song. Despite the fact that their feet are stepped on, their gowns wrinkled, and their sensibilities injured, the place of song is not so threatened as Calidore's land of Pastorella or so remote as Milton's Eden. On one hand, the place of the performance is detached from the familiar and the ordinary and like all such sanctuaries has something of the strange and marvelous about it: the song of Adonis concerns a realm of demigods and natural fertility well beyond the normal. On the other hand, the song contains much that housewives can carry back when it comes time to fix dinner for one's churlish Diokleides; its cycles of life and death concern everyone. In return, the common lives of the housewives test and pass judgment on the song's mythic fictions.

Such digressions that turn out to be a complex negotiation of opposed realms are not far off the mark as models of poetic irrelevance in general. Other Theocritean idylls, too, by exploring the collaborations of labor and otium, the ordinary and the marvelous, the poetic and the practical, suggest the circuitous path by which fictions detour through reality by way of imaginative distortions. Like Sterne's view of the artist's waywardness, they make a roundabout approach to death, love, and certain social transactions; and while they do not take us very far into the details of these matters, they at least keep them in sight across the borderline that separates fictions from their social contexts.

Even so, it is not always easy to separate fictional from statement-making discourse. Informational and realistic fictions are less parenthetical than others, more like nonfiction. Although the difference can still be seen in the distinction between what Merleau-Ponty calls "use" objects and objects *en soi*, that distinction is less than absolute and consistent. Many strategic or useful statements have become literature under the right circumstances, and certain creative works may in turn be put to use. Indeed, for virtually anything to assume aesthetic qualities, it has only to disappear from sight and reappear in a new setting— as when a Sears catalogue ages, undergoes a metamorphosis, and yields something akin to found poems. A cast-iron stove in an antique shop is not what it originally was in a house; once it has been removed from its surrounding tables, windows, and bodies to be warmed on cold mornings, its parts are recycled in aesthetic perception. While such items may have a definite function for homo economicus, as aesthetic works they beckon the viewer to a different sort of contemplation. As John Crowe Ransom suggests in "The Tense of Poetry," nostalgia is popular with poets: they recover "out of the past the specific experience" in their sharper, "dramatic, brilliant" retrievals and thereby alter the former existence of things, which was more furtive, from which our full "attention was withheld."[29]

The recovered past that poems offer warrants a commitment of feeling and cognitive intensity that useful statements often lack. But again the categories are not mutually exclusive. Almost any reclaiming of the past, even the stories of governments and battles, owes something to one or another form of distancing: narrative logic imposes itself on historiography, heroic myth on chronicle. By a process similar to that enshrinement of use objects, Aeneas and Ulysses are reappraised by Homer and Virgil; Arthur and Henry V return as fictive characters in

Malory and Shakespeare. We insist on both their integrity as poetic creations and on their footing in history, however ghostly their remnant of actuality may be. Conversely, statements that were issued initially as poems, novels, or plays are also capable of losing their aesthetic standing and reverting to ordinary discursive statements, especially if they are not particularly good as fictions—or if the information they provide as documents is of timely and special interest. No aesthetic object is completely detachable from the world in process, as an old kerosene lamp, when the electricity goes out, ceases to be merely a decorative relic. The harder we look at such objects, the more they pass back and forth from their stand in the present to their former settings, the more they conjure the past not as transparent messages but as stylized symbols.

Some of the things that happen in this transit of objects from one condition to another depend upon the interpreter and his purposes. Each kind of interpretation does something different to the text it singles out for attention. Consider these, for instance.

Kinds of Texts	Kinds of Retrievers	Governing Principles
Legal	Judges	
Instructional	Users or consumers	Pragmatism
Scientific	Chemists, physicists	Curiosity
Scriptural	Preachers, laymen	Pleasure
Philosophical	Lay and professional philosophers	Scientific analysis
Historical	Historians	
Artful	Critics, poets, performers	

Since several sorts of interpreters can approach several kinds of texts, the conceivable reconstructions of past documents are numerous. A comprehensive account of historical retrieval would have to take that variability into account and ask, for instance, what sort of continuity results from each contact of a text by each party. What sort results from survey courses in literature, courses in the history of science, browsing in the library?

When we have recourse to the law, to choose one instance, we discover binding precedents within a framework quite different from the one we find in consulting the "Thou shalt nots" of scripture or the even less binding didacticism of a moral treatise. When a ruling judge applies a legal precedent to a specific case of misbehavior, he cannot be too careful in deciphering the intent of the text: his interest is decidedly in the letter of the law and its immediate applicability. He thereby seeks to bind the past and a contemporary act in a single paradigm, so that if a given crime has occurred, its appropriate punishment follows. In contrast, "Thou shalt nots" from scripture are more easily avoided, unless they are reinforced by law. A citizen who commits adultery will not be seized by the clergy and tossed into prison. (At worst, a preacher may seize his conscience and toss it into a state of guilt.) Yet scripture nonetheless has a binding power among believers, as in Christ's version of the Last Judgment, in which the power of the law returns with vengeance, raised to eschatological proportions. The difference is that belief is requisite to the interpreter's sense of the binding paradigm, whereas in the law, a social consensus has removed the individual right to disbelief.

At the opposite extreme from an expounder of the law, still freer than the exegete, is the reader of imaginative literature, whose text may or may not urge changes of consciousness. Presumably the task of an interpreter of Homer is simply to understand and evaluate, not to apply Homeric advice. Neither historical distance nor latitude in reading means that the critic is not moved by the text; but he is moved precisely by fictions and symbolic models—by empathy with characters through a suspension of disbelief—not by inescapable precedents.

Such variables in our approaches to texts admonish us not to accept too readily Schleiermacher's notion that the interpretation of all texts follows the same hermeneutic principles. Any selection of texts by readers of different sorts automatically changes the ground rules of interpretation and even the nature of the discourse to some extent. It is equally true that the intent we bring to a text may be changed by it, as when we casually browse our way into something that turns out to be important, or when some text that meant little to us yesterday assumes vital significance today. Nor can we willfully declare fictions to be accurate histories if they are not or pretend that a legal transcript is a fiction. It is also true that our establishing a canonical literature to be interpreted is not totally subject to contingencies and individual whims. The preacher chooses his text, the critic his masterpiece, and the lawyer his legal precedent for reasons urged not merely by expediency and taste but by general practice and common consent. Moreover, the selection of any given text from the library affects the reading not only of that particular text but of others, if only by rendering the others momentarily unread or misinterpreted. Our canonical texts—legal, scientific, literary, religious—have by and large been preselected and interpreted by that consensus, just as our musical scores have been chosen and rendered for us and our art masterpieces have been hung on the wall and screened through guides. Even the reading of our personal subconscious drives and dreams is directed by codes, tables of recurrent symbols, named psychotic tendencies, and training in methods.

These are perhaps sufficient instances of the waywardness of literature's temporality and our retrieval of texts to suggest the difficulties of diachronic study. I will not elaborate on them further at this juncture but will return to similar matters in the last chapter. In the meantime, I want to proceed to problems in genre and consider certain pluralistic devices of replication and change. My contention is that each literary kind that gains acceptance proceeds by its own temporal laws and resists blending into any uniform social movement, period norm, or other kind, though it interacts with these. Its relative discreteness helps it gain a perpetuity and repeatability achieved by very few other things that civilizations throw off. Any decision by either a reader or a writer to retrieve a text must include an acknowledgment of the kind and how its practitioners have developed it. Nearly every good new poem is both a culmination of the potentials of its genre and a break from some of its orthodoxies. An author's personal stockpile of structures, styles, metaphors—his credits in the literary bank, his citations, his allusions, echoes, footnotes, even his parodies—engage the ongoing expressive forms of his culture in ways that no pragmatic activity could. Encyclopedic works like *Paradise Lost* are consummations of a pointed and focused past that gathers for the occasion—not in spite of the work's isolation and boundedness but because of it.

In the context of their predecessors, such works appear as new energy systems, or balancings of old and new. In Milton's case, we find the past of the sonnet, pastoral, epic, and tragedy collecting in each new performance. His own career may also be gathered up there, as *Lycidas* is rewritten by *Paradise Lost* in a greatly enlarged cycle of lost and regained paradises. Similarly, Virgil anticipates his own epic in the eclogues and then fulfills the promise of the eclogues in the epic, which of course recollects Homer as well. Spenser, in recalling the pastoralist he has been as he proceeds to a "far unfitter task" in *The Faerie Queene*, brings his and the tradition's past forward to be juxtaposed with the larger undertaking of allegorical romance. Such culminations and retrievals redefine the literary past in works sufficiently like their predecessors to make literary chronology meaningful. That chronology is composed foremost of like performances seated among a host of recurring social institutions and learned responses.

CHAPTER 2

Recurrence, Institution, and Literary Kind

*All actions men put a bit of thought into are ideas—say, sowing seed, or mak-
ing a canoe, or baking clay; and such ideas as these work themselves into life
and go on growing with it, but they can't go apart from the material that sets
them to work and makes a medium for them. It's the nature of wood and stone
yielding to the knife that raises the idea of shaping them, and with plenty of
wood and stone the shaping will go on. I look at it, that such ideas as are
mixed straight away with all the other elements of life are powerful along with
'em.*

Goodwin at the Philosophers' Club, *Daniel Deronda*

I TAKE THE POINT OF Goodwin's treatise on social change to be that no
preconceived set of forms or ideas escapes deflection in those innumerable strokes of specific labor, those encounters with circumstance
that are our daily doing (or undoing). Each performance pits ideas
against the materials at hand. For the maker of artifacts and poems, as
for the sower of seeds or fashioner of canoes, most of the ideas he puts
to use consist of conventions and inherited forms. They repeat the past.
But Goodwin passes over that aspect of making and goes on to another.
The problem I want to raise here is similar: By what chemistry do specific forms of making and their general cultural surroundings react to
one another? What sort of mutual flow do they create in their successive moments? And rising to their highest stature as heralds, what do
critics have to offer in describing that mix?

There seems to be no nimble and expeditious way to answer such
portentous questions, partly because they are embedded in the total
psychology of learning and social continuity in which heritage, individual mind, and the present aggregate of social forms all whirl about together. Although a significant part of the repossessable past in our reserve of forms comes to us through novels, poems, essays, and plays, it
is not very clear what it means to have it there. One thing is evident,

however: as Joost Meerloo indicates, personal growth involves much more than the formal acquisition of an ancestry through books; it includes all means of instruction and a combination of faculties that conduct "a journey along the evolution of the race." It is guided by the processes of symbolization in general: "Just as the history of evolution is condensed and stored in the genes as bearers of genetic memory, the history of human thinking and communication is condensed and stored in human symbols ... Man captures time and duration through his creative acts, his rhythms, words and cadences, his mathematical figures, poems and historical dreams. Thus the symbol as a historical communication [becomes] the inherited psychological gene and time-binding messenger of ancient traditional concepts."[1] As Raymond Williams also notices, literature is but one of many ways we have of pulling remote experience into our particular domains. In addition we have "history, building, painting, music, philosophy, theology, political and social theory, the physical sciences, anthropology, and indeed the whole body of learning," not to mention what we get outside formal study from "institutions, manners, customs, family memories."[2]

Probably no one would dispute either this or the proposition that among the many forms of storage, condensation, and digestion, fictions occupy a unique if limited position. Freed of certain constraints that limit discursive modes, they can be charged with an epitomizing centrality, stripped of incidental matters, shaped for comprehension, idealized, and rendered memorable. Duration does not have the same effect on them, and age is something different in a work of art from what it is in other cultural phenomena.

In fact, since all cultural components age differently—some evolve, some decay, some recur in cycles—we require something like George Kubler's concept of "systematic age" to measure the distance between points in the overall chronological line. Although a uniform cultural calendar obviously has its uses, it tends to place all things at the same distance from us, whereas the Elizabethan social order may be much farther away generally than reperformable Elizabethan dramas specifically; Keats may be immediate in the systematic age of the lyric, while history's horse-drawn carriages are distant in the systematic age of technology. What systematic age measures is the distance something has traveled in terms of relative positions "in the pertinent sequence" of its kind alone. It "requires that we relate each thing to the several changing systems of form in which its occurrence belongs."[3] Aging depends on frequency of recurrence and the wider or narrower circle of cultural phenomena that influences the changes in something. A given kind may recur infrequently and endure long periods without change or be thickly dotted on the temporal landscape and quickly come to fruition. Thus tragedy is comparatively sparse through most of Western history, but it clusters heavily at certain times and changes quickly. Epics are widely scattered (almost one good one per culture), and yet they change radically with each occurrence, as though each epic demanded a rebirth or transformation of the mode.

Moreover, all systems interact; nothing ages in a vacuum. Hence in any such view of systematic perpetuity, what both historians and poets have to deal with is a related set of common forms developing or decaying at their own rates, having recognizable qualities, and possessing stable if not unvarying organizations. For the sake of simplicity, let us simply call everything with a systematic age an "institution," by which I mean any self-perpetuating idea or organization that dwells under a habitual title and has a footing in the common dictionary—including such things as motherhood, parliaments, Christmas, and the middle-class household, and such rarer things as kingship, the country estate, and the pastoral elegy. All identifiable classifications, class names, and kinds become institutional whenever their content maintains enough similarity from occurrence to occurrence to empower us to speak of transitions and to focus on itineraries. All such things have momentum. To a large extent, education consists of identifying a great quantity of them and displacing or transferring elements of the unconscious and the libido to them, as in transferring some of the primitive feeling that we have for family members to surrogate institutions such as government, big business, and the church. Our capacity to shift among categories and attach networks of feeling to them makes it immensely difficult to trace the course of any given institution. But only by gauging its direction, change, and degree of displacement within its own systematic progression can we make sense of its turns, revolutions, and contrasts or begin to identify the entries by which one suborder gains access to another.

It is axiomatic that literary history thrives only when it is permitted to look beyond literature to outside institutions that literature imitates or refers to. When it is limited merely to the reactions of one text directly to others in its category, as in the history of kinds shorn of their modifications and specific topical content, it obviously loses a good deal. To realize its full potential, it requires the freedom to consider not only genetic conditions and reception but the history of ideas, political and military events, and biography. This would go without saying were it not that the preshaped institutions and general headings of the social context are sometimes disallowed in criticism as pure externals, not only by formalist critics but also by advocates of one branch of historicism over others.[4]

One legitimate reason is that whatever specific, literal, datable experience lies behind a text is usually unavailable to readers after a time. But what can be known almost always are institutions prominent and enduring enough to gather significant, articulated bodies of testimony. With a caption such as "kingship" in hand, for instance, the historian can move up and down the scale of abstraction, linking specific events to general practice and providing a bridge from such things as Shakespeare's plays to their chronicle sources.[5] Because certain institutions recur in several genres (as kingship turns up not only in Shakespeare's history plays but in his comedies and tragedies, in Jonsonian masques, Sidney's pastoral romance, and Spenser's allegory), they provide some grounds for a comparative analysis of forms. And because in literature they gather in many of the motives of psychic life—as when the king functions as a father—they may come to us charged with special significance: they do not remain merely neutral facts or exemplifications of repeatable things but register on us as evocative symbols. Thus the local and the personal are connected with the public and the general. (There need be nothing mystifying about the expansion from the immediate precincts of the self to public entities in this way. As F. Smith Fussner points out, in the development of historiography itself, family heraldry and genealogical studies played a role in the broadening of historical documentations; history writing moved into national fields from family history, into larger institutions from smaller.)[6]

Comparatism, too, obviously thrives on the concept of institutions, on national cultures and their subdivision, genres, common themes, grammatical entities translatable from one language to another, topoi, and theoretical precepts. The concentration of certain kinds of institutions in certain periods enables literary history to escape the squeeze of narrower sorts of genre study and conceive of movements. In pursuing an institution like the kingship and its impact on dramatic, epic, pastoral, lyric, and other forms, the historian can suggest trends and styles that coincide with it. Thus in the context of his stand on kingship and its surroundings, Milton inaugurates new versions of forms that Sidney, Spenser, Jonson, and Shakespeare handled in describably different ways. The kinds of poetic statement that "Arcades," Comus, and Paradise Lost make can presumably be understood better if we follow Milton's reactions to feudal and royalist-dominated forms of praise and to the heroic modes that manifest them—that is, if we approach them from a context that social historians describe in terms of an evolving republicanism.

What the historian has mostly to work with, then, are general headings. This is perhaps not astounding news to anyone, but a commitment to such intermediate social and linguistic forms as institutions represent does force us to abandon two common habits of literary theory: one is to assume the hegemony of one or another defined institution, such as the means of production in Marxism; the other is to find everything outside the poem total chaos, possessed of no shaping influence on the self-constituting miracle the poem is. Both of these conditioned reflexes seem to me distortions of the sort of sets that poets have to work with. The kingship for Shakespeare exists outside the plays and suggests certain values and arrangements inside them; it influences characterization, plots, decorum, and the sense of closure. On the other hand, even an institution as prominent and powerful as the kingship does not impose a definite structure or value on the work but encounters in it competing and reinforcing sets, such as the inherited forms of comedy or tragedy and the playwright's individual predispositions and talent. Neither the literary nor the social institution is entirely self-generated or lacking in common elements.

Actually, several subdivisions of settled institutions are conceivable, and each offers itself to texts differently. One useful division, for instance, is E. D. Hirsch's distinction between provisional and intrinsic kinds, or kinds still open to crucial development and more or less settled kinds.[7] For the moment, however, I want to pursue a quite different classification that divides institutions into ideas and functioning orders on the grounds that ideas pass easily into texts while other things do so less easily. Ideas live primarily a linguistic life and follow the course that rhetoric and dialectic dictate. They travel from treatise to treatise under the regulations of formal discourse. Although functional orders may be imitated or talked about in literature, they exist outside our statements about them.

Ideas first: to be historic, an idea must be isolatable, like anything else we might regard as an institution. As an instinct enters the genealogical inheritance only after a set pattern has settled into the reflex system, so an idea becomes codified only after it reaches a certain stage of recognition. The idea of progress is typical. It is sufficiently separable from fellow travelers both to pass from writer to writer in the processes of analysis and to impose certain regulations on its handling. It can almost be said to initiate a method and a discipline of its own by which it is further tested and defined. Historians can therefore find it in this or that thinker, demonstrate its migration, and make comparisons among periods and national settings on the basis of its differences. In Virgil, the transfer of empire in *The Aeneid* and the millenarian thrust of the Fourth Eclogue touch upon it with sufficient persuasion to offer leads to Christian thought, which in turn combines linear notions of its own with it. Comtean progress and Darwinian evolution carry it along a somewhat errant but still traceable path. Again the individual psyche and the general culture find some common ground in the institution, since progress construed ontogenetically becomes personal development.

However, significant ideas proceed also by subdivision, reversal, and opposed pairings. The idea of progress is no exception. It splinters, gathers subordinate notions under its general caption, and is opposed by theories of historical cycles and decline. Wherever one of these rival theories ascends, the notion of progress necessarily gives way, as various forms of progress dominate the earlier nineteenth century and bring about such ringing declarations as Tennyson's "Better fifty years of Europe than a cycle of Cathay," but then yield to the theory of decline (as Tennyson in "Locksley Hall Sixty Years After" seriously modifies his hopes and anticipates Spengler and Toynbee).[8] The great chain of being, to take an equally noteworthy example, is paired with companion ideas throughout its history. Already strong in Platonist cosmology, it dominates medieval and Renaissance orthodoxy in combination with certain Christian doctrines. Many eighteenth- and nineteenth-century thinkers return to it in modified form, as in the evolutionary tree of those ever-higher evolving species. In this concept (as for instance already seen in Raphael's promise in *Paradise Lost* that Adam and Eve might advance to virtual angelhood), it gains reinforcement at certain points from the idea of progress. Or again, in the concept of Circean metamorphosis in the Florentine Platonists, it combines with the idea of the Fall and the downward spiral of the theory of decline.

Much of the history of ideas consists of new combinations of such tried and tested ideas as these. But ideas need not be prominent enough to attract a history all to themselves before we acknowledge their impact or their existence as institution. One cannot speak of a "traitor" or a "hero" without implicit reference both to the ruling concepts behind the words and some sense of how a given instance matches up with the consensus. All ideas are packaged for a new writer by the texts he has read or utterances he has heard previously. For the analyst of social dynamics, the itinerary of such ideas in their systematic aging has its obvious value: their lasting general shape discloses the common ground among periods, while their local changes require detailed research. Tracing the path of debate and the inroads that related matters make upon it, the scholar of ideas both periodizes and compares periods. Again this intermediate level between chaos and one or two dominating forces gives us the wherewithal to conceive of a literary history seated within social history. Unfortunately, very few institutions once entrenched ever get flushed entirely away. They exist as dormant residues ready to spring up again, just as the notion of a flat earth survives somewhere in England and sustains a certain number of devotees slouching toward Bethlehem to be reborn. Nothing is too absurd to preclude a second or third coming.

The captioned topic or idea is both independent as an idea and applicable to functioning institutions. Ideas and pragmatic orders intermingle constantly, of course, just as George Eliot's Goodwin in *Daniel Deronda* suggests in the figure of the woodcarver. The great chain, for instance, has connections with feudal society in Renaissance Italy's courtly circles. It makes possible a number of analogies between cosmic and social orders that are directly useful to vested authority. Despite that, the great chain as an idea or set form retains its distinct character, almost as an archetypal container into which a variety of new experiences can be poured when the time comes around again, or through which experience can be repeatedly monitored whatever its immediate circumstances. Thus when freed from its Italian captivity, it lends itself to Milton and an entirely different social theory and politics. It then goes on its way, providing one of the bridges from early to later Renaissance texts and from courtly to Puritan and then to Augustan poetics. Most of the discussable topics of intellectual history—the cogito ergo sum, the subject-object problem, universals and particulars, freedom and necessity, the concept of nature, the theory of species and classifications, and so on—lead a double existence, unfolding as pure arguments, yet counseling actions.

Even so, the course of pragmatic, functional orders differs in one essential way from that of ideas: while the one exists primarily in discussion, the other leads the full-bodied existence of logistics, memberships, training periods, political actions, geographical places, and social conditions. If one exists almost exclusively in the domain of words, the other lives both in charters and codes and in representative conduct. It enters literature not as a set of shaping definitions but as an assumed world of mimetic content. Functional orders include not only all rule-abiding organizations but all the teachable professions (medicine, law, labor, business, the military, and the ministry). Among sciences they include the distinguishable applied disciplines; among the arts, the studio skills in instruments, painting, dance, cinema; among more abstract or theoretical study, such departments as philosophy, economics, and history, insofar as these have not merely ideas to work with but national organizations of their own.

I remarked earlier that we cannot understand the internal dynamics of chartered organizations without knowing something about the transmission of energy that messages make among their members— messages from inside and outside. Many suborders are possessed of self-interested, self-perpetuating educational systems designed to convey their orthodoxies to new members. Thus the performing arts transmit techniques from professionals to novices; the study of literature proposes stages toward the Ph.D.; the legal, medical, engineering, and military fraternities organize their training academies. The perpetuity of civilizations obviously depends on the indoctrination of subgroups in accumulated knowledge and specific codes that shape one generation to another. The functioning conservatism of a social order occurs at the dinner table, in the flute lesson, in the grammar drill, and in the science laboratory—not primarily in the political arena or the bureaucracy. In order to be both continuous and discrete, a given organization must transmit not only its practical experience but its prevailing ideas and an implicit theory of its structure; and to be teachable in this broader range, it must make a gesture toward an abstraction of principle from praxis. Ideas and functional institutions are linked again in this development of method and theory at the level of abstract, theoretical study, which is promulgated mostly at universities. In fact, education repeats virtually all the rest of society but in detached indirect form, as methods and ideas. It not only enables citizens-to-be to carry into future suborders news of other realms but is itself sufficiently instituted to have its own histories, theories, methods—its study of study.

Failure to understand the built-in momentum of self-perpetuating, intermediary institutions underlies many of the miscalculations and missed prophecies of social change such as Flinders Petrie's, Pitirim Sorokin's, Vico's, and Marx's. As I suggested earlier, for instance, it is risky to assign hegemony to economic elements in an industrial age, when all institutions are active in self-governance and when their total is so large. As Trotsky himself remarks, although culture is generally responsive to economic change, it does not become instantaneously bourgeois or proletarian when those classes dominate.[9] The reason is that our total legacy of attitudes transcends economic status. If some single center of all institutions at a given calendar moment *were* conceivable, it would have to be a galvanic idea capable of generalized infiltration. It would have to influence relatively discrete areas by a common set of terms.

Whether such a center ever truly comes into being or is the invention of historians after the fact is debatable. To be sure, wherever several institutions pool their resources, they multiply their power. But to succeed, a Zeitgeist must not merely create an additional energy of its own but discover kinships among institutions and accelerate exchanges among them. Dominating ideas such as the idea of progress do permeate a good many suborders and individual ways of thinking; and their impetus, in radiating from institution to institution, gives some credence to the notion that one can discover a basic cause of social change—can systematize a period or movement. But it is always a mistake to ignore the temporal lag of the rest of a cultural cross-section, which is not always so dormant as the idea of the flat earth. Any given period contains too many relatively unsynchronized units from different points of origin to be very uniform.[10] No contemporary institution truly regulates all residues that coexist at a given moment. For instance, though the theory of biological evolution spread through several disciplines in the mid-nineteenth century, and though the theory of class conflict spread through a great deal of social thought after Marx and

Engels, neither of these fused into one system everything that surrounded them; they did not manage to drive out such significantly large residues as the bourgeois family or classical and Christian ethical norms.

"Zeitgeist" is thus perhaps best taken as a name not so much for a genuinely blended group of systems or an absolute reigning power as for a dialectical principle: one sphere contends with others and attempts to move them in a certain direction, but it in turn yields something to them. They cannot abandon their own histories—merely establish analogies and mutual grounds with it. The social analyst finds eventually that the terms of the presumed Zeitgeist slip loose from areas that seemed momentarily to have been bound by it. Evolution in one institution proves eventually not to resemble progress in another; nor can the class struggle of a manufacturing system in nineteenth-century England and Germany explain the social relations among races, sexes, teachers and students, or even colonizers and colonized in twentieth-century technological societies. When analogies that momentarily seem to unlock social dynamics shatter, we are left with an interpretive vacuum, decentered once again: the Zeitgeist moves off as the phantom it is.

The velocity of broad social change derives both from the nature of its departments and from the nature of the self-interested assimilation that suborders make of one another, which in turn depends upon their teaching methods and expressive powers. Active institutions not only indoctrinate initiates but seek to transcend technical matters and capitalize on analogies with other sets—on similarities in structure, idea, and function. In fact, since nothing is perpetuated without a medium of transmission, we can almost legitimately boil the collectivity of institutions down to their presence in signs and capacity for exchange. If the study of language has recently become central to institutional analysis, it is because we cannot know what symbolic models do until we have assessed the medium through which they travel—their capacity to epitomize reality, for instance, or to influence our perspectives, redirect attitudes, and blueprint changes.

Unfortunately, not all the vital elements of historical actions lie on the surface ready to be expressed. Some aspect of an institution's charter are normally private and invisible to documented study. Because living institutions tend to spread beyond their necessary functions and form comprehensive models of behavior, they inevitably touch upon moral and emotional complexes. Their members carry these within them into other arenas, generalizing and comparing as they go, but unconsciously and secretly in part. Thus a given institution nearly always contains a much more unsystematic mix than it shows on the surface and is vulnerable to change as its incoming ingredients urge. All institutions such as marriage, the church, or democracy are darkly allied with uncharted, untaught accompanying residues, each as complex in chemistry as the amalgamating minds and nervous systems of their members. As each initiate takes in the methods, ideas, and practices of an institution, he subjects them to that subtle chemistry of the inner self. If the hidden part of an order grows too large or important, we cannot readily codify it or write its history.[11]

Subrational connections are perhaps more powerful than we realize even in well-documented institutions. Any likeness in sound or thought, any nearness in the conditions of storing away, transmission, frequency of association or recall, or simply wayward and fortuitous accident may link things in the mind and draw them into a complex. Of all the agencies of invisible collectivity, analogy is perhaps the most mysterious, powerful—and literary. Not all analogies among subsystems are close or explicable. When Yeats cites Phidian sculpture and Cuchulain as ideal companions of Pearse in the Dublin Post Office (in "The Statues"), he is constructing a theory of historical connections that ordinary logic cannot approach. He crosses temporal and logical gaps on a bridge of analogies. Although other Yeatsian poems and *A Vision* offer some access to those analogies, the density of metaphor and the number of interwoven sources that the poem draws upon prevent any easy reduction to paradigms.

The means by which we form networks from relatively discrete institutions are often not even as definable as metaphor and analogy; they may be simply syndromes and aggregates made up of the loose materials of common experience, convened by unconscious mental and social sets far more numerous than the usual Freudian vocabulary suggests. The getting-rid-of syndrome, for instance, in any given situation may have a number of levels—physical, moral, spiritual, social, religious, literary, rational. Insofar as relief in one such sphere parallels relief in others, it provides a concealed reinforcement for its analogies. Thus, under the right circumstances, throwing off a sickness on the bodily level might suggest the riddance of guilt on the moral level, the removal of an enemy, catharsis, or the refutation of a mistake, all of which have in common the removal of a malfunction in an otherwise harmonious system.

For the weight of one level to be felt in another, no formal analogy need actually be stated: the nexus may remain totally covert. Because a word like "riddance" applies to many situations, it is capable of blurring individual levels and thus of exciting the imagination with echoes of one level in situations dominated by others. Or to take a similar example: "clicking into place" makes its secret pact with a multitude of experiences, as in the good fit of a well-made machine part, the rightness of aspects of a plot or story, the correctness of conclusions in logic, moral certitude in ethics, the coming home of the saved, all of which have the feel of perfection or of a teleological principle roosting where it should. Still other examples: lurking in the neighborhood of a good riddance and perfection one finds more ambiguous adhesives such as the balancing of hostile factors that cannot be either perfected or shunted aside. A compromising and flexible order, for instance, might silently urge another to recognize right not as that which has purified itself of antagonisms but that which has adjusted, as Manichaeanism offers a balanced good and evil; or as paradoxes propose a balance in rhetoric.

In multiplying examples of conglomerates and syndromes, one could include such actions and ideas as starting out and arriving; turns and reversals; rupture, surprise, intrusions of the unknown; the absurd; alienation or lostness; addition, complication, and refinement (in making and changing conglomerates); masking and unmasking. These are not quite institutions in their own right, but as tropes they approach archetypes in their recurrence and governing power. I would deny that such subterranean connections are at all precious and unhistorical. On the contrary, their transmission of energy is real and common. They are the formative stuff of motives, ready to slip into innumerable situations where they can generate new kinds without our being aware of them.[12] They are portable pieces of equipment capable of working many fields. Thus, though no one belongs to an active party of riddance, the "sick and tired of this or that" vote usually figures in conservative and radical extremes: every Republican platform contains some items of self-preservation and good riddance. The psychology remains the same, though the titles that the issues go under change from year to year.

Without necessarily being encapsulated in open definitions or paradigms, then, any of these reiterated mental clusters—set together by image and word—may seize an event or idea, associate it with a vaguely familiar company of fellows, and infuse one instance with the collective force of others. It is probably safe to say that no computer can ever be programmed to sort out all the associative laws by which we entangle our institutions in the web of experience that constitutes both the individual self and the collective enterprise. They are not describable as the neuroses or mechanisms of repression and displacement to which psychology gives entitlement. Nor is a formalist concentration on communicative means and methods likely to explain the dynamic contact they make among organisms. We must first know the preparedness—the structure, function, and habitual motives—of institutions before we can assess the impact on them of either covert or explicit messages.

Unhappily for neatness, the history of a conglomerate has all the connections that the minds in it have made with all other aggregates, which carries collectivity far beyond the descriptive capacity of any ordinary theory of cultural change or historical method. Certainly the full history of an entire period or movement cannot be limited to a recording of its manifest actions. What is willed into action is only a small part of the social complex and of the total sensibility of individuals that we might like to know about. Much that is not manifest and is strictly personal finds no mode of storage beyond memory, and even memory shelves most of its contents out of immediate reach. Part of the domain of the repressed is the vast unnameable, which is simply unavailability to coded storage. The discrepancy between experience and the little that messages make historical gives some indication of the leakage of our best containers. Though systematic study has pulled many a dark perception squirming from the shadows and fixed it in an illuminated lineup of fact and theory, much still escapes the best of retrieval systems.

Genres

My aim in suggesting this sample of institutional categories is partly to substantiate the claim for multilinear principles of historical study and partly to suggest that for the disclosure of the motives that make up a collective network we require sensitive registers of the means by which institutions are connected. All the more reason not to turn away from the past that fictions reflect and create. Short of sortilege and divination, perhaps only fictions can deliver sufficient private worlds to enable us to guess what they were and how they came forth to join institutions that other documents have halfway prepared us to see. A general history should not only line up the itineraries significant institutions have taken but also ask: Do we not in fact inherit different perceptions and find them arranged by a different logic when fictions serve as their vehicle? Are such ideas as progress and such institutions as kingship not extended to us differently by Tennyson or Shakespeare than by Trevelyan? Do we not see in Shakespeare secret analogies between familial and civil structures that would not likely be traceable by some other method?

How are literary forms keyed to the variety of institutions that form their contexts? Is the novel geared to bourgeois life, the country house poem to rural squires, in such a way as to make these forms expressive extensions of what they mirror? Where the association between a literary form and an active social order is very close, sociological criticism obviously occupies a privileged position in answering such questions. But does the looser association of Spenser's fairyland to Troynovant afford it the same privileges? From another angle: does the accumulated practice of pastoral from Theocritus and Virgil to the sixteenth century deflect the momentum of those social forms that fed into it—say in Italian courtly entertainments—so that the literary product is not an expressive form for the social order but a complex, distorting analogy to it and a critical commentary on it?

Whatever the specific answers to such questions, acknowledging the momentum of social institutions is among the first steps a historian has to take in tracing their transformed images in fictions. If cultural entities cluster, collide, form leagues, and bring about swerves and dodges in each other's courses outside literature, they may be supposed to maintain some of that energy inside as well. Certainly neither social nor literary forms go their own way without altering course upon contact with one another. The language of literature derives much of its force from what it gathers contemporaneously; it borrows the charters and the preshaped tendencies of surrounding institutions. Or to put it the other way around, no tone, attitude, plot, image cluster, or characterization makes sense except in terms of writer's and reader's trained reaction to actual matters to which a text refers. To say this does not totally fly in the face of what I said earlier about literature's waywardness and the eighteenth century going its way with or without Defoe; it merely points up the other side of the parenthesis: one way of getting at mainline happenings is precisely by seeming to detour away from them.

What are the groupings and associational principles by which literary kinds make contact with those external systems and institutions? What aspects of the past can they capture and reinstate? In part at least, the answers can be the standard ones: we group literary texts and associate them with subject matters mainly by conventional and recognized forms, by periods and nationalities, by styles. The difficulty has usually been not that texts wander into the wrong company and get misclassified but that we do not sufficiently adjust the concept of imitation and of historical movements to what a given kind does with its temporality or what it allows by way of retrieval at different stages of its own systematic aging.

In the interests of a compressed view of major kinds and a clustering of their hitchhiking materials, let us consider two diagrams, the aim of which is to associate literary genres roughly with typical materials. The first borrows from Northrop Frye (with an assist from Paul Hernadi).[13] The second, which can be imagined as the reverse side of the first, suggests that the complex that an educated self forms is as important to literary kinds as it is to the make-up of functional institutions.

One reason for placing the self and literary forms back to back as though on opposite sides of a sphere is their common use of masks: both individual texts and kinds can be treated as extensions of the performing self. However, an existing self is significantly different from those performances to which we give discrete titles as texts. Outside of artful performances, we are deflected by circumstances from the plots

GENRES

SUBJECTIVE

PRIVATE

PUBLIC

OBJECTIVE

romance modes
fairy tale
parable
allegory
etc.

lyric

comedy

tragedy

novel
anatomy
satire
biography
etc.
realistic modes

epic

SELF

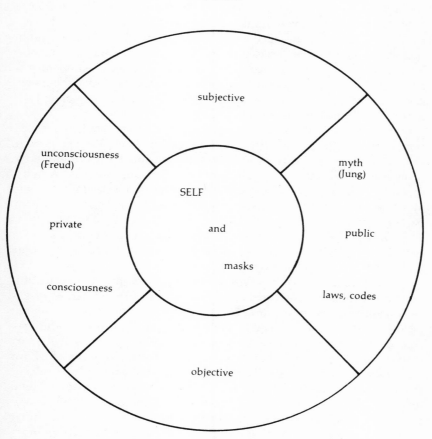

we would enact, which are seldom consummated with all the satisfactions of poetic justice. We constantly break down old clusters and kinships and form new ones; and we carry the habitual practices and recurrent traits of our collective reservoir forward into new circumstances among which we must be pragmatic and reactive. In contrast, artful performances are relatively bounded; and even though no literary kind as a whole is fully discrete or beyond change, a finished work is one of our most unalterable and revivable institutions, despite the stylistic variability of individual performances. Also, some forms, such as romance, tend to hold to recurrent psychic patterns even among scattered authors and are shaped more by predecessors than by their particular settings. Although romance alters as it travels from Hawthorne to Kafka, it is comparatively immune to specific historical detail. In contrast, such forms as the documentary novel, topical satire, and public rhetoric respond more directly to the social context and its changing idioms and are more accessible to diachronic theory. Although the novel makes use of formal strategies that have existed since the invention of narrative, in its realistic and naturalistic versions, it is thoroughly implicated in social history.

Similar distinctions can be pursued in other forms. Tragedy , for instance, joins with epic in its preoccupation with Greek, Roman, French, or English dynasties; the heroic prototypes of both forms often derive from real models such as Achilles, Aeneas, Roland, Lear, and Antony. In contrast, comedy and lyric usually take leave of specific cases and move respectively outward to recurrent buffoons, scapegoats, tempters, parasites, misers, and gulls; and inward to recurrent feeling. In its concern with personal experience as opposed to public deeds, however, tragedy joins lyric rather than epic (although epic, too, may welcome lyric moments, as in Milton's invocations).

Literary kinds ally themselves not merely with preexisting institutions but with other intermediary forms. Most of the materials of encyclopedic epic, documentary novels, and topical dramas are taken not directly from unfiltered experience but from other forms of writing—chronicles, histories, letters, newspapers. Drama reminds us "with particular vividness," as Northrop Frye remarks, "of analogies to ritual, for the drama in literature, like the ritual in religion, is primarily a social or ensemble performance." Forms that lean toward the antihistorical tend to take their cues from myth and bear some resemblance to ritual and dream. Myths themselves, as when they convert solar and lunar rhythms to story form, do so not directly but with assistance from other forms of expression. As Frye says: "The myth accounts for, and makes communicable, the ritual and the dream. Ritual, by itself, cannot account for itself: it is pre-logical, pre-verbal, and in a sense pre-human . . . Myth is more distinctively human."[14]

But these observations in taxonomy quickly reach a dead end; in any case, we cannot explore very many of the interactions of individual literary forms and social settings here. Instead, I propose to narrow from generic institutions in general to a representative pair and then to specific examples. Since so many forms of poetry mix myth and history, the distinction between them is a plausible place to begin. One function of widely encompassing forms like epic, for instance, is to interpret the universal forms and emotions of myth in the light of specific social codes and systems and in turn to reveal the impact of mythic formats on historical cultures. Comedy similarly mixes its means: it may combine fashionable references to the beau monde with disguised versions of the mating ritual, eternal cycles of young replacing old, and masquelike contests of lunar and solar powers, order and disorder.

However, given the nature of these elements, perhaps *logos* and *mythos* would serve better as our generic pair, since history is only one of the discursive kinds that logic and information dominate, and "myth" is a less useful term than one that encompasses not merely a specific narrative format but a way of thinking. The poet's handling of mythos and logos tells us something about the interaction of literary kinds and social institutions across a spectrum of more particularized kinds. I mean by these terms basically what Susanne Langer means by discursive and nondiscursive modes: logos opposes mythos roughly as ratiocination opposes intuition. Rather than restricting the workings of symbolic expression to explicit, rational language and assigning the rest to irrational feeling, Langer recognizes them as descendants of a single parental stock, one manifested primarily in the workings of theoretical and practical reason, the other in the visual imagination, dream, myth, and ritual. Logos, like the discursive mode in general, makes an explicit or denotative use of signs and includes all rationalized theories of succession, cause and effect, classification, enumeration, and inventory.[15] It is often the function of logos to apply daydream, or to specialize the individual or collective dream by putting it to work. It operates in such kinds as the elegy (despite the elegy's mythic components) when the poet seeks theological or philosophical consolations for certain losses. Dialectical, rhetorical, meditational, and metaphysical modes of poetry are heavily indebted to logos, if not so totally as a high-information mode such as the novel.

In contrast, the ways and means of mythos are less easily classified and less definitively linked to history's course of visible ideas and functional orders. Mythic narratives are less governed by explicable logic and less well integrated into the labors of our waking hours. All expressions of mythos insist upon a residue of irrelevance and symbolic play. Such kinds as the saga, romance, ritual, and dance descend into the unconsciousness of mythos as a source of archetypes. It is up to acts of critical explanation to translate these into intelligible principles and thus to provide some of the working labels, categories, and definitions of logos. Criticism in this respect is to mythos as psychoanalysis is to dreams: the labor of making is not complete in the text itself, as far as intelligence is concerned, only in its displacement. As Mircea Eliade remarks, the personal and the racial past, too, can be recovered by psychoanalysis as well as by archaic means, or it can be destroyed by willed forgetting and then recreated. As *Cosmos and History* contends, archaic societies that are dominated by myth make every effort to disregard the eventful, linear course by which the past is ordinarily sorted out and repossessed: "In the particulars of his conscious behavior, the 'primitive,' the archaic man, acknowledges no act which has not been previously posited and lived by someone else . . . His life is the ceaseless repetition of gestures initiated by others."[16] Even conscious memory cannot retain historical events beyond the span of a few generations except insofar as it transforms them into archetypes (p. 46). Thus mythos is one way of making history itself memorable, though in an altered, unspecific state.[17] It works largely with covert analogies and networks beneath explicit tribal codes. Its deep structures are scarcely codifiable at all and are not easily translated into moral commandments or plans of action. They are repeatable psychic patterns by which collective affairs are coordinated and reissued as tribal customs.

It seems to follow that no sophisticated poet can escape into the realm of pure mythos even if he wants to, because the act of writing automatically imposes on him certain considered aspects of thought and composition. In their union in written mythopoesis, myth and poetry both undergo transformations: myth is caught up in the articulations of plot, style, and drama, while poetry is pried part way loose from didactic or topical purposes. When mythos deviates into such literary forms as tragedy, epic, or romance, it takes on an explantory phase in axioms, theorems, theses, intelligible dialogue, characterization. Thus a text like *Sir Gawain and the Green Knight* combines a good deal of social realism and explicit interpretive commentary with a residue of vegetation myth. Such poems as *Lycidas* and *Comus* displace basic myths of metamorphosis, death, and rebirth with rationalized Platonist and Christian definition.

The recollective strategies of mythopoeic texts, too, are mixed. At the encyclopedic extreme, they may offer us something like a Proustian inventory of social manners and appointments. At the mythic extreme, they suggest a timelessness that is neither personal nor social but is built into the ubiquitous presences of sun, vegetation, and animal law. Most literary forms tend to read history's *res gestae* in the light of such recurrences; they bring the human congeries home to universals. In fact, the great middle ground between cyclical or repeatable versions of the past and linear or unique versions is the most natural domain of literature,[18] which extends from cosmic archetypes to recurrent folly, from religious handlings of birth, death, and rebirth to the tones and attitudes of topical satire. While pursuing his digression, a poet measures reality against the standards of mythic distance; or in reverse, measures some recurrent dream against the limits of reality.

Most written literary forms, then, are not myth, although they may have mythic elements. One shortcoming of Frye's theory of archetypes is that it holds the evolution of literary forms aloof from the impact of intellectual, social, and technological factors and makes myth less undisplaced in literature than it usually is. It seems an exaggeration to say as Frye does in *A Study of English Romanticism* that "at any given period of literature the conventions of literature are enclosed within a total mythological structure."[19] It would perhaps be closer to the truth to say that myths, literature, historiography, and other kinds of writing overlap but remain distinct. However, in assuming the primacy of myth over discursive forms, Frye has influential allies, and none more so than Ernst Cassirer, who maintains: "In the relation between myth and history myth proves to be the primary, history the secondary and derived, factor. It is not by its history that the mythology of a nation is determined but, conversely, its history is determined by its mythology." In this view (which I personally find mystifying), myth does not define its subjects by cause and effect or general laws and processes but "lives entirely by the presence of its objects—by the intensity with which it seizes and takes possession of consciousness in a specific moment." Or more fully and still more boldly:

> Myth knows nothing of that kind of objectivity which is expressed in the mathematical-physical concept or of Newton's absolute time which "flows in and for itself, without regard to any outward object." It knows historical time no more than it does mathematical-physical time. For even the historical consciousness of time contains very definite objective factors. It is based on a fixed chronology, a strict distinction of the earlier and later, and the observation of a determinate, unequivocal order in the sequence of the moments of time. Myth is aware of no such division of the stages of time, no such ordering of time into a rigid system where any particular event has one and only one position . . . The stages of time—past, present, future—do not remain distinct.[20]

Where mythic thought treats its objects as animate forces (making the sun into Apollo or Re, and fire into Vulcan), science treats even persons as things; it demythologizes and unromanticizes both the human personality and nature.

Either way of thinking, scientific or mythic, seeks to block off the interaction and mutual modification of mythos and logos. But they cannot always remain aloof even outside literature. Although myth may be hostile to history and unimpressed by science, we insist on proposing scientific studies of it and anthropological theses about its functions. The gradual conversion of myth into science is of course one tendency of Western intellectual history—sometimes a dangerous tendency, as Kenneth Burke suggests in *A Rhetoric of Motives*: "It is but a step from treating inanimate nature as mere 'things' to treating animals, and then enemy peoples, as mere things . . . In the systematic denial of what one knows in his heart to be the truth, there is a perverse principle that can generate such anguish."[21]

Still other concessions must be made to logos even in mythos-dominated literature. The development of traditions, for instance, systematically translates myth into convention. One of the ways we get from E. D. Hirsch's provisional to his intrinsic kind is precisely along that path of codifiction. When pastoral, to take an obvious case, focuses on figures such as Diana, Venus, or Pan or causes both the human and the supernatural to conform to a system of artifices and habitual practices, it moves from myth to formulaic convention. In the course of time, nearly all its elements become formalized: a given pastoral dwells in a world of recognized predecessors. Its long-forestalled amatory affairs, its metapoetic concern with song itself, its special friendships and ceremonies, and its oblique way with moral and political allegories are all subordinated to the poet's initial commitment to the kind's formulae. In this respect, pastoral keeps both myth and history at a distance. While a branch of science might develop in a relatively tight chain of researchers and analysts reacting to preceding fact and opinion, or while myth might develop cults of adepts or tribal centers of belief, pastorals develop echoic fraternities of metropolitan poets masquerading as shepherds. Even in folk forms, ballads, and sagas, the literary text or performance is individuated as a work of art: its proponent is neither a shaman nor a legislator but a craftsman practicing his skills, his *techne*.[22]

To sum up: the temporal layering of literature is complexly keyed to the identifiability of institutions, some of them social, some intellectual, some modal or stylistic. These have their own momentum and their own ways of joining into provisional networks. When we juxtapose various kinds of creative literature with preexisting institutions, we can begin to sort out the likely marriages and analogies, though gauging the impact of two or more kinds in aggregate is always a difficult and sensitive task, all the more so because all kinds—social, linguistic, literary—are on the move. Contacts among them may result in finished specimens that we can contemplate in their niches and display cases; but the business of historians is not merely with them but with their linear courses and the deflections they make as they spill out one after another.

Two Illustrations: Donne and Yeats

Virtually any text of any dimension should illustrate some aspect of the mixture of logos and mythos, the intersection of digressive viewpoints with ongoing historical moments, and the consorting of working institutions with kinds of fiction. The major odes of Keats would do so, for instance, as would Wallace Stevens' poems (if we were to turn these sets of terms around to accommodate Stevens' "imagination and reality"). But let us first consider Donne and Yeats, both of whom exploit admirably the poet's advantages with historical and mythic elements. Such poems as "The Good-morrow," "Goodfriday 1613. Riding Westward," and "Easter 1916," for instance, operate close to the center of literature's special temporality—close enough at least to suggest certain representative patterns.

Let us begin with "The Good-morrow" and a minor generic note. The poem is basically a commemorative lyric and a morning song. It pulls something formerly lodged in dream into the open and into definition, in the dawning of a new consciousness. The speaker launches a career in love just as the poem's definition of that love articulates love's perceptions. It suggests not just a beginning, then, but the emergence of a career into historicity from untraceable sources beyond documentation. Before the lovers can greet one another in this new light, they must weather a long unenlightenment.

Logos and mythos seem at first unbalanced in that awakening, which leans decisively toward the current, the rational, and the analytic. Most of Donne's lyrics in fact leave very little directly to myth. The kinds that they manifest are of a definable sort that draw upon the intellectual storehouses of Renaissance Platonism, alchemy, the business world, and the professions. Donne's speaker is usually a witty man of the world who might have been a courtier; he is always rational or at least pretends to rationality. Donne's poems have virtually nothing to do with classical mythology, and even their versions of Christian thought are controlled by theological precepts. "The Good-morrow" nonetheless presumes that love has a residual element of the mythic. It ends, for instance, with a defiance of ordinary time that carries beyond analytic limits and earned explanations:

> I wonder by my troth, what thou, and I
>   Did, till we lov'd? were we not wean'd till then?
> But suck'd on countrey pleasures, childishly?
>   Or snorted we i'the seaven sleepers den?
> 'Twas so; But this, all pleasures fancies bee.
> If ever any beauty I did see,
> Which I desir'd, and got, 'twas but a dreame of thee.

And now good morrow to our waking soules,
        Which watch not one another out of feare;
For love, all love of other sights controules,
        And makes one little roome, an every where.
Let sea-discoverers to new worlds have gone,
Let Maps to others, worlds on worlds have showne,
Let us possesse our world, each hath one, and is one.

My face in thine eye, thine in mine appeares,
        And true plaine hearts doe in the faces rest,
Where can we finde two better hemispheares
        Without sharpe North, without declining West?
What ever dyes, was not mixt equally;
If our two loves be one, or, thou and I
Love so alike, that none doe slacken, none can die.

Perhaps the best way to make sense of that final claim is to say that the discovery of the beloved coincides with the mind's awakening to some eternal form now locatable in temporal life. Although a great deal of intellectual ingenuity goes into the liberating of the mind from logic, the analytic act is ultimately placed in the service of a constituent myth: as the soul's discovery of love controls all other seeing and gives it command over the world's miscellany, Donne exploits reason to defy reason. This compressing of the great into the small is a mythic habit of thought that enables the mind to counter its former mistaking of corporeal for spiritual forms and its pursuit of inadequate dreams. When its matching form appears in the beloved, the mind discovers simultaneously the meaning of an epitome and the limits of reason: one place can be an everywhere; identification of all things cancels their differentiation and their dispersal, as love exemplifies and opens up an awareness of the world reduced to possession. In one place, the speaker recognizes the mystery of his other possessions; by analogy he conquers. And if the objects of space yield to his grasp, so might things dispersed in time. The miracle knows no bounds. As "The Sunne Rising" says even more pointedly, "Love, all alike, no season knowes, nor clyme, / Nor houres, dayes, months, which are the rags of time." Love is beyond enumeration, calculation, classification. It brings everything that matters into a single room, where "She'is all States, and all Princes, I, / Nothing else is."

Conversely, in "A Nocturall upon S. Lucies Day," the disappearance of the beloved takes the world away and renders "a quintessence even from nothingnesse." The lover returns to origins, rebegotten of "absence, darknesse, death; things which are not." Something similar also underlies the fourth stanza of "The Canonization" in its contrast of the pretty rooms of sonnets to the chronicles and half-acre tombs of the great. Though the resurrection of Donne's "dead" lovers is not equivalent to the journey of departed spirits to far abodes, it has more than a token mysteriousness:

> Wee can dye by it, if not live by love,
> And if unfit for tombes and hearse
> Our legend bee, it will be fit for verse;
> And if no peece of Chronicle wee prove,
> We'll build in sonnets pretty roomes;
> As well a well wrought urne becomes
> The greatest ashes, as halfe-acre tombes,
> And by these hymnes, all shall approve
> Us *Canoniz'd* for Love.

In one way, this variant of the theme proclaims merely that by comparison to the memorability of love, ordinary standards of historical significance and fame are deficient. But the word "canoniz'd" forges a more radical likeness of lovers to saints and of poems to holy relics. Like martyrs who die and rise transcendent and thereby supply their legendary models to the future, the lovers and their poems achieve a miraculous eternal presence. To do so, they must demand their time and place apart, like the lovers of "The Sunne Rising": the rooms they inhabit must be isolated from a world where lawyers and courtiers go about their business. In a way, to capture the king on the stamped face of coins, as the first stanza hints, is a perversion of the possession that words make of the lovers and their world. Money must be spent to command its products; it perishes in itself to bring in articles of exchange, and all the king's men cannot restore it without a return of goods. In contrast, love requires that one sacrifice the world and purchase nothing with it; but paradoxically, possession of the beloved, especially as enshrined in the words of the poem, brings back the lost world itself. The sonnet too is coinage; it purchases esteem and perpetuity. It is by the hymns of lovers that readers shall find them canonized. The moment apart reduces the macrocosm outside their sanctuary to their size; the world is distilled and purified as they pull it in and epitomize it.

In this respect, poetry as a celebration of love's supposed irrelevance matches love's own retreat from the active life: it defends that retreat by a satiric devaluation of other forms of exchange and stages in it the miracle of lover's rebirth in expressive forms. Hence, just as Sterne's apparent digressions prove to be a concealed progress, the lovers' aloofness provides a model that others will consult; if they draw apart, it is only to become available.

What the beloved sometimes reveals to the awakened soul in Donne is its circuit from temporality to timelessness, or something like a prefiguration of blessedness—though not with the same aura of mystery and grandeur that Dante and Petrarch find in Beatrice and Laura. Thus

in "The Good-morrow," love is more than an emotion; it is a reconstruction of the self and a discovery of a world permeated by the sacred. Were the sacred not in it, love could not bring to itself the lost
world or stamp itself on the poet's verbal coinage for perpetual circula-
tion. The moment and the place of the awakening are intersections of
the celestial and the earthly, which is roughly equivalent to the special
moments and places in myth where epiphanies occur. Once delivered
by individual love from busy activities, lovers have no need either of
the excursions of explorers roaming the globe or the discursiveness of
the world's rational goings and comings. The miracle of love is precisely that seeing is possessing. It is effortless and exuberant.

What is the nature of the poet's own career thereby? Is it too a withdrawal that is not a withdrawal, like Theocritean pastoral or Milton's
nonpolitical politics in *Paradise Regained*? If we follow Donne's biogra-
phers, the conversion of a personally disadvantageous marriage into a
career as a poet suggests something like that, in the sense that Donne's
being waysided in one career as a courtier forwarded his other career as
a poet. However, despite the claims that he makes for love in "The
Good-morrow," "The Sunne Rising," and "The Canonization," he obviously did not finish his career with these poems, summary as he
makes them seem at the moment. Love too has a career and goes
through stages, as "Love's Growth" argues. Because life goes on, it constantly confronts new situations, such as departures ("A Valediction:
Forbidding Mourning") and deprivation ("Nocturnal"). Hence the
career of both man and poet brings changes. Ultimately for Donne it
brought a redefinition of the object of reverence. The religious poems
redefine the myth of love, or more accurately replace it, as the lover discovers that only Christ can perform the miracles that the poet of *Songs
and Sonnets* attributed to love.

"Goodfriday, 1613. Riding Westward," for instance, completely re-
defines both secular and religious careers. Donne again assumes a ri-
valry between what the poet holds sacred and the practical world, as he
does in "The Canonization." But this time, as the man of affairs goes
westward, the native motion of the soul forces it to circle back. Casting
recollection eastward to the Crucifixion, the soul finds another time still
present, at least in memory:

> Let mans Soule be a Spheare, and then, in this,
> The intelligence that moves, devotion is,
> And as the other Spheares, by being growne
> Subject to forraigne motions, lose their owne,
> And being by others hurried every day,
> Scarce in a yeare their naturall forme obey :
> Pleasure or businesse, so, our Soules admit
> For their first mover, and are whirld by it.

> Hence is't, that I am carried towards the West
> This day, when my Soules form bends toward the East.

The poem is again the ally of this apparent withdrawal from the active world: as an instrument of meditation, it draws the mind out of its westward business. It is a countermotion, a throwing back, as the soul's form and the poem's both seek their perfection in an image from another plane. That its image happens to have been historically implanted by the Incarnation enables the poem to fuse mythos and logos: its ultimate reference is divine and nontemporal, but its imagery and occasions are historical. In the more common terms of Sidney, poetry transcends history and seeks lasting forms that please the soul. Or as Bacon remarks:

> The use of this feigned history hath been to give some shadow of satisfaction to the mind of man in those points wherein the nature of things doth deny it, the world being in proportion inferior to the soul; by reason whereof there is, agreeable to the spirit of man, a more ample greatness, a more exact goodness, and a more absolute variety, than can be found in the nature of things. Therefore, because the acts or events of true history have not that magnitude which satisfieth the mind of man, poesy feigneth acts and events greater and more heroical.[23]

Both the motions of the soul and the discipline of the poem involve acts of discarding that excise all ordinary connections; most of what the traveler acquires in his westward movement must be defined as deformity, to be burned off. The act of recollecting that finds Christ on the Cross is an act of forgetting or putting aside, a retrogressive movement to essence. In facing God directly, the poet will ultimately find the original Maker's image reestablished in him:

> Burne off my rusts, and my deformity,
> Restore thine Image, so much, by thy grace,
> That thou may'st know me, and I'll turne my face.

In this variation, the myth of the eternal return counters other itineraries of the soul. However, rather than celebrating a good morrow for the soul's awakening, the poem assumes a history that still intervenes and must be recurrently faced down. The soul does not actually return to origins or abandon its westward course; it merely prepares, and offers a petition while remaining in the midst, examining its rival directions, looking toward the point at which the divine image may lift it free.

The rearward or wayward movement of thought in Donne also tracks certain currents in the history of ideas that are recognizable outside the poem. The poem's sense of the soul's form is not merely its own; it is united with that of an institution, with Easter rituals, detailed exegesis of scripture, and a legacy of attendant books, since as we know, not merely the poem but an entire way of thinking favors the digressive track away from routine business that Donne's memory takes. Yet the poem is justified as a personal expression of those fixed ideas. It establishes them in the context of a new discovery and dramatizes the moment at which a particular wayward soul gets reoriented. What the poem, as opposed to a theological treatise, offers is precisely an enacted paradigm and hence an image of apparently scattered and miscellaneous motives realigning themselves under the magnetizing force of a Christian pattern. In offering us repeatable abstractions, a treatise would be more likely to sacrifice to a systematic logos the dawning moment of intuition in which the myth is grasped. The poem seeks the living presence of the original sacrificial image in a form that will seat it in the perpetuity of art, as the sonnets of the lovers are the vehicles by which they are recurrently brought to us.

Although Yeats's juxtaposition of logos and mythos is comparable, it does not have a similar framework of doctrine to fall back upon. Also, Yeats turns the relationship between mythos and logos around: whereas Donne appears dedicated to the analytic powers of logos but subordinates them to a centralizing myth, Yeats appeals constantly to a variety of myths but remains entangled in the enumeration of historical phases and narration of topical occurrences. Even though he promises to "restore to the philosopher his mythology," he is in fact an extraordinarily historical poet who not only cites a good many actual events but constructs a systematic reading of history as a whole. For instance, by comparison to Donne's Easter return to orientation in "Goodfriday, 1613," Yeats's Easter rebellion is more caught up in political affairs than Donne is in business. Yeats insists in "Easter 1916" that the ordeal of the Dublin Post Office has so molded its participants that it has lifted them out of their habitual, casual comedy. But they do not repeat some earlier cycle as they might be supposed to do in the later Yeats. They merely contribute a page to the chronicle of modern politics. While seeking an explanation for the waste of sixteen executed people and a failed insurrection carries the poet beyond political and social surfaces, Yeats does not automatically find sure signs of an overseeing destiny. Rather, he moves from the ordinary to the aesthetic, as though the intensity of a tragic sacrifice forced events across the borderline between the muddle of history not to myth but to art.[24]

Several transforming agents stand between the event as failed politics and the event as tragedy. One is simply the form of song itself; another is nature's ceremonial and acceptable change:

> Hearts with one purpose alone
> Through summer and winter seem
> Enchanted to a stone
> To trouble the living stream.

> The horse that comes from the road,
> The rider, the birds that range
> From cloud to tumbling cloud,
> Minute by minute they change;
> A shadow of cloud on the stream
> Changes minute by minute;
> A horse-hoof slides on the brim,
> And a horse plashes within it;
> The long-legged moor-hens dive,
> And hens to moor-cocks call;
> Minute by minute they live:
> The stone's in the midst of all.

That ordinary people should become their heroic masks seems no more startling under this trope than that clouds should alter before a wind; passions of the heart are no more or less disturbing than the stone in the midst of the stream. If in fact all things proceed by contraries, as Yeats elsewhere insists, turbulence is inevitable and necessary in the order of things. It is an application of patterns generated beyond the historical process, like the time that rushes from the narrow gateway of "A Needle's Eye":

> All the stream that's roaring by
> Came out of a needle's eye;
> Things unborn, things that are gone,
> From the needle's eye still goad it on.

However, because its focus remains on a particular event and those who took part in it, "Easter 1916" does not proceed very far into myth. We do not glimpse in it, for instance, creatures like Zeus in "Leda and the Swan" or the dark shape that moves so ominously in "The Second Coming." Its conversion of the muddle into acceptable form is primarily a matter of enumeration, description, roll call, and valedictory attitude. That the poem is so self-consciously a song and so closely patterned (it is divided, for instance, into units of four lines arranged in symmetrical groups of 16, 24, 16, and 24 lines) gives it much of its detachment—whatever added distancing it finds in mythos:

> I write it out in a verse—
> MacDonagh and MacBride
> And Connolly and Pearse
> Now and in time to be,
> Wherever green is worn,
> Are changed, changed utterly:
> A terrible beauty is born.

This transformation of cataclysmic events into art is typical of other poems in which the poet remains rooted in topical affairs while suggesting those spiraling, alternating contraries that turn the larger historical wheels. Though it is seldom clear what the initiating source is (Yeats seldom deals with myths of beginning or ending, generation or apocalypse), the laws of ancients do return. He reiterates the pattern of contraries and antitheses again and again and makes the pluralism of historical institutions conform to a single dance. His panoramic view brings, if not authentic myths, at least metaphors for poetry.

One of the more remarkable examples is the "Fragment" (from *The Tower*), which gives us one of Yeats's few versions of a beginning. That he uses Genesis ironically in it, however, indicates that Eden is not a place from which all things flow but a point of reference, or a fiction by which we may judge modern reality.

> Locke sank into a swoon;
> The Garden died;
> God took the spinning-jenny
> Out of his side.

Locke is of course historical and sufficiently identifiable with the industrial revolution to contrast sharply with Adam. In the difference between them, Yeats finds basically two modes of thought, one rationalistic and the other mythic. The story of Eden is not necessarily a believed myth, but it is at least a sanctuary of the imagination. If the dream from which Keats's adamic poet awakens to find truth has not completely perished since Locke, however, it lives a precarious life in the midst of the labors of intellect and home manufacture. Whereas Adam was presumably not asked to apply his mind to practical tasks, the new age puts him in harness: when the cycle of the seasons turns, it must yield a steady flow of products.

This is of course no more than a preliminary sketch of Donne's and Yeats's handling of the tension between mythos and logos; my intent has been merely to suggest their blends of these elements and the presence of certain institutions in them, one of which is the recurrence of literary forms. The differences among poets are measurable finally only by the juxtaposition of like poems in sequence. Part of what is at issue in such a juxtaposition is how events and institutions are absorbed into larger designs—primarily linear, teleological, and derived from tradition in Donne; cyclical and personal in Yeats. Under such systems of retrieval, memory, monuments, legends, and literature represent what happens at one moment for the benefit of other moments.

II

REVIVALS AND CONTINUITY

CHAPTER 3

Poetic Recollection and the Phantomized Past

The days gone by
Return upon me almost from the dawn
Of life; the hiding-places of man's power
Open; I would approach them, but they close.
I see by glimpses now; when age comes on,
May scarcely see at all; and I would give,
While yet we may, as far as words can give,
Substance and life to what I feel, enshrining,
Such is my hope, the spirit of the Past
For future restoration.

WORDSWORTH, *The Prelude*

O NE SYMPTOM OF THE SHIFT in literature's absorption of the past that has taken place since the Renaissance is the rise of the professional writer or maker of fictions. Such a maker brings about a more decided separation of fictions from other things. As long as a modified mimetic doctrine holds and the poet's creations are presumed to be analogous to something preexistent, the historical and natural world offer themselves to the writer as his main concern. As Harry Berger, Jr., has pointed out, we can see an analogous difference in the theater's progress from the medieval cycle play to Elizabethan drama. The drama moves from what Berger calls a first world, reenacted in ritual, to a created or second world. The staging of plays symptomatically moves from the church to the church porch, then to inn yards, and finally to theaters—or from the God-made to the manmade Globe and from holy day to holiday. Accompanying that shift is a new professionalism in acting and staging and an emphasis on realistic representation, since the set-apart world of fiction has to establish its own connections to the external world by presenting it in detail. Meanwhile, the audience pays for tickets, walks into a special arena, and sits down to take in a performance by people who make a living pretending to be what they are not.[1]

As a poet who is edgy about his acceptance (such as Spenser, for instance, in *The Shepheardes Calender*) seeks to establish a name and develop a recognizable style, the fictional work comes to be shaped less by traditional norms and more by characteristics that will set the present performance apart. The interceding ego of the writer is noticeable not only in Spenser, but in Milton, Donne, Jonson, George Herbert, Henry Vaughan, Robert Herrick, and others. However, these Renaissance poets, and some dramatists and fiction writers as well, manage to negotiate their way back into the fold. Their subjects include common Christian and Platonist types and classical topics; and their genres are more or less commonly accepted and recognizable, though they experiment with them freely. We cannot, of course, say as much of the romantic poets, who recognize the problem of subjectivity, isolation, and personal as opposed to collective time. When days gone by return to Wordsworth almost from the dawn of life, he means *his* life; he seeks for the secrets of man's nature in his own recollections. The romantic no longer expects his poems to join a community of classics. The collective past is always there, and it returns unavoidably in one form or another; but the question is what to make of it.

Actually, the problem of gaining enough freedom from the burden of the past to write as one wishes is an old one and is related to the poet's freedom from affairs of the day as well. Pastoral again provides convenient examples because of its habit of sealing off an artificial, expressly recreative world wherein the poet-shepherd is momentarily able to avoid the responsibilities of the bard. For instance, in the First Eclogue, Virgil grants the placid Tityrus a certain charmed circle amid a course of troubling events that stem from the Roman capital. The capacity of the poet to maintain himself apart is challenged, however, by the traffic on the road that runs by. Meliboeus, who has been forced out of his homeland and now makes up part of that traffic, has not been so fortunate as Tityrus:

> Meliboeus
> Tityrus, here you loll, your slim reed-pipe serenading
> The woodland spirit beneath a spread of sheltering beech,
> While I must leave my home place, the fields so dear to me.
> I'm driven from my home place: but you can take it easy
> In shade and teach the woods to repeat "Fair Amaryllis."[2]

The decisions that lie back of the evictions, like those that have saved Tityrus, are social; they stem from the collective order of the city. Thus on the one hand, the poet-shepherd seeks to remain aloof from a stream of events that spreads from Rome to Africa, Britain, Scythia, and "the chalky spate of the Oxus." On the other hand, what the eclogue itself concerns is not the recreative moment or the quality of the free life but the challenge of the historical process.

The combination of romance and pastoral in works such as Sidney's *Arcadia* and Spenser's legend of Courtesy points up similar dangers to the equilibrium between the poet as a singer, apart from his surroundings, and the unavoidable intrusions of history. The poet cannot remain a Colin Clout piping on a mountain if he requires an audience; and he also needs patronage. The poet who relies on his craft for a living, as Theocritus complains in the sixteenth idyll and Spenser in the October eclogue of *The Shepheardes Calender*, appreciates rewards as well as the next man. And in serving highly placed men, he cannot avoid singing of heroic deeds; in offering panegyrics for princes, he automatically takes sides in certain struggles. Hence the mythic hankerings of a Colin Clout must be set aside or exploited to meet the requirements of praise laid upon the professional poet. To put it another way, try as it might, even pastoral, the most escapist of poetic kinds, has difficulty developing as a self-contained mode following its own historical succession and its own subset of rules and regulations. As part of the times, it carries the burden of the times. The poet's developing career and the entire chain of productions of poets of like kind are influenced by the overall progress of the social order and its specific problems of the moment. Behind Virgil's career and Spenser's we hear the drum of Roman and Tudor empires, both Troynovants in their time; behind Tityrus we catch the rumble of those not-so-distant disturbances that have exiled Meliboeus from his *dulcia arva* and will send him to the remotest provinces on the Roman map. Hence with or without an ideology that makes his dreaming responsible to the world of affairs, the poet of whatever period or place finds himself burdened with a double historical load—the legacy of expressive forms within which he works and the world he accounts for outside his door or in history books.

However, it remains true that the nature of the historical burden and ways of handling it have shifted significantly since the Renaissance. Reinforced by dogma and a Platonist confidence in universals, the Renaissance poet reengaged key events of the past in a special way. By resetting portions of the past in the present, poetry shared in a general redemption of time. Thus in Donne, Herbert, Milton, Fulke Greville, Sidney, Spenser, Richard Crashaw, Thomas Traherne, Vaughan, and others, poetry sought, at times at least, to repossess a divine presence and traces of a providential purpose that extended from beginning to end and clarified the historical world between. That repossession was assisted by written records and documents. As far back as the beginning, the past was articulate; human kind sprang forth in Eden with an intact language and was summed up in a reliable book that did not presuppose ever-receding cycles of lost civilization, as modern archaelogy does. This reduction of the world to writing did not automatically enable the Renaissance poet to integrate historical and mythic functions, but it helped, and it chastened his independence even while it sustained him. The historical record pointed decisively to a complete cycle from the golden age to the present and thereby established itself in a mythic totality of which he became a part as soon as he discovered his vocation. Nature itself was suspended between historical and mythic functions as a secondary or ancillary book, often referring to the historical Christ, for instance, as the center of all books.[3]

The appeal to the Muses and the problematic setting forth of the writer on new enterprises were crucial reengagements, in the moment of writing, of that general order and its sanctions. Beginning outside, the poet moves inside the tradition in the act of writing. Thus in *Arcades, L'Allegro, Il Penseroso, Comus,* and *Lycidas,* Milton moves from the local, individual, and natural to the archetypal, from the historical to the mythic. He does not claim for nature absolute powers of revelation; but groves and landscapes do prepare for the manifestation of special influences, "Sent by some spirit to mortals good, / Or th'unseen Genius of the Wood." In fact, the poet makes his deepest historic and prophetic discoveries in the book of nature under the spell of ancient haunts of Muses. He is specially gifted to make those discoveries, and once he does so, he rejoins his predecessors. Even when he eventually seeks out a hermitage in *Il Penseroso* he may sit therein and

> rightly spell
> Of every Star that Heav'n doth shew,
> And every Herb that sips the dew;
> Till old experience do attain
> To something like Prophetic strain.

Equally telling about the historical process and its integration with nature, but more outside its normal records, is Marvell's reading of signs in "Bermudas," "The Garden," *Upon Appleton House,* "Clorinda and Damon," *The First Anniversary,* and other poems. Although Marvell finds nature a barrier between the sensory man and the divine in "A Dialogue between the Resolved Soul, and Created Pleasure" and "On a Drop of Dew," on other occasions the poet discovers strong signs of providence in nature's bounty. He receives hieroglyphic transcriptions of the past from the forest:

> Out of these scatter'd *Sibyls* leaves
> Strange *Prophecies* my Phancy weaves:
> And in one History consumes,
> Like *Mexique Paintings,* all the *Plumes.*
> What *Rome, Greece, Palestine,* ere said

> I in this light *Mosaick* read.
> Thrice happy he who, not mistook
> Hath read in *Natures mystick Book.*
> (*Upon Appleton House,* 577-584)

Both nature and sacred script are analogous to the permanence of art, as the mosaic leaves are like both paintings and testaments. Thus if Marvell cuts easily through the trauma of a burdensome, anxiety-ridden past, it is because the past dissolves and reconstitutes itself outside the library and outside monumental art, in the figuration of leaves or a forested icon of blessedness. Not only is the book of nature delightful, but it is teasingly mysterious and gives the poet as intermediary a function that salvages his vocation. His language in turn may be oblique, his anticipation raised to a pitch of surmise. Marvell may still have literary predecessors even at this moment, then, but the function of his wanderer's waywardness—his laziness or otium, his casual play of "phancy"—is to allow him to dodge the more serious matters of allusion and plagiarism. Behind this mask, he is delightfully independent and at one with both nature and the grandeur of high civilization.

How Marvell intends this consumption of history by nature is suggested again in "Upon the Hill and Grove at Bill-borough" where the grove absorbs the military exploits of Fairfax and places them under bark:

> For they ('tis credible) have sense,
> As We, of Love and Reverence,
> And underneath the Courser Rind
> The *Genius* of the house do bind.
> Hence they successes seem to know,
> And in their *Lord's* advancement grow;
> But in no Memory were seen
> As under this so streight and green.
> (49-56)

In this commerce between great lords and their trees, the topographical poem is an easy-going cousin of epic and the romantic nature excursion—easy-going in the sense that it does not drive a wedge between human institutions and the bardic figure. The readable open book stands between. The poet locates his job in his valedictory function. However, in the moving, whispering breeze of "Upon the Hill and Grove at Bill-borough" and in the oracles that trees speak is perhaps a hint of ghostly presences from the past that romanticism will take up, and a suggestion in Fairfax's retreat of a loss of connection with current affairs. In Marvell's imagery, nature moves closer than before to the interior landscape of memory and mental echo, and his playfulness underscores the fictive pretense of treating nature in this way at all.

Nature's blending of the historical and the divine did not come to an end with Marvell or Milton, nor did the poet's reintegration with previous makers of books. English topography for some time served comfortably enough beside history and scripture in a general association of monumental and sacred matters. Pope, for instance, exploits likenesses between Eden and Windsor Forest to read local events as part of the typology of sacred history. The poet's historical vocation is to interpret the script of rivers, plains, hills, and woods. That script has nothing arbitrary about it in Pope's eyes: the poet traverses the present landscape as though crossing the past. A perfect harmony reigns between the mind as a generalizing instrument, the laws of nature, and their originating power. Myth and logic are united; both descend far enough into the details of history and landscape to hand the poet all the signifiers of the Creator he needs. The result is a kind of palimpsest or locodescriptive technique that carries the imprint simultaneously of immediate time and a deeper time, local place names and typical repetitions of a common tradition.

Among other things, these are examples of the imposing of governing rules from one institution (religion for instance) on others (nature, science, descriptive poetics) that have a conservative braking effect on change. The patterns of recurrence of both medieval and Renaissance poetry derive from theological and philosophical universals in which local phenomena are rigorously interpreted according to reigning principles handed down from Plato, Saint Augustine, Plotinus, Saint Bonaventura, and scripture. For the traditionalist poet—even if he does conceive of himself as an independent, professional writer—going backward is virtually equivalent to pulling historical records into poetic form.

In sum, let us imagine the relationships between history and myth in earlier periods to be something like this:

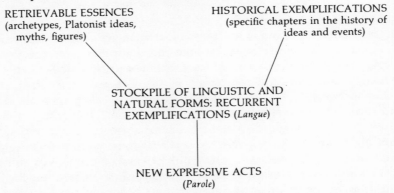

RETRIEVABLE ESSENCES
(archetypes, Platonist ideas,
myths, figures)

HISTORICAL EXEMPLIFICATIONS
(specific chapters in the history of
ideas and events)

STOCKPILE OF LINGUISTIC AND
NATURAL FORMS: RECURRENT
EXEMPLIFICATIONS (*Langue*)

NEW EXPRESSIVE ACTS
(*Parole*)

As I have indicated, even the first tier of retrievable essences is not preverbal to the Renaissance poet, though it contains ideas, myths, and archetypes of such force as to be thought privileged beyond any particular expression. Just so, an ardent neo-Platonist considers the One and the Beautiful, and a Christian considers the Word, which no single book of gospel, poem, or exegesis has totally in hand. The special force of those privileged centers carries into chronicle events and into less privileged types that partly veil the Word. As *Upon Appleton House* suggests, they carry into the leaves of the forest where those who are thrice blessed may interpret them. It is primarily through a culture's intermediary texts—its treatises, poems, and classics (which of course contain much more than first-tier realities)—that a poet receives his past and finds his identity as someone justified to stand before an audience.

I have dwelt upon Renaissance poetics primarily to suggest that point and to get some comparative leverage for understanding the romantic difficulty in establishing such a collective history, and hence in justifying the poetic vocation. We find that difficulty even in such poets as Coleridge and Shelley, who believed firmly enough in Christian and in Platonist universals, respectively. The problem with romantic reconstructions of either a real or an imagined past of tangible, distanced, intelligible institutions lies in the general discrediting of those second-level forms in the stockpile of conventions.[4] The Renaissance poet gets hold of both retrievable essences and historical exemplifications primarily through expressive means of the culture—in the common topics, emblems, literary forms, and readings of nature. The collective wisdom of the classics, of science, the church fathers, and of philosophers gives him these forms, as do poetic predecessors. All those sources are more dubious for the romantics. This may be one reason for the peculiar ghostliness of the romantic past, which is the phenomenon I am setting out to explain by roundabout. In some of the romantics, the first tier itself becomes problematic; in Keats, for instance, it drops out of sacred books and their hermeneutic traditions and defined doctrines and falls into the realm of dream. In other romantics as well, the second tier loses ground by comparison to its status among the neoclassicist library of masters, in whom the principles of nature and the supernatural are dressed to advantage and formalized.

Divergences of Myth, History, and Nature in Shelley

Whereas Renaissance poets have confidence in at least scripture and nature and manage to associate local deities, estates, and even political figures with them, Wordsworth writes concerning records and English history :

> 'Tis true, the history of our native land—
> With those of Greece compared and popular Rome,

> And in our high-wrought modern narratives
> Stript of their harmonising soul, the life
> Of manners and familiar incidents—
> Had never much delighted me. And less
> Than other intellects had mine been used
> To lean upon extrinsic circumstance
> Of record or tradition
> (*The Prelude*, VIII.617–625)

What does offer delight are those local legends and landmarks that are still evident in the landscape and seem almost an extension of one's personal past. They are a form of reminiscence that stimulates the imagination and yields some concrete imagery. As Georges Poulet remarks concerning the onset of personal recollection and the transcendent powers that break into it: "Begotten by feeling, imbued more and more with feeling, the thought of the century which is ending becomes more and more apt to discover in the depths of its vibrant actuality the interflowing images of reminiscence and premonition. Always isolated in the moment which gives it form, it seems this moment incessantly invaded, overwhelmed, transfigured by states of mind from beyond." Those luminous spots of personal remembrance that punctuate time do so almost in defiance of communal holdings; and since duration "based on affective memory" offers little that can be held to, every moment becomes potentially revolutionary. "Romantic nostalgia," as Poulet continues, "appears thus as the forlorn desire of a life that the mind can never give itself fully in any moment and that, notwithstanding, it sees from afar, there, beyond both ends of the moment, in the elusive realm of duration." To the normal "sadness of the past" that this brings may be added "the anguish of the future": "And so there opens, at the center of man's being, in the actual feeling of his existence, an insupportable void which real existence borders on every side. . . . The romantic effort to form itself a being out of presentiment and memory ends in the experience of a double tearing of the self."[5] The linearity of personal experience thus becomes insurmountable, as Wordsworth once distant from the shores of childhood cannot return in the same way that Milton or Herbert can to the Word or the racial origins of Adam himself.

If both romantic and postromatic poets have difficulty binding themselves to common continuity, it is partly because the poet has become aware of the unpoetic factuality of historiography in ways that would not have occurred to Milton, Marvell, or Spenser. The poet's deeper past is not publicly authenticated in Blake, Shelley, Coleridge, Wordsworth, or Keats, or again in Tennyson, Yeats, Stevens, Frost, or Eliot (among others). The personal past, which has its own sort of authenticity, cannot be readily linked to racial history as Milton conceives of it. If the poet offers portraits of originating gods, they are likely to be obviously fictive, like Endymion, Hyperion, Apollo, or Prometheus.

Why this separation of second-tier institutions and chronicle history from first-tier essences? We get some idea from the disagreement between Shelley and Peacock over the nature of history and the poet's relation to it; this quarrel, as I interpret it, points up the separation of the historical from the mythic and the poetic. Certainly Shelley's dispute with Peacock (whom he does not answer directly) hinges on the character of historical progress and the poet's handling of it.

Peacock's charge is basically that poetry began as defective history writing: assigned in primitive societies to celebrate famous deeds and perpetuate the fame of leaders (who not incidentally provided room and board), the poet was originally a kind of high-toned propagandist who enabled the barbarian warrior, once he became a chief or king, "to disseminate the fame of his achievements and the extent of his possessions." This organ of publicity and fame was liquor-inspired, skilled in panegyric and "brief historical notices" and tumid with hyperbole. Having no rivals in command of the facts, he reigned alone, taking to himself the functions not only of history writing but of science and theology. But the areas left for poetry shrank as science and true historiography laid its myths to rest; and now the poet has become so separated from his own times that "the march of his intellect is like that of a crab, backward."[6]

Cut off as they were from science, industry, and public institutions, Peacock's contemporary poets gave him some reason to believe that the past they proposed was pure invention, and in at least this much, Shelley does not take issue. In his version of the poet's past, the poet does not seek to be a spokesman for human achievements, either identifiable from records or exemplified in current matters. Instead, he traces an invisible and essentially eventless spirit whose traces are beyond most forms of discourse. Such timeless abstractions as liberty, truth, and beauty are either disembodied or touch down historically here and there by no determinable logic and certainly by no principle of cause and effect. In bringing eternity into time through his contact with such terms, the poet in effect neutralizes time's linearity and works counter to those progressive myths of fall and racial redemption that occupy Renaissance poetry. Although poets do point toward new societies and are "the institutors of laws, and the founders of civil society, and the inventors of the arts of life," they build those future projections not out of a demonstrable historical logic but by a "certain propinquity with the beautiful and the true, that partial apprehension of the agencies of the invisible world which is called religion." The act of composition is itself an extrapolation by which beauty is revealed in its paradigmatic essence. The poet has no need for stories any more than he has for facts: "Time, which destroys the beauty and the use of the story of particular facts, stripped of the poetry which should invest them, augments that of poetry, and forever develops new and wonderful applications of the eternal truth it contains." The sort of history that Peacock has in mind is thus to Shelley merely a "catalogue of detached facts, which have no other connexion than time, place, circumstance, cause, and effect."[7]

This is not to say that Shelley assigns poetry no truly historiographical functions. He salvages enough of Milton and enough of the Renaissance defense of poetry to think that poetry catches from the record at least scattered images of the eternal. Homer's epoch and the century preceding the death of Socrates left illuminating records, for instance, records "stamped . . . visibly with the image of the divinity in man." In fact, not documents as such but "poetry alone, in form, in action, and in language has rendered this epoch memorable above all others, and the storehouse of examples to everlasting time" (Brett-Smith, p. 34). The final answer to any connection between the poet and the historian is that what the poet finds memorable, by his very act of discovery, is liberated from its setting, even if it initially resembled chronicle fact. Proper names and singular objects mean little to the poet, who deals with exemplars. Nothing could say more clearly that the intermediate tier of social and linguistic forms, which used to deliver news of the deeper past, has been discredited; it interferes with visionary perception. Only when the poet takes leave of the ordinary do familiar appearances become wonderful and his paradise arises "as out of the wrecks of Eden" (pp. 44–45). Poetry then "arrests the vanishing apparitions which haunt the interlunations of life, and veiling them, or in language or in form, sends them forth among mankind" (p. 55).

Despite these ringing phrases, however, the poet's capacity to recall past moments of glory, or capture present ones, is not beyond question for Shelley. Indeed, actual poems are but a "feeble shadow" of their originating inspiration. The words of the poetic record are not, as it turns out, real poems at all but deformations of unworded perception and "vanishing apparitions." Having undermined all other records and historical remains of the spirit, Shelley thus comes very close to making poetry, too, a collection of traces betrayed by its own imagery. In contrast, the radiance of disembodied intellect is an unworded blankness, an unstoried eternity.

Shelley's position on the trackless, arbitrary descent of Ideas from an atemporal realm is extreme among the romantics, but it points up a typical severance of levels. Since visionary moments come strictly to individuals and not to collective societies—or come to societies *through* gifted individuals—it is easier for the poet to discover other privileged receivers than for whole societies to restore some golden past or take a definite course toward its future restoration. Only insofar as the poet succeeds in propagating his vision can he gather sufficient momentum to bring history into line, and no poet has that demonstrable power. Where Shelley's fellow Platonists Spenser and Marvell feel some tension between the activist and the poet in retirement, Shelley so reshapes that tension that the poet has no legitimate competition among historical figures at all—as he does in Spenser's queen and Marvell's Fairfax and Cromwell. In this respect, Shelley takes an antitemporal stance as extreme as Milton's in *Paradise Regained*—except that he does not propose a Christocentric location in which glory and the Creator's image are established on historical footing, to be repeated later in disciplined imitations.

Wordsworth and the Ghost behind the Object

As Shelley's "apparitions" suggest, the poet's "interlunations of life" are haunted by vacancy, just as, in looking forward, poets are the hierophants of an unapprehended inspiration, mirrors for gigantic shadows. The confidence of other romantics in concrete images and specific temporal moments is obviously stronger than Shelley's. But each poet has his own problems in joining the lower tier of personal experience to the upper tier of transcendent principles without going through history's stockpile of intermediate forms, types, and conventions. Wordsworth, for instance, seeks avatars frequently in single, discrete objects, as Frederic Garber reminds us,[8] and these can be far from self-explanatory. Certainly nature is not part of an ancillary book in which a providential intent can be deciphered by an informed initiate. In fact, paradoxically, the stronger the object's singularity, the more forcefully it sounds the depths of absence, just as the solitary reaper, because she is separate and alone, conjures remote geographical regions at the edge of consciousness. Actually, two sorts of absence can often be sorted out when Wordsworth isolates proper names, objects, or places—one recollective and the other transcendentalized. In "Tintern Abbey," the first of these takes the form of memory's images, which thoughtless youth·has absorbed through the unconscious eye; the other appears as a pantheistic spirit locatable not merely in that specific setting and not exclusively in nature at all but in all things, and simultaneously in the recollective mind.

Recollection and transcendence are of course closely related. Wordsworth sometimes feels, in observing his own creative processes, that only what is past is truly haunting and truly transcendent. As he remarks in a poetic fragment, "I look into past times as prophets look /

Into futurity." The parallel that the "as" assumes between forward and backward perception is telling, as the context suggests.

> For me,
> When it chanced that having wandered long
> Among the mountains, I have waked at last
> From dream of motion in some spot like this,
> Shut out from man, some region—one of those
> That hold by an inalienable right
> An independent Life, and seem the whole
> Of nature and of unrecorded time;
> If, looking round, I have perchance perceived
> Some vestiges of human hands, some stir
> Of human passion, they to me are sweet
> As lightest sunbreak, or the sudden sound
> Of music to a blind man's ear who sits
> Alone and silent in the summer shade.
> They are as a creation in my heart;
> I look into past times as prophets look
> Into futurity, a [?] of life runs back
> Into dead years, the [?] of thought
> The [   ] spirit of philosophy
> Leads me through moods of sadness to delight.

Ernest de Selincourt speculates that these lines might have been intended as an introduction to "Michael" or may have been "an 'Extempore Effusion' on a theme dear to Wordsworth."[9] Whatever their potential use, they clearly suggest that important to the wandering poet, as to the prophet, is a removal of limiting evidence: both past and future contain hints of transcendent and deep-rooted causes that enter the temporal stream from outside—causes that leave traces not for antiquarian science but for the reconstructor of legends working with relics and symbols. Both past and future extract from the poet an impassioned style and a dramatic approach to "higher truths," which are neither totally embodied nor totally disembodied. In this respect, Wordsworth does not follow Shelley in discrediting words and images, though he doubts that words can fully give "substance and life" to "the spirit of the past." Instead, the poet searches for tangible monuments, and if he is fortunate, nature, history, and art collaborate in producing a legend or the equivalent to an epiphany. In this personal mythologizing of a region (which Stevens' *Comedian as the Letter C* attempts quite differently), the communion of scene and heart recreates paradise and undoes the preterite: the past falls into place with the impact of surmised things to come.

Wordsworth's reading of the past as futurity is basically a way of perceiving traces in an unscripted landscape, in states of heightened receptivity among objects that are always there but usually seem commonplace. (How and toward what end the poet seeks the ghostly past in such traces has perhaps been best explained by Geoffrey Hartman in *The Unmediated Vision*.) The past in one sense merely carries us a step toward a renewed realization of the tension between surfaces and an oceanic calm underneath. It is a portal. To put it another way, calm is to the ribbed, divided, many-colored surface of a landscape as present detail is to generalized recollection; or again, as the senses are to the inner spirit and mind that carry recollection. Saying that one is particular and the other universal, however, does not quite get at the full truth, which requires also a distinction between kinds of cognition and kinds of expressive modes. Thus the senses, the present, and the surfaces of landscapes are deliverable in the descriptive accuracy of noun and adjective, in placement, boundary, and definition, as these are part of the knowability we ascribe to nature.

But they do not always reach as far into the knowable as the spirit wishes. The poet has within him a deep felt need not merely for the classifications and relational acts of analysis that reason and science perform (within second-tier mediations) but for unity and a sense of moving forces operating on another plane. To arrive at these, he must translate surfaces into signs not of a created order but of an underlying essence that must be seized as a totality. Exact naming would dishonor that essence. The most the poet can say about it is that the faculty best suited to discern it is imagination, assisted by memory. Imagination requires assistance from memory precisely because nature has appeared more forcefully to the poet in his youth, in certain localities that he must now revisit. Transcendence must be approached through reverberations. Hence to some extent, the poet is imprisoned in an adjective-dominated description: he cannot reach his goal except through the enumeration of recollected scenic elements, which set him off and going. A past incident or visitation is an arch or threshold to pass through. What comes forward in the right epiphanic moment, as one passes through the entry after wandering aimlessly, sleepwalking among mountains, is an unwilled, unpremeditated orientation.

Wordsworth's is essentially a new mode of retrospection, then, in which the first time around, experience is incomplete. At a certain stage, time and place are remote enough not to dominate, and the poet then finds "types and symbols of eternity" or "characters of the great apocalypse" in the measured distance.

Unfortunately, what to prophecy would be a rising rhythm becomes, in recollection, a decline or perhaps a ghostly disappearance, or at best, as in the Intimations ode, a mixture of blessings and losses in an elegiac benediction. Certainly, personal recollection is not easily connected with documented history, though that is a slightly different problem. A landscape here and now draws the poet aside from the collective course that seems to provide substance and verification for one's surmises about the past and its privileged moments. He is not directly answerable to empire but is perpetually provincial, or on the margin. Epic he reduces from an account of public power to the cycle from youth to lost or impaired imagination. Again, one's immediate poem demonstrates not the founding of civilizations but the return of a personal past. It constitutes the poet's only historical document, the only really privileged text. In terms of the waywardness of poetry, the journey into one's own past is an excursion of great length and a pause in midcareer to get one's bearings. If such excursions turn out to be central and not peripheral it is because they make their own orientation; they do not discover it in a fund of experience matured elsewhere. Thus the poet's impaired state in London shows him to be relatively crippled and ineffective at the capital, when he is caught up in movements; his moments apart, in provinces and remote places, are his best. Even so, he cannot really be satisfied with autobiographical narrative. He yearns to stretch memory into history, which is one of the things that legends begin to do. Insofar as all men are similar, his personal experience can also be representative; but even beyond that part-for-whole epitomizing, he seeks specific monumentalized links with fragments of the European heritage.

No single statement of Wordsworth's retrospective inclinations does justice to all these ramifications, but another variant deserves attention here before we look at a poem or two. In the well-known passage on recollection in "Preface to Lyrical Ballads," poetry is said to take its origin "from emotion recollected in tranquility: the emotion is contemplated till, by a species of reaction the tranquility gradually disappears, and an emotion, kindred to that which was before the subject of contemplation, is gradually produced, and does itself actually exist in the mind. In this mood successful composition generally begins." By making the poet's own rekindled feeling the generative moment of poetry, Wordsworth suggests that what counts in recollection is an internal chemistry by which primary experience is transformed. As though by an organic process, words replace sensory and affective materials without passing through dependence on other poets, methodical thought, or the training one has received in rhetoric and poetics in school. The new feeling simply filters into the shape left by vacated old feeling, as minerals replace the substance of bone in forming fossils. This is of course not a theory of the past or its redemption but a description of the creative process. But it suggests the coalescence in poetry of separate points in the chronological spectrum and a congress of universal feelings that the poet shares with his former self and with readers. Wordsworth leaves to our speculation what may be different about that recollection. That the event is past, however, is crucial to the evocation of the new feeling, because in composition a poet who treats of "absent things as if they were present" does so not by pretending that no interval has come between but by exploiting whatever interval there is. He recaptures in altered form an experience that a reader whose "mind be sound and vigorous" can repeat through the medium of words.[10] A poet who is distinguishable from other men by a "greater promptness to think and feel without immediate external excitement" is singularly equipped for that resurrection.[11]

Several instances point up the difficult suturing that Wordsworth undertook in bringing together old and new feeling, local chronicles (often of a more or less folkloric nature), and personal experience. It is a suturing both like and unlike Milton's. As the tutelary guardian and exponent of sacred places, the Miltonic poet follows the office of a mediator and celebrant. He may link local powers and deities (such as the Countess Dowager of Derby in *Arcades*) to the force that moves the spheres; he may return Lycidas, now a type of the resurrection, as a guardian genius of the local shore; or he may find spiritual paradigms in the distances of the scriptural past. None of these sorts of historical and local placement does Wordsworth seriously attempt. In *The Prelude*, recounting an earlier search for a poetic subject, he toys momentarily with the past subjects that attracted his predecessors and thinks naturally of Milton and Spenser:

> Time, place, and manners do I seek, and these
> Are found in plenteous store, but nowhere such
> As may be singled out with steady choice;
> No little band of yet remembered names
> Whom I, in perfect confidence, might hope
> To summon back from lonesome banishment,
> And make them dwellers in the hearts of men
> Now living, or to live in future years.
> Sometimes the ambitious Power of choice, mistaking
> Proud spring-tide swellings for a regular sea,
> Will settle on some British theme, some old
> Romantic tale by Milton left unsung;
> More often turning to some gentle place
> Within the groves of Chivalry, I pipe
> To shepherd swains, or seated harp in hand,
> Amid reposing knights by a river side
> Or fountain, listen to the grave reports
> Of dire enchantments faced and overcome
> By the strong mind, and tales of warlike feats.
> (*The Prelude*, I.158–176)

But clearly none of these subjects would have suited what one thinks of as typical Wordsworthian revisitation. "Tintern Abbey," the Intimations ode, the Lucy poems, "Michael," and other poems deal with moments when expectations and immediate joy or love have passed (or are about to pass) and must be experienced as loss—as "the memory of what has been / And never more will be." Nature in general, on the other hand, is "always," not "then" or "to be." In scenes of beauty, the poet is reminded both of the sublimity that resides in it and the passing of those moments when he had readier access to that sublimity. Where the common materials of nature and religion enter, they are merely aspects of recollective complexity or dimensions of a cognitive layering.

Perhaps the best single example, especially to set beside the groves of Marvell and Milton, is "Yew-Trees."[12] Rather than considering "Tintern Abbey" or the Intimations ode as complete statements of his theory of recollection, I settle on this lesser poem because it does not proceed too quickly to its first-tier speculations. It pauses on local historicity and suggests the intervention of an intermediate national history of a kind Wordsworth ponders in the little band of names he might summon back in the passage from The Prelude. It thus affords an opportunity to see the poet deploy deeper times beyond the personal past in a landscape that supplies the monuments and legends that the prophetic past requires. In brief, "Yew-Trees" does not translate its ghostly half presences into intimations of a spirit so infused in all things as to put aside all problems of temporal separation and interval.

The suggestion of an eventful national history in the yew tree of Lorton Vale makes it specifically monumental, but this memorability of the tree's past is also contested by a deeply rooted melancholy and a sense that the events of nations are now distant echoes. Though not a whispering historian of the sort that Marvell's grove is, the Lorton Vale yew is ancient enough to have furnished

> weapons for the bands
> Of Umfraville or Percy ere they marched
> To Scotland's heaths; or those that crossed the sea
> And drew their sounding bows at Azincour,
> Perhaps at earlier Crecy, or Poictiers.

I agree with Riffaterre that these names are not in themselves significant except as they suggest the possibility of things specifically memorable (whereas some general term like "ancient battles" would not). But at the same time, these particular names are full of tradition (as Gene Ruoff has pointed out) and are part of a national history that an informed audience recognizes. They fill out a rhetoric of praise that belies the solitude and discreteness of the surviving tree: that something has lasted in addition to it changes the reception of a text that sketches an implicit map of Europe and a temporal chart of England. Although we do not know their names, quite literal ghosts may hover around the tree, much as the spirit of Greek antiquity once hovered about the marbles, schools, and wandering rhapsodists that Wordsworth finds remarkable in *The Excursion* (in a passage that may have had some influence on Keats's view of the Grecian urn[13]):

> a SPIRIT hung,
> Beautiful region! o'er thy towns and farms,
> Statues and temples, and memorial tombs;
> And emanations were perceived; and acts
> Of immortality, in Nature's course,
> Exemplified by mysteries, what were felt
> As bonds, on grave philosopher imposed
> And armed warrior; and in every grove
> A gay or pensiv2 tenderness prevailed,
> When piety more awful had relaxed.
>   (IV.735–744)

If warriors, philosophers, poets, and priests are to be drawn together, something of longevity and centralizing authority must hold their lingering spirits to the locality. Wordsworth thus celebrates the continuous life that endures in places of local genius despite the "blind walk of mortal accident." But this specificity of historical people and places raises immediately a lament for transience. While that life is "From diminution safe and weakening age," man himself "grows old and dwindles and decays":

> And countless generations of mankind
> Depart; and leave no vestige where they trod.
>   (IV.761–762)

"Yew-Trees has a little of that lament for transience as well. In the presence of a tree that Wordsworth surmises must have been alive in the Christian age and perhaps before the Flood, endurance reminds him of the perishability of other things.

What strikes him more forcefully about the grove, as opposed to the Lorton Vale yew alone, however, is the holiness that comes of perpetuity and the accumulation of spirits that have gathered around it. The ghosts of this particular place (unlike the pageant of warriors of "An Evening Walk" and Percy's troop) are not really historic, and in fact they quickly give way to generalized shapes of allegory and fantasy— Fear, Hope, Silence, Foresight, Death, Time—at the opposite end of the linguistic scale from "Percy" and "Azincour." Unlike monuments built to commemorate specific achievements, the yews of Borrowdale draw the poet toward an inhuman grandeur and abstraction. Perhaps even more than transience, these wash out the present and disconnect it from the specific past. What the grove destroys in fact is high noon and the acuteness of specificity. The instant in which the observing "I" might be expected to exist most fully lapses into vagueness. The grove has the power always to be there, but it is never entirely there at any one time; it exists in its total span, stretching toward an unstoried eternity, almost in defiance of linear time, as Gene Ruoff suggests. Wordsworth appropriately finishes the poem with the sounds of a mountain stream "murmuring from Glaramara's inmost caves," fading from distinctness, echoing and reechoing in sympathy with the temporal distances of the trees.

Echoes are important in another way as well—echoes not of events on distant battlefields but of literary forms and particularly of Milton's descriptions of Eden and the wilderness.[14] These echoes, too, tend to make the "I" of the poem less precise. Actually, we hear reminders in the style not of Milton directly but of Milton through his eighteenth-century variants, which impose still another layer of pastness on the poem:

> Huge trunks! and each particular trunk a growth
> Of intertwisted fibres serpentine
> Up-coiling, and inveterately convolved;
> Nor uninformed with Phantasy, and looks
> That threaten the profane.

These stylistic ghosts, too, are a source of implicit melancholy. Where some allusions bridge distances between poems, the sounds of Edward Young, James Thomson, and Milton come forth as though extracted not by the landscape but by a shelf of accumulated expectations. The effect of all phases of the past—the fields of Azincour, the abstractness of Silence, Foresight, Death, and the verbal echoes—is paradoxically to fulfill one aspect of the poet's need (his wish for depth and wide circumference) while depleting another (his need for personal centrality as an observer). Ironically, where a Renaissance poet might think of nature as a book and read all that *"Rome, Greece, Palestine* ere said" in its mosaic of leaves, Wordsworth tries to maintain the independence of nature for its own sake only to surrender it to stylized language; nature is not a book, merely bookish.

This intrusion of past styles suggests that we should give more than passing importance to the apparent drop-in that Wordsworth allows verbal mediation in *The Prelude:*

> and I would give,
> While yet we may, as far as words can give,
> Substance and life to what I feel, enshrining,
> Such is my hope, the spirit of the Past.
> (XII.282–285)

It is up to the poet to give substance and life not to things themselves but to what he feels in their presence. But words may not be equal to the task. They must be wrapped around the subject ("inveterately convolved") like the figures and icons that adorn Stevens' rock:

> In this plenty, the room makes meanings of the rock,
> Of such mixed motion and such imagery
> That its barrenness becomes a thousand things
>
> And so exists no more.[15]

Wordsworth has cured the barrenness of the trees at the expense of the self whose new symbols and variants on old ones should yield the joy of making and recapturing.

Keats's Paradigms and Chronicles

Unlike Wordsworth, Keats turns frequently to imagined historical settings for embodiments of what amount to personal first principles. That embodiment is strangely tangible and sensuous on the one hand and illusory on the other; it registers with all due particularity on the senses but has the fragility of dream and visionary pageant.

No poem is more bewitching in its illustration of that paradox than *The Eve of St. Agnes*. Its medieval ambience is as vital to love's coming forth from dream as are the eve's magical rites. But both of these eventually prove to be merely stages to be cast aside. As the poem separates the living from the dead and the half dead, Madeline and Porphyro pass into the enchantments of a special world beyond our seeing. Like Wordsworth's better moments of recollection, their retreat is essentially private: it requires the abandoning of parents and the chivalric world of the castle. However, even as the poem lets the lovers escape, it dwells on the cold ashes of the Beadsman, the deformed face of Angela, and the strewn bodies of the warrior guests, and hence on the historical distance between us and the legend. The physical burden that settles upon the insensitive guests of the Baron represents an unredeemable shell of history.

From the reader's standpoint, an analogous retraction takes place upon the departure of the lovers as he finds confirmed the purely fictive and paradigmatic nature of the romance, and in this respect Keats shares in Wordsworth's phantomizing of the past. He clearly cannot carry the lovers through marriage, children, and a comfortable old age in Italy; as they depart for warm southern moors, hoping to find immunity from the perils of the wind-haunted castle, they become distant spirits:

> They glide, like phantoms, into the wide hall;
> Like phantoms, to the iron porch, they glide;
> Where lay the Porter, in uneasy sprawl,
> With a huge empty flaggon by his side:

> The wakeful bloodhound rose, and shook his hide,
> But his sagacious eye an inmate owns:
> By one, and one, the bolts full easy slide:—
> The chains lie silent on the footworn stones;—
> The key turns, and the door upon its hinges groans.

Though the hound finds them not altogether invisible, in fact familiar, they pass outside the narrator's field of vision: "They are gone: aye, ages long ago / These lovers fled away into the storm." Thus a kind of romantic estrangement descends between the past and the present; the dream that has become real in Madeline's chamber is enfolded within another dream that is the fiction. As Laurence Lerner writes: "Instead of telling us something about the lovers, [Keats] tells us something about the way he has told the story. That is why it was appropriate to finish with the Baron's nightmares and Angela's death: we now take these details as confirmation of what we've suddenly been made aware of, that all this is the world of once upon a time."[16]

Other Keatsian figures are similarly drained of tangibility as they enter the realm of legend wherein the imagination houses its paradigms. Keats's initial point in *The Fall of Hyperion* is that whatever else may have historical perpetuity, dreams drop immediately into darkness if they are not "trac'd upon vellum or wild Indian leaf" and given "the shadows of melodious utterance." Unfortunately, as these phrases suggest, they remain shadowy even then. Dreams come in more than one kind. Some are the solipsistic illusions of fanatics; others, according to Moneta, vex the world and make their appearance to dreamers who are "distinct, / Diverse, sheer opposite" to the poet. The problem in all such visions is the break between waking moments and desire's intangible world of images and myths. It seems again that it is the lack of middle-level cultural presuppositions that renders the mythological past so ghostly. The poet's identity is not located in but theatened by predecessors, with whom he does not share sustaining forms and ideas.[17] In the Hyperion poems, the gods are stalled in wreckage, lost to their own past, unidentified by act, without concerted plots. In the ruined sanctuary in which the dreamer finds himself at the beginning of *The Fall*, for instance, the twilight of the gods casts a long shadow:

> what I had seen
> Of grey cathedrals, buttress'd walls, rent towers,
> The superannuations of sunk realms,
> Or Nature's rocks toil'd hard in waves and winds,
> Seem'd but the faulture of decrepit things
> To that eternal domed Monument.
> (I.67–70)

Dreams cannot unriddle these relics or solve the mysteries of ancestry. Nor have Keats's gods acquired knowledge with the passing of their powers: they are bewildered and groping. The evolutionary logic that presumably prevails over them is in abeyance for the moment, and the interval between the fall and the discovery of its purpose is filled with agonizing:

> As when upon a tranced summer-night
> Forests, branch-charmed by the earnest stars,
> Dream, and so dream all night without a noise,
> Save from one gradual solitary gust,
> Swelling upon the silence; dying off;
> As if the ebbing air had but one wave;
> So came these words and went . . .
> Long, long those two were postured motionless,
> Like sculpture builded-up upon the grave
> Of their own power. A long awful time
> I look'd upon them: still they were the same;
> The frozen God still bending to the earth,
> And the sad Goddess weeping at his feet,
> Moneta silent. Without stay or prop,
> But my own weak mortality, I bore
> The load of this eternal quietude.
> *(The Fall of Hyperion, I.371–390)*

The mainspring of a potential plot has broken and what remains are fragments of dialogue and descriptive portraits. As the "pale Omega of a wither'd race," even Moneta is but a gloomy memory.

In all this, Keats appears to be groping for, among other things, a tangible concept of periods and historical movement. The phases he suggests in the Hyperion poems can almost be equated with literary movements, since presumably the succession of gods tells us something about the succession of kinds of poets. The difficulty is that one group is antithetical to another without being moved into action by it. Some dynamic principle is missing, which we can perhaps attribute to Keats's own ambivalence toward ancestry. Certainly he wishes to revere the past as represented by Spenser, Dante, Shakespeare, and Milton, all of whom he imitates; yet he cannot merely redream their old visions or live entirely within their imagined worlds. He wishes the modern poet to move current actions and thus to absorb, revitalize, and replace his inherited myths. But so far the formula that would unlock the present and send it forward is missing. What the poet-dreamer sees before him is a paralyzing ruin, beginning in *Hyperion* with Saturn himself "Upon the sodden ground" (17).

In *The Fall*, under Moneta's guidance, he comes upon the same pano-rama, and its significance in both cases is partly that it generates no new cycle. If the wreckage is a sign of anything, it is the endless war of gen-erations. In any case, Clymene fears an evolution that will leave them obsolete. Hyperion himself appears to be more a threshold of light than a realized Apollonian sun. As Coelus (the fathering heaven) sees him, he is stretched "in grief and radiance faint" on a horizon awaiting the day. Though nothing fully explains this short tenure of the gods, Oceanus' version of the creation myth offers a reason for cycles in general: Creation is not finished but ongoing, and as earth and heaven are fairer than chaos and blank darkness, so "on our heels a fresh perfection treads" and will excel. To excel means to replace, since "first in beauty should be first in might." Clymene adds testimony to that in finding that her own talent for melody has been surpassed by the "new blissful golden melody" she hears in the distance. A transfiguration of forms kills off the old; "a living death" comes on each new "gush of sounds."

As Keats imagines the morning brightness of a new poetry, then, he does so not with great hope but with the anxiety of those who are displaced by it and cast into the shadow of dreams. That anxiety is surely heightened by the poet's discovery that he does not share the recurrent forms and standards of his predecessors. None of the recurrent Platonist and Christian types are transferable to him, for instance, and certainly not the overall logic of the genesis-to-doomsday cycle. Hence the poet cannot serve as herald to a future already determined by the past he has fixed upon; he cannot collect the past as his sustenance. Instead, what he sees of Eden and Miltonic epic, for instance, is their wasted forms. The dreamer himself identifies with the sick and the fallen, and when Apollo comes forth, his point of departure is still another vision of ruin. Gods and humans alike are goaded into song not by the onset of a dreamed ideality but by the surface of chronicle change and the leavings of former poets and architects:

> "Names, deeds, grey legends, dire events, rebellions,
> Majesties, sovran voices, agonies,
> Creations and destroyings, all at once
> Pour into the wide hollows of my brain,
> And deify me, as if some blithe wine
> Or bright elixir peerless I had drunk,
> And so become immortal."
> (*Hyperion*, III.114–120)

Unfortunately, the only product of that Apollonian forthcoming is a shriek. Nor does Apollo's descent into suffering reclassify him as a mortal or carry *The Fall* from myth into history. The entire upper realm of Keats's war in heaven, with its myths and archetypes, has at best an enigmatic bearing on the native realm of the poet.

It is worth noting in passing that this separation is in at least one respect in keeping with the doctrine of the enlightenment historians whom Keats had read. Whereas Milton interprets no sphere in the human enterprise without reference to the ultimate designs of Providence, the antiquarian history that Keats knew put its institutions, its rules and orders, and its social sphere in isolation: it separated sociological disciplines from theological precepts.

A similar separation of knowledgeable historiography from the sort of truths that Keats's dreamer seeks is evident in "Ode on a Grecian Urn." What seems to be missing again are the guiding principles that would provide the observer with keys by which to interpret the urn. In some sense, he *can* read it; but what he finds in the lovers, for instance, are the barest outlines of universal desire, frozen at a moment of near-fulfillment. The story of the figures requires unfolding in time, as in the approach to love and its consummation, the hearing of music, the progress of happiness in its experiential state. But even as these things suggest living sequences, we find them fixed and paradigmatic as visual models. The contrast here is not between the realms of mortals and gods (who seem to the observer indistinguishable) but between art and historical inquiry. No dieties "perne in a gyre" to lift the poet into some artifice of eternity. Instead, the urn raises lines of inquiry that a scholar might pursue and then immediately frustrates them. Is the scene in Tempe or Arcady? In the history of art, would such shapes be gods or men? What customs are reflected in the pursuit? Such sociological and cultural questions obviously misuse art as an avenue to archaic culture, and the urn refuses to answer. Whatever the figures depict, they must stand on their own. They rest in eternity, not in historical culture and expressive forms. Thus, turning away from the antiquarian's approach to explication, Keats finds that these flowery tales can no longer be deciphered. In supplying guesses from his own experience, the observer cannot help being struck by the insurmountable barrier between historical existence and the timelessness of art. If true historical rescue is not the accurate naming of something but the movement of feeling toward "another heart / And other pulses" as Keats elsewhere suggests,[18] ordinary historical inquiry would be insufficient even if the evidence were firmer and more abundant.

In addressing the urn and its figures as though they could answer, the observer heightens the discrepancy between what we want from historical contact and what the cold record allows. Nothing could be quieter than marble, nothing more chastening in its endurance or less human. Cut off from the vitality of the past, the poet turns to timeless philosophy as art's more bracing partner. If it cannot establish singular, live events, art can at least gesture toward absolute beauty and truth. In making that radical change, Keats again demonstrates the lack of mediating levels between the specific life that the urn depicts and the high universals it announces as concluding axioms. If indeed all one knows is that beauty and truth are identical no matter what, specific recollections of the past are discardable. The figures on the urn are forced to become pure art, and art becomes pure shape and attitude without referential functions. As it does no good to approach eternity by stages, so it does little good to ponder art's absolutist message. With that realization, the poet denies art access to historical substance and phantomizes its content, not gradually, as in some recession of weakening memory, but categorically, as a discrepancy between what moves and lives and what has perpetuity. Nothing endures that is not translated into immobility; nothing lives and breathes that is so translated.

On perhaps only one occasion was Keats able to dissolve these and similar contradictions between the present one lives through and a fictive past where ideals are staged in a pageantry that proves to be inaccessible. In "To Autumn," he sets aside recollections of the past for a present that entirely fulfills the poet's desire by its sheer natural abundance and by the delight of its slow maturity. Or to approach from another direction: rather than inaugurating a new history, as Adam does in awakening from his paradisal dream, the poet completes the harvest of just fulfilled things. Essence is construed as the moment of completion in which Ceres grants the defined shape of things. Thus the poem is totally given over to objects beyond prophecy and recollection—objects that merely are. And rather than placing himself in an allegory of the emerging psyche, the poet assumes that the maturing of autumnal blessings is his maturity also; he is no longer an initiate among mysteries, straining at the threshold of the realms of the gods. He is not a professional poet seeking muses or internal paramours to guarantee his stature. He is an observer merely, more negatively capable than dreamers. The self-consciousness that comes of awakening from dreams will not be required by these acts of perception. The understanding, meddling intellect is devoted exclusively to commemoration. The poet practices not recollection, then, but collection. Certainly he discovers in autumn nothing of the wasted summer fruits of *The Fall*:

III
Where are the songs of Spring? Ay, where are they?
   Think not of them, thou hast thy music too,—
While barred clouds bloom the soft-dying day,
   And touch the stubble-plains with rosy hue;
Then in a wailful choir the small gnats mourn
   Among the river sallows, borne aloft
      Or sinking as the light wind lives or dies;
And full-grown lambs loud bleat from hilly bourn;
   Hedge-crickets sing; and now with treble soft
   The red-breast whistles from a garden-croft;
      And gathering swallows twitter in the skies.

This sequence of stir and rest is closer to rhythmic pulsation than it is to linear or cyclical movement: sheer abundance overpowers our awareness of the one-way, life-to-death processes of lambs, crickets, and swallows.

"To Autumn" manages to be a full-bodied poem without a trace of romantic ghostliness only because of its dismissal of personal and cultural pasts. Its focus narrows to a present-tense close-up of natural sequences, and its course of feelings is pinned to descriptive riches and the associations that come naturally with Ceres' delivered blessings. In this respect, it stands apart both from Keats's predecessors and from the main Keatsian influence. It betokens at one and the same time a setting aside of the Keatsian dreamer's high ambitions for bardic responsibility and the deliverance of what is perhaps Keats's most curative blessing for the suffering mankind that Moneta admonishes the dreamer not to forget. If it seems a pure adamic dream in its way, it is only because it succeeds so well in disciplining the urge to think about stages before and after the present, or Edens that are not here now. The difference between the living processes depicted on the urn and those that "To Autumn" celebrates drives home pointedly the inability of language, memory, and imagination to collaborate in retrieving a substantial past. The urn drops the specific past in order to philosophize on a high plane; "To Autumn" drops all notions of transcendent beauty and truth in order to commemorate what is harvestable by the senses.

The quandary of the Hyperion poems is obviously not solved thereby: namely, how one can use the antithesis between present and past to generate a new future. If nature has its ritual recurrences in "To Autumn," it is devoid of those levels of mythos that reinstitute archetypes. The icons of "To Autumn" are almost purely natural despite some personification; they do not gesture toward a realm of ideas that give form and purpose to linear time as in Milton's lost and regained paradise or Marvell's pilgrimage to the paradisal harvest of "Bermudas." As it refuses to have a past or a future, so it refuses to become involved in the library of poets.

Yeats, Eliot, Hemingway: Hosting Other Phantoms

> The host is riding from Knocknarea
> And over the grave of Clooth-na-Bare;
> Caoilte tossing his burning hair,
> And Niamh calling *Away, come away:*
> *Empty your heart of its mortal dream.*
> *The winds awaken, the leaves whirl round,*
> *Our cheeks are pale, our hair is unbound,*
> *Our breasts are heaving, our eyes are agleam,*
> *Our arms are waving, our lips are apart;*
> *And if any gaze on our rushing band,*

We come between him and the deed of his hand,
We come between him and the hope of his heart.
(W. B. Yeats, "The Hosting of the Sidhe")

"To Autumn" predicts a modernist tendency to fix upon landscapes in the present moment (a tendency that recurs, as we shall see, in William Carlos Williams, Wallace Stevens, and Richard Wilbur, who move on occasion toward a special privileging of objects). But it is not particularly typical of romanticism in general, especially romanticism's unresigned, questing, historically ambitious branch, which I want to explore for the moment. Three examples—Yeats, Eliot, and Hemingway—will be if not reasonably representative at least about all space affords. Needless to say, each is quite different from the others. I have chosen them not to set a thesis in concrete but to raise questions and suggest a spectrum of possibilities concerning the postromantic canceling of certain intermediary norms.

Of the three, Yeats is the most explicitly romantic and has the most fully elaborated version of the past, although Eliot's version too is obviously substantial. Actually, both Eliot and Yeats profess belief not only in an upper tier of universals but in the cultural mediation of secondary forms. To the extent that this profession is genuine, neither is truly romantic. In other ways as well, Yeats especially is only marginally a romantic and even less a modern. For instance, he takes Swift's side in the battle of ancients and moderns. He marches forward waving the banner of Shelley in one hand and the banner of eighteenth-century ceremony and custom in the other—before he drops both and picks up his Renaissance and his Byzantine insignia.

With respect to Yeats's Swiftean phase, old world literature, he remarks in *Explorations*, has at least one great advantage over modern literature in that the world was not changing so quickly then, and there was nothing to draw the writer's "imagination from the ripening of the fields, from the birth and death of their children, from the destiny of their souls, from all that is the unchanging substance of literature." In this apparent championing of the good old days, Yeats's preference for what abides is far from casual; the creative energy of former writers, he finds, depended upon the belief that they have within them something immortal and imperishable, and so he would like to believe any good poet has to have.[19] We remember of course how he chided Maud Gonne for marching forward under alien insignia inscribed with political causes and mere opinions. The poet and indeed anyone who wishes the blessings of the horn of plenty and a peaceful spirit must not do that. All that is timely and arduous is inimical to art. As he remarks in the preface to *Essays and Introductions*, he has received his own subject matter "from the generations, [as] part of that compact with my fellow men made in my name before I was born. I cannot break from it without breaking from some part of my own nature, and sometimes it has come to me in supernormal experience; I have met with ancient myths in my dreams, brightly lit; and I think it allied to the wisdom or instinct that that guides a migratory bird."[20]

That the past influences the present so directly and returns to it so substantially is one difference, at least in degree, between Yeats and his romantic predecessors and between Yeats and most moderns. He is also more systematically and subtly a theorist of recurrence than any of the romantics. (I refer of course to the later Yeats.) In his system, powers of the first tier reenter history regularly in its determining moments and in different guises so that every coming is a second or third coming. The poet, in Yeats's view is therefore confronted not with a single tradition, as Eliot believes, but with cross-referenced collaborations among several phases. Born out of phase, a certain type may find his closest correspondence in the surviving images of another era. This makes art more than an incidental ornament to such a person; it becomes a counterproposal that conveys the forms of another period to him as a prepared receiver. Indeed, if the historical process is not to be blind, it must allow access to a total vision of all cycles; and only relics, statues, poetry, and perhaps philosophy can do that with any adequacy.

In this way, art is both revolutionary and reactionary at the same time: a key instrument in the interchange of the gyres, it is a casting back and a lurching forward. As Yeats writes in one of his final statements on a subject that occupied him all his life, everything returns again, from particulars to universals:

Now that I am old and live in the past I often think of those ancestors of whom I have some detailed information. Such and such a diner-out and a charming man never did anything; such and such lost the never very great family fortune in some wild-cat scheme; and such and such, perhaps deliberately for he was a strange, deep man, married into a family known for harsh dominating strength of character. Then, as my mood deepens, I discover all these men in my single mind, think that I myself have gone through the same vicissitudes, that I am going through them all at this very moment, and wonder if the balance has come right; then I go beyond those minds and my single mind and discover that I have been describing everybody's struggle, and the gyres turn in my thoughts. Vico was the first modern philosopher to discover in his own mind, and in the European past, all human destiny.[21]

Despite the "cracked tune that Chronos sings," the gyres turn with regularity. History, Yeats confesses "seems to me a human drama, keeping the classical unities by the clear division of its epochs."[22] The rises and falls of the ages are regular, as every age unwinds the thread another age has wound: before Phidias, Persia fell; and for Byzantine glory,

Rome fell.[23] The particular way of the poet is to move from specificity to a sense of that pattern and back again, to leave history and approach myth, but to return to history again. As Yeats remarks early in his career, "To the greater poets everything they see has its relation to the national life, and through that to the universal and divine life: nothing is an isolated artistic moment . . . But to this universalism, this seeing of unity everywhere, you can only attain through what is near you, your nation, or, if you be no traveller, your village and the cobwebs on your walls."[24]

In one sense this means that one may take all things as potential insignia. Whereas Wordsworth looks for avatars of transcendental being in revisited landscapes, Yeats looks for the articulate traces of specific talents and intelligences in the customs, books, and objets d'art that make up a civilization; and around these as the field in which they are stationed, nature stands with all her universal rules and cyclical passages from one state to another. Everything carries some mark, some piece of heraldic proclamation; nothing is merely deadened matter, like the inert scraps and residue left by gods who have abandoned Keats; nor is the natural field, without its still-reigning statues, towers, and mosaics, sufficient and bountiful in itself, as Ceres is to the resigned poet of "To Autumn." Rather, the past stands available for penetration. Its statuary does not hold off and tease us with its marble eternity as the Grecian urn does but dances to the lively movement of returning spirits. Figures in mosaic descend to be the poet's singing masters. When Yeats thinks of Leda's Zeus or of Byzantium or of mythical beasts, they are already descending into time and stirring with the revolution of the gyres.

With all this particularized recurrence and respect for the mediating forms of past discourse, art, and thought, it might seem that Yeats would be relatively free of the phantomizing that besets the romantic escape from specific times and places to abstractions and universals; and comparatively speaking, he is. But as we noted earlier, he cannot automatically reconcile mythos and logos, which we can often translate into the paradigmatic on one hand and the historical or the topical on the other; and he is not always confident of the poet's ability to reseat the past's ideal forms in the present just when he wants to. Although all things are potentially insignia or demarcations of history's revolving forces, they are not necessarily scaled to human size and control.

The poems of *The Tower* illustrate with particular cogency the poet's difficulty in this regard. It is true that art offers certain guidelines if one chooses to follow them, as Sato's gift of an ancient sword represents to the modern possessor some five hundred years of history. Yeats hopes that such a symbol might moralize one's days out of their aimlessness (in "My Table"). When changeless works of art pass from father to son, they mold the "soul of generations" into similar patterns of beauty that spread outward into daily affairs. Yet this continuity is only one side of a complex meditation on ancestry and the place of counterthrusts in history's cycles. In other poems, Yeats finds it all too likely that one's heirs will "lose the flower" through either weakness or too much business with the passing hour. The tower itself, with all its cracks and its rooflessness, is reminiscent of old romantic places—except that the phantoms that appear there are far more vigorous and more destructive than their predecessors. As they whirl into the present, they provide violent antitheses for the current times, as though the broken mainspring of Keats's Hyperion plots had been mended. Things are once more on the move:

> A puff of wind
> And those white glimmering fragments of the mist sweep by.
> Frenzies bewilder, reveries perturb the mind;
> Monstrous familiar images swim to the mind's eye.
>
> 'Vengeance upon the murderers,' the cry goes up,
> 'Vengeance for Jacques Molay.' In cloud-pale rags, or in lace,
> The rage-driven, rage-tormented, and rage-hungry troop,
> Trooper belabouring trooper, biting at arm or at face,
> Plunges towards nothing, arms and fingers spreading wide
> For the embrace of nothing; and I, my wits astray
> Because of all that senseless tumult, all but cried
> For vengeance on the murderers of Jacques Molay
> ("I See Phantoms of Hatred and of the Heart's Fullness
> and of the Coming Emptiness")[25]

Yeats's vision of "innumerable clanging wings that have put out the moon" (p. 204) climaxes in "Nineteen Hundred and Nineteen," a demon-haunted poem that lacks the consolations of either tragic joy or formal art. In several sections that range from meditational probings of the extent of evil to chantlike descriptions of universal ruin, he misses the kind of continuity that other poems celebrate. Art is one of the first things to be destroyed in the turning of the gyres:

> Many ingenious lovely things are gone
> That seemed sheer miracle to the multitude,
> Protected from the circle of the moon
> That pitches common things about. There stood
> Amid the ornamental bronze and stone
> An ancient image made of olive wood—
> And gone are Phidias' famous ivories
> And all the golden grasshoppers and bees.
> (p. 204)

So senseless a fury can pervert even Yeats's favorite symbol of the dance, as the vicious phantoms of the past force their way into the present and move it to the pattern of previous upheavals:

IV

We, who seven years ago
Talked of honour and of truth,
Shriek with pleasure if we show
The weasel's twist, the weasel's tooth.
(p. 207)

The unwinding bobbins of other poems translate here into a ribbon dance reminiscent of both Symon's dance of Herodias' daughters and Yeats's own "Hosting of the Sidhe":[26]

When Loie Fuller's Chinese dancers enwound
A shining web, a floating ribbon of cloth,
It seemed that a dragon of air
Had fallen among dancers, had whirled them round
Or hurried them off on its own furious path;
So the Platonic Year
Whirls out new right and wrong,
Whirls in the old instead;
All men are dancers and their tread
Goes to the barbarous clangour of a gong.
(Collected Poems, pp. 205–206)

Having experimented several times with gong-tormented images, Yeats here settles on one that expresses perfectly the cyclical unwinding of antinomies. As embodiments of the violent winds, the Sidhelike dancers return a past as unlike the current times as possible.

The final image of the series is of a depraved phantom riding slowly forward—"That insolent fiend Robert Artisson"—about whom Yeats writes: "The country people see at times certain apparitions whom they name now 'fallen angels,' now 'ancient inhabitants of the country,' and describe as riding at whiles 'with flowers upon the heads of the horses.' I have assumed in the sixth poem that these horsemen, now that the times worsen, give way to worse. My last symbol, Robert Artisson, was an evil spirit much run after in Kilkenny at the start of the fourteenth century. Are not those who travel in the whirling dust also in the Platonic Year?"[27] The clangor of the gong and the dance grow quiet at the reentry of this creature, who brings a sinister end to prophecy, coming as though in the aftermath of history's creative-destructive fury:

Herodias' daughters have returned again,
A sudden blast of dusty wind and after
Thunder of feet, tumult of images,
Their purpose in the labyrinth of the wind;
And should some crazy hand dare touch a daughter
All turn with amorous cries, or angry cries,

According to the wind, for all are blind.
But now wind drops, dust settles; thereupon
There lurches past, his great eyes without thought
Under the shadow of stupid straw-pale locks,
That insolent fiend Robert Artisson
To whom the love-lorn Lady Kyteler brought
Bronzed peacock feathers, red combs of her cocks.
     (p. 208)

As the rhythm slackens to a dying fall in "Nineteen Hundred and Nineteen," we may hope that it is time to settle into common reality; but if so, we are disappointed: what the new turn brings is the inevitability of vulgarity and further evil, not a clarification or a new purpose. The past does not fade and will not finally be weakly phantomized, but neither will it be explicable when it returns; overturning all phases of chivalry, it steps forward as a parody of lady love and knighthood, a perversion of warfare, and the worst of art reiterated.

The overall direction of *The Tower* sequence and the vision of Robert Artisson constitute perhaps Yeats's gloomiest descent into the senselessness of cyclical change and the spinning of history out of inhuman powers. Unlike Keats's succession of Saturn by Hyperion and Apollo or Wordsworth's inland exile from the radiant shores of youth, Yeats allows no sanctuaries beyond the ruins, not even in this case the elegiac art that attends the ancient Chinese in "Lapis Lazuli." From *The Tower* onward, Yeats alternately rejoices in and laments the cycles of waste and rebuilding, just as he moves back and forth between the helpless passivity of art and its shaping force and drops one set of banners for another.

Despite this courting of opposite moods, he comes back to one repeated preference: the quiet reinstatement of ideals in private retreats, which he prefers to public action. In that preference he is perhaps influenced by William Morris more than by the romantics. As a boy he read parts of *The Earthly Paradise* and *The Defence of Guenevere*, and although he did not value the poetry itself highly, he confessed later that he would rather have lived Morris' life than his own or any other man's. The imperturbable Morris, in his view, was basically inactive and contemplative in repossessing the choice moments of art and of history. Despite his antithetical place in modern consciousness, he bore his exile from his native ideal with serenity. The portrait of Morris by George Frederick Watts that Yeats had hanging over his mantlepiece spoke clearly of that calm amid total difference: "Its grave wide-open eyes, like the eyes of some dreaming beast, remind me of the open eyes of Titian's 'Ariosto,' while the broad vigorous body suggests a mind that has no need of intellect to remain sane, though it give itself to every phantasy: the dreamer of the middle ages . . . the resolute European image that yet half remembers Buddha's motionless meditation, and has no trait in common with the wavering, lean image of hungry speculation, that cannot but because of certain famous Hamlets of our stage fill the mind's eye."[28] In its conjuring of the medieval mind and its ranging through fantasies of the past—even in its remembering of Buddha—the portrait reveals that images from the past may take a peaceful form.

Yeats's ambivalence toward the passivity of art is given full rein in "The Statues," which asserts that art's transmission of ancient ideas and forms has an immediate impact on political activism, while artworks themselves remain formally static and fixed. An original Phidian image comes to modern perception not only through Cuchulain but through a passive contemplator who (as Vivienne Koch points out[29]) closely resembles Morris. As a lasting ideal, that image has resisted the many-headed confusion of Asiatic disorder, reversed the direction of civilization (moving north and west toward Ireland), and seated itself in the Buddhistic pose of Morris's knowing passivity:

> One image crossed the many-headed, sat
> Under the tropic shade, grew round and slow,
> No Hamlet thin from eating flies, a fat
> Dreamer of the Middle Ages. Empty eyeballs knew
> That knowledge increases unreality, that
> Mirror on mirror mirrored is all the show.
> When gong and conch declare the hour to bless
> Grimalkin crawls to Buddha's emptiness.
> (*Collected Poems*, p. 323)

However, all that is worthwhile in Phidian or other art, though an instrument of history's antinomies, is out of phase in the contemporary world and may be swept away at any time. It is insubstantial enough to suggest the phantoms of the romantic past and the shades that torment "Byzantium." Indeed, in one sense what Yeats has done is regularize the appearances of Shelley's floating apparitions, which descend by less determinable principles in Shelley's version of history. For Yeats, both the reappearance and the wreckage of ideal forms are certain.

In proposing that cyclical displacement, Yeats explores one aspect of the romantic dilemma, in which the acuity of the present is undermined by what is absent and unattainable, or by the force of things unseen in general. In this he is both like and unlike Eliot. For Eliot, what is valuable in former periods also returns, but as part of the intellectual tradition of modern Europeans rather than as the generative power of cycles moved by spirits, phantoms, or ideals embedded in art. It returns knowingly, as consciously retrieved poetry, philosophy, history, and style. Although Eliot's modern poet, too, may be antithetical to his times, the result of his repossession of past literature is an amalgamation or complex attunement of differences and similarities between himself and it. His possession of his full inheritance ideally involves a discovery of the essential oneness of the European mind, which is celebrated on Eliot's chief banner. Unlike Wordsworth's personal recollection, the range of that backward reach is chronologically extensive. Eliot does not propose phases of growth and revolution like those of either Keats's Hyperion poems or Yeats's *A Vision*. Nor is the poet's spiritual home limited to the reincarnation of a particular phase, though Eliot himself prefers Dante, the Elizabethans, and the metaphysicals as models. Instead, the poet acquires a past of conscious scholarship, and he should do so broadly:

> Tradition is a matter of much wider significance [than mere repetition]. It cannot be inherited, and if you want it you must obtain it by great labour. It involves, in the first place, the historical sense, which we may call nearly indispensable to anyone who would continue to be a poet beyond his twenty-fifth year; and the historical sense involves a perception, not only of the pastness of the past, but of its presence; the historical sense compels a man to write not merely with his own generation in his bones, but with a feeling that the whole of the literature of Europe from Homer and within it the whole of the literature of his own country has a simultaneous existence and composes a simultaneous order. This historical sense, which is a sense of the timeless as well as of the temporal and of the timeless and of the temporal together, is what makes a writer traditional. And it is at the same time what makes a writer most acutely conscious of his place in time, of his contemporaneity.

Although the poet cannot take the "past as a lump, an indiscriminate bolus," neither can he "form himself wholly on one or two private admirations."[30]

It is predictable that the author of "Tradition and the Individual Talent" would ponder in poetry also the returns of the past, but it is perhaps surprising to find the past there as distant and elusive as it is. In effect, Eliot's past, too, is phantomized despite its guaranteed presence in the library of classics. Its literature is neither fully usable nor part of a single order, at least in his poetry, where it raises echoes, revenances, and plangencies. In presupposing the superiority of central myths now beyond reach, it collides with the poet's own times. Actually, Eliot's later prose commentary on the nature of classics also points up the difficulty of bringing the past within reach. The maturity of mind and language and the comprehensiveness required of an authentic classic effectively stifle reiteration in latecomers: "Not only every great poet, but every genuine, though lesser poet, fulfills once for all some possibility of the language, and so leaves one possibility less for his successors." Seemingly, then, some form of aberrancy or deviation is forced upon latecomers that carries them away from the centrality of the empire to which classics give expressive form. If Aeneas is a symbol of Rome and Rome commands Europe, Virgil stands at "the centre of European civilisation," in a position that no other poet can share. What later poets are left cannot be essential Europe; they are forced to become provincial, which is to say, partial, eccentric, different. They must distort some values and evade or corrupt others.[31]

Eliot is less emphatic about Europe's progressive disfigurement in *The Classics and the Man of Letters*, where he is willing to allow a different station, at or near the center, for those who are capable of grasping the whole of literature without trying to copy its center. As we noted earlier, the realm of letters includes men of second or third or lower ranks as well as the greatest, and "These secondary writers provide collectively, and individually in varying degrees, an important part of the environment of the great writer, as well as his first audience, his first appreciators, his first critical correctors."[32] They provide the continuity of literature amidst the discontinuity it suffers between classics. They assist the purveyance of texts and thereby extend the principles of the center to the marginal public of readers, critics, and lesser writers. That does not, of course, change essentially the dilemma of the forestalled, would-be major poet, who must escape the used-up language that classics have left behind and yet recapture the maturity of European letters. In any event, one thing that the poet must not do is develop his own private mythology—as in Eliot's eyes Yeats did with his "highly sophisticated lower mythology" and his spirit-ridden Celtic world. The main struggle of our times, as *After Strange Gods* insists, should be to concentrate, not dissipate, certainly not to proliferate new myths.

Several poems nonetheless suggest that the poet sees about him in the twentieth century far more scattering than gathering. In "Burnt Norton" Eliot returns to beginnings that are both racial and personal, for instance, as the poet follows the echoes of the rose garden into a first world and discovers there traces of both beginnings and endings. But he writes from the midst and even more drastically than Wordsworth finds the chronic backward view draining the present of its authority. Also, since no one's past is automatically anyone else's, Eliot's version of the main line necessarily requires that he put other versions aside and discredit much of the present as illusory or third rate. Christopher Caudwell has some justification in saying that, though Eliot believes "he has discovered a common social world, that of literary tradition ... the common world-view of literature is in fact an illusion. Unless there is a common world-view of reality, there cannot be a common world-view of literature."[33]

Although such a notion denies the centrality of classics, it does so no more forcefully than Eliot's own poems do at times. They summon at best only fragments of the European whole, and they do so largely as measurements of modern deviations from classic or near-classic texts. To some extent, the question boils down to the competition between personal, unique moments and universal patterns that we perceive to be the property of great texts and their exhaustive language. Whereas "Tradition and the Individual Talent" and "The Function of Criticism" skirt that competition, "Burnt Norton" dwells upon it and sacrifices passing moments to enduring patterns; it suggests that since individual exemplifications of a pattern are always moving, they are always imperfect and perhaps always provincial. Hence on one hand, the poet must build upon tradition and reconstitute it if he is to survive beyond the first blush of his talent (and a people as a whole without history "is not redeemed from time, for history is a pattern / Of timeless moments"); on the other hand, history is redeemable only at the cost that universals exact when they command total allegiance and pull us out of the immediate moment.

Only in his version of the Logos as Christ does Eliot's past endure in the tangible fullness and immediacy that his criticism champions. But even this medieval and Renaissance version of a redeemed timelessness by no means ends the poet's difficulties with cultural recollection. The poet himself, after all, is not the Logos, merely a maker of verbal constructions. Although he labors in the shadow of Dante, Milton, and Donne, he can make no claim to their prophetic offices or their renewed epiphanies. He is haunted, not fulfilled, by their seeming proximity to the Logos. What the modern poet renders is not an achieved recollection of the European experience, then, but a search for it. The past gains a footing in present thought only in a discursive, abstract way. Although it gives depth to the poet's sense of history, it remains unformulated and unfixed, just as older genres become unsettled and subject to parody in new versions such as *The Waste Land*. Eliot consistently keeps the past *in* the past despite the simultaneous existence it should have with the present; it is something to be echoed and yearned for among its modern fragments.

The present is haunted by the past and carries its imprint, then; but the time that we truly experience is a casual procession of changes that essentially deny the grip of the past upon us:

> In succession
> Houses rise and fall, crumble, are extended,
> Are removed, destroyed, restored, or in their place
> Is an open field, or a factory, or a by-pass . . .
>
> there is a time for building
> And a time for living and for generation
> And a time for the wind to break the loosened pane
> And to shake the wainscot where the field-mouse trots
> And to shake the tattered arras woven with a silent motto.[34]

In keeping with this *ubi sunt* lament, in the medieval dance of "East Coker," Eliot describes that cultural solidarity in a lost language, set to the "weak pipe and the little drum," in demonstration that some literary styles too are now quaintly distant. Although the dance itself "betokeneth" a "concorde" and a marriage under old rustic or georgic rituals, in the end, "the dancers are all gone under the hill." The poet can only hold on as a moment of absence passes and await some sort of renewal. Meanwhile, as "Little Gidding" says, he cannot escape the coming and going of ancestors:

> We die with the dying:
> See, they depart, and we go with them.
> We are born with the dead:
> See, they return, and bring us with them.

Thus time brings a return of sorts to Eliot, but only in speculative form. In the absence of clear manifestations of the total myth of Europe, the modern poet is conscious of a vacancy that cannot be filled adequately by captains, bankers, statesmen, civil servants, or industrial lords, who drop into "vacant interstellar spaces." The rose garden, the sound of birds, and the landscape testify to something hinted in them, but more for the imagination than perception. The absence-in-presence of romanticism creeps into all annunciatory moments. As we can watch the stillness of eternity only through its opposite—the moving spokes of the wheel—so we can know the passage we did *not* take to paradise only by the path we *did* take. The music we hear in the garden in "Burnt Norton" is the natural, lowly music of birds who in turn respond to music we cannot hear, a ghostly music that must be divined. Though perhaps no more than the music of spring, the bird's song romantically triggers the perception of lost times, including in the furthermost distance the first Garden itself. It is always in a corner of the eye that we glimpse lost selves and lost parents. If we hear too evidences of the Word, the recurrent authority of all times, it is in echoes of other poets. Thus a romantic sense of the marginal and the inconceivable invades what the essayist Eliot prefers to be a less fragmented heritage.

In all of this, Eliot crystallizes the romantic problem of absence and the almost palpable ghosts of the past: the poet offers networks of association and finds the present at the edge of a large sea. But his method for registering such glimpses and echoes is not a Wordsworthian portent of wholeness (centered in a single landscape or spot of time); it is a reflection of fragments in fragments. Whatever haunts the bird's song and the turning wheel does so in quickened intuitive glances, refracted through reminiscence and meditation. Its fragments can be made into a single construction, if at all, only by the unifying thrust of the poet's own composition, as an interweaving of motives and a building of sequences toward a work that may never be totally realized. The basic function of verse is to turn those fragments over and over in constant re-vision.

A more oppressive sense of desertion and emptied substance begets Prufrock and Gerontion and of course *The Waste Land*, with its fragments of the romance-quest and lost heroic paradigms. Prufrock is perhaps Eliot's most salient example of a hapless modern caught up in phantomized recollection. Taking a cue from Dante's visitation to the underworld, Eliot makes Prufrock's mind extraordinarily elusive and ghostly among its literary precedents. The suggestion is again not so much of the continuity of the European mind as its division into many things, each too weakly sustained for Prufrock to exploit it in warding off his own anxieties. Certainly he lacks the comparative satisfaction that the *Quartets* take in sampling eternity's stillness (though in retrospect we can see how little Eliot needed to alter to reach the relative assurance of the *Quartets*). Prufrock's re-visions are a shrinkage of visions with which he tampers until he has reduced them to size.

Despite its nostalgic recollections, Prufrock's song obviously differs in important respects from Wordsworthian revisitation. For one thing, it does not progress toward a point of recognition in the present or stake a claim to spiritual transcendence. Prufrock's urban setting leaves him without the avatars of the Wordsworthian landscape. Without the crescendo of romantic epiphany—or with it scattered into smaller rises of feeling—Prufrock's itinerary is a fluctuation, a coming on of passions and insights quickly cut back by irony. His losses are scaled down to an elegiac minimum. In his sort of recollection, the past neither circles back again nor contains a thrust toward something definite. Instead, when Prufrock looks up from the impressive world of, say, *The Divine Comedy*, he confronts a panorama less orderly, less intense, more vulgar, less possessed of itself than the past affords, less able to locate a normative human sacle.

The modern prose writer is at an even greater disadvantage than Prufrock in mastering a time-deepened field, because his focus on the surface of present settings and social affairs almost precludes his finding roots in artistic and intellectual sources of the kind that Eliot champions. Compared with Eliot's European past, for instance, Hemingway's personal experience is lacking in the echoes and shadings of tradition, flattened in tone, burdened by its matter-of-factness. In this respect, Hemingway's past, too, seems at first something quite different from romantic ghostliness. Does one not after all concern oneself with cafés, the current wars, and the arenas of contemporary Europe? The difficulty lies in the tendency of everything to move toward one of two extremes: either flattened enumeration or significant but receding personal memory. This is so even in earlier works; while we might expect passages like the following to appear in *Across the River and into the Trees,* they come as a surprise in a novel as generally taut as *The Sun Also Rises:* "We paid for the beers, we matched and I think Cohn paid, and went up to the hotel. It was only sixteen francs apiece for Bill and me, with ten per cent added for the service, and we had the bags sent down and waited for Robert Cohn."[35] The narrative strains to lift such minutiae into some redemptive showcase of art, but nothing could be farther from the symbolic objects that turn up in romantic landscapes. Even the drive into Spain that follows reads at times like notebook material or marginalia to a journey of no great consequence:

> We were going through farming country with rocky hills that sloped down into the fields. The grain-fields went up the hillsides. Now as we went higher there was a wind blowing the grain. The road was white and dusty, and the dust rose under the wheels and hung in the air behind us. The road climbed up into the hills and left the rich grain-fields below. Now there were only patches of grain on the bare hillsides and on each side of the water-courses. We turned sharply out to the side of the road to give room to pass to a long string of six mules, following one after the other, hauling a high-hooded wagon loaded with freight. The wagon and the mules were covered with dust. Close behind was another string of mules and another wagon. This was loaded with lumber, and the arriero driving the mules leaned back and put on the thick wooden brakes as we passed. Up here the country was quite barren and the hills were rocky and hard-baked clay furrowed by the rain.   (p. 105)

No one would deny the vividness of parts of this passage despite its repetition. With a little stretching, it could be said to suggest the tradition of lake-poet excursions or travel diaries that the romantics both kept themselves and read in others. But as Hemingway assumes the memorability of commonplace observations, he is again caught between modes and cannot apply the rescuing capacity of narrative to an inventory without portent. For instance, the sighting of first one mule train and then another has no particular resonance; nor does the observation that a string of mules consists of one behind another! It should go without saying that if the rocky hills sloped down into the fields, the fields in turn go up the hillsides. Part of this repetition is careless, but the rest is seemingly the result of an attempt to ritualize, to load in significance by reiteration, where no real reason to recollect suggests itself.

To say that no Proustian or Jamesian intelligence comes forward to absorb these details in some rendered perspective is both to evaluate and to mark the borders of Hemingway's style. But we need not go outside Hemingway himself to find a standard against which to measure this draining away of significance:

> In the late summer of that year we lived in a house in a village that looked across the river and the plain to the mountains. In the bed of the river, there were pebbles and boulders, dry and white in the sun, and the

water was clear and swiftly moving and blue in the channels. Troops
went by the house and down the road and the dust they raised powdered
the leaves of the trees. The trunks of the trees too were dusty and the
leaves fell early that year and we saw the troops marching along the road
and the dust rising and leaves, stirred by the breeze, falling and the sol-
diers marching and afterward the road bare and white except for the
leaves.[36]

As the tangible surface of the landscape crystallizes in the memory and
is cherished by repetition, the rhythmic pace and sequence of the observations convince us that recollection can be meaningful without the
deeper resonances of an intellectual inheritance. Despite the palpability
of details in such passages, Hemingway's art at its best suggests the failure of recovery and hence the weight of what is there to be missed. Its
nostalgic stoicism refuses to turn explicitly elegiac, and in that it sometimes rises to the maturity of a classical style, which is hostile not to the
unstated in general but to the mysteries of the unstatable. As Hugh
Kenner remarks, Hemingway often wishes to perpetuate perfect moments in settings that never recur and can never be reexperienced.[37] Beyond that, the quest for lost perfection points toward the futility of a
prose rendering and thus to the limits of a specifically literary summoning. Unlike Wordsworth's confidence in the usefulness of poetry as
recollection, Hemingway's stoicism implies that talk is of minimal
value. The difference in *A Farewell to Arms*, or at least in this passage, is
that the description manages to be evocative and finely shaded without
suggesting attendant forces beyond the natural. As always, Hemingway
resolutely limits recollection to the reservoirs of untranscendental
memory: nothing metaphysical or mystical intrudes. If anything is to
benefit from the golden halo of recollection, it will be merely the minor
satisfactions of daily rituals, wine, and courage among hardships.

Less obviously attuned to memorialization but no less concerned
with what one can and cannot repossess on that limited scale is the
opening of "In Another Country":

> In the fall the war was always there, but we did not go to it any more. It
> was cold in the fall in Milan and the dark came very early. Then the
> electric lights came on, and it was pleasant along the streets looking in
> the windows. There was much game hanging outside the shops, and the
> snow powdered in the fur of the foxes and the wind blew their tails. The
> deer hung stiff and heavy and empty, and small birds blew in the wind
> and the wind turned their feathers. It was a cold fall and the wind came
> down from the mountains.[38]

In a movement toward passivity, a general giving over, Hemingway's
maimed officer turns away from the war only to find in Milan other
causes for stoicism. What the opening section details are some of the
things one should not lose; indeed, a man should search for "things he

cannot lose." Unfortunately, so exclusively bound up in particular experiences is the image of perfection that it escapes the renewability of language and memory: it cannot be generalized or raised to transferable principles.

Unlike Proust, Hemingway does not fall back on the interior continuities of the recollecting self. Where he allows a degree of interiority, the emphasis falls on isolation and the melting away of some portion of the physical world that was once sustaining, as in the following first-person passage from *The Sun Also Rises*:

> Across the square to the hotel everything looked new and changed. I had never seen the trees before. I had never seen the flagpoles before, nor the front of the theatre. It was all different. I felt as I felt once coming home from an out-of-town football game. I was carrying a suitcase with my football things in it, and I walked up the street from the station in the town I had lived in all my life and it was all new. They were raking the lawns and burning leaves in the road, and I stopped for a long time and watched. It was all strange. Then I went on, and my feet seemed to be a long way off, and everything seemed to come from a long way off, and I could hear my feet walking a great distance away. (pp. 192-193)

The focus holds so long on the terms of the comparison that the city square recedes and the returning hero walks through a landscape of ghostly objects in a body that itself seems half phantom. As a revisiting of a life of sensations, the passage reconstrues a reality that "seems to be a long way off"; and as one's feet walk at a great distance away, so one's memory (and typewriter) bring forth a set of traces no longer intimate, yet incapable of giving way to other presences. The past is neither prophecy nor safe repository. Whereas Wordsworth finds in revisited scenes evidence of a partly hidden spirit and of memories, Hemingway's revisitation raises mostly echoes of the lost self in the midst of a European architecture that delivers no reminders of enduring forms. All intellectual Europe—its monuments, poetry, doctrines, types, and archetypes—are lost to Hemingway's expatriates, who possess neither a bracing provincialism like William Carlos Williams' nor a Roman tradition like Eliot's. Whereas that Europe will not let the present rest in Eliot and Yeats without reminding us of modern barbarity, Hemingway's new barbarians are aware only of their incompleteness—not what might cure it or what realized ideals might rescue them. These have become too intangible even to haunt their hotels and countrysides.

The Momentous: Tennyson and Stevens

Hemingway's draining of the present is an offshoot of romantic recollection in the sense that it points up in another way the separation of chronicle fact from totalizing myths and first principles. When we look backward from Hemingway or simply across to other modes from the sort of prose inventories that *The Sun Also Rises* renders, we discover a confusion at the heart of the romanticism itself: it is never quite clear in Wordsworth's or Keats's dealings with the past where the borders lie between real things, their observers, and literary borrowings. In Milton's retrieval of Adam's past or Herbert's of Christ's past, recurrence does not claim strictly personal merits; the poet does not reinvent the past but recasts it. In contrast, when the supernatural collects in Wordsworth's privileged times and landscapes, it overrides normative logic and overpowers the objects through which it erupts. It comes directly to the poet through agencies that others have passed by without noticing. Or so we are led to believe. But as romanticism experiences difficulty in providing expressive in-between forms (in the scale between the minutely personal and the transcendental), so it sometimes loses sight of the distinction between what is personal and what is traditional.

Georges Poulet remarks that essential to nearly all the romantics is a "belief in the continued existence of the past, in the wonderful possibilities of its revival."[39] But in fact, romanticism is ready to mistake the inspiration gathered from the past for a kindling spark of another sort. Or to look at it another way and set aside literary borrowing specifically, what Augustine attributed to divine inspiration or Plato to preexistence, the romantics often attribute to gift or vocation. Recognizing that and resisting it, Eliot argues for reducing once again the role of personal imagination: what may seem one's own he reasorbs into one's cultural sources. Thus as we noticed earlier, when Wordsworth turns to the yew trees and describes them with Olympian detachment, one source of his attitude toward them comes from outside the objects themselves and his own experience—namely, from previous verse. We hear similar Miltonic echoes, more finely tuned, in Tennyson, and more pensive in William Cullen Bryant's "Thanatopsis," which is also romantic in the implicit animism of its landscape:

> The hills,
> Rock-ribbed and ancient as the sun,—the vales
> Stretching in pensive quietness between;
> The venerable woods—rivers that move
> In majesty, and the complaining brooks
> That make the meadows green; and, poured round all,
> Old Ocean's gray and melancholy waste,—
> Are but the solemn decorations all
> Of the great tomb of man. The golden sun,
> The planets, all the infinite host of heaven,
> Are shining on the sad abodes of death,
> Through the still lapse of ages.

That Bryant is able to exploit nature's baritone moments is due to his carrying forward of a force embedded in the rhythms and phrases of a certain body of a blank verse and elegiac sentiments.

The repetition of styles and kinds is not entirely ignored among the romantics, and certainly it becomes a conscious problem later. Tennyson in "The Lady of Shalott," for instance, glances at it in exploring the limits of representation and what it is that words can preserve. As the lady, a figure of the artist, is isolated in her tower, her indirection is roughly equivalent to afterwords, or to the poet's choice of far-off Arthurian legends for parables. It is as though poetry must avoid direct contact with contemporary affairs, at the risk of making the poet's realm a shadow empire. The lady surely speaks for other postromantics when she laments, "I am half sick of shadows." What lies beyond her grasp in the concrete life of curly-haired shepherds, troops of damsels, and village churls is everything that passes in the instant—the unique, colored quality of things flashing by in sensory forms on their way to memory. Copied from the mirror, the act of retrieval changes reality and attaches to it the regret of the elegy that so characterizes the life-in-death of Victorian afterimages.

The classic statement of that loss—when what has once been expansive drops into the realm of phantoms and returns as shadow thought—is "Tears, Idle Tears," in which the perception of objects is sharpest just as they disappear from view. The lacrimae rerum theme of the poem may be a repression of belatedness (as Harold Bloom suggests); but more explicitly, the poem makes a statement about the powerlessness of all modes of expression to seize their occasions. The margin between the present and the past is the most revealing location of that regretful perception, and it marks the difference between reality and poetic repossession. Though the theme is itself a common property of poets, it suggests in this case not recurrence or plagiarism but singularity: objects refuse to become anything other than what they are. The "divine despair" of such occasions is an impenetrable burden. In the principle of Keats's "Ode to Melancholy," the poet's felt personal sadness confirms a mystery and intensifies a puzzle:

> Fresh as the first beam glittering on a sail,
> That brings our friends up from the underworld,
> Sad as the last which reddens over one
> That sinks with all we love below the verge;
> So sad, so fresh, the days that are no more.

Similarly, dying people with failing eyes and ears hear the sounds of dawn in a bird's piping and see the "glimmering square" of a casement. If in the background are Keats's odes and Wordsworth's Intimations ode, in the offing are Eliot's *Quartets* and Prufrock's plangency. But unlike these, Tennyson's lament translates sorrow into metaphors that intensify the protest against phantomization itself: "Oh Death in Life, the days that are no more!"

This aspect of recollection does not change when the object moves from the immediate past to the intermediate past (as in Arthur Hallam's case) or the greater distance of the *Idylls:* any stage of recollection from any distance generates the same ancestral veneration and tears for lost moments, including no doubt the lost opportunity to be first in empire, to be *there* with King Arthur. Thus in the dedication to the *Idylls,* one phase of disappearing vestiges of things is joined to another as Tennyson identifies Arthur Hallam with King Arthur and reiterates the theme of "Tears": "I dedicate, I consecrate with tears— / These Idylls." Not until "we have lost him" and "he is gone" can poetry take up the task of commemoration—not because of poetic proprieties and conventions but because the poet requires the perception of loss before he can station the past poetically. Similarly, within the tales, when the grail descends into Arthur's realm, it becomes most manifest precisely at its last appearance. Its departure from the earth is then again like the dropping of some mysterious being over the edge of sight. That being, as Percivale suggests, we see precisely, and at the same time do not see:

> From the star there shot
> A rose-red sparkle to the city, and there
> Dwelt, and I knew it was the Holy Grail,
> Which never eyes on earth again shall see.
> Then fell the floods of heaven drowning the deep,
> And how my feet recrost the deathful ridge
> No memory in me lives.
> ("The Holy Grail," 529-535)

This phase of recollection too, of course, places poetic representation on the verge between presence and absence.

In prophecy, romantic recollection is turned around in that, rather than disappearing over the verge, reality comes forward "fresh as the first beam glittering on a sail." But not all the way forward: a prospect almost upon the poet is as favorable to romantic surmise as something dropping away. In fact, as Wordsworth's view of recollection-as-prophecy suggests, a grammar of romantic retrieval should include a supporting notion of forward surmise. "Ode to the West Wind" would provide one suitably enough, but perhaps more useful as specific ballast for Tennyson's dawning cry in "Tears" is Stevens' exemplary "precollection" in "Not Ideas about the Thing but the Thing Itself." There Stevens explores an ever-adjusting balance of definition and surmise, ripeness of observation, awareness of reason's boundaries, and the wonder that lies beyond them. "The thing itself" is one of the modern poet's answers to pastness in any form. Though the observer in Stevens is near the same margin as the dying perceiver in the third stanza of "Tears," he experiences not fading perceptions of a disappearing reality but a growing impression of reality coming on. The object is increasingly available to his waking mind without filtering through mythologies of the past:

> That scrawny cry—it was
> A chorister whose c preceded the choir.
> It was part of the colossal sun,
>
> Surrounded by its choral rings,
> Still far away. It was like
> A new knowledge of reality.[40]

Growing into definite knowledge at the onset of choral words is obviously quite different from passing into estrangement. The sun is familiar as well as grand, and it is growing more so—growing in enlargement, certainty, and powers of enlightenment. It implicitly provides one sort of answer to Keats's twilight of the gods and his concept of melancholy as a necessary condition of beauty. It calls for no help from Apollo or Hyperion in taking its course away from mystery toward the mind's satisfied seizing of its perceptions. The sublimity of the colossal sun is in keeping with the halo of the extraordinary that surrounds objects in the romantic field of vision; but though the mind does not reach regretfully after disappearing essences, it waits, and while it waits, measures the changing distance between earlier doubts and the certainty of its oncoming reality. By comparison, looking backward, Tennyson marks a two-way passage of objects into mere consciousness and of consciousness toward baffling estrangement:

> Ah, sad and strange, as in dark summer dawns
> The earliest pipe of half-awaken'd birds
> To dying ears, when unto dying eyes
> The casement slowly grows a glimmering square;
> So sad, so strange, the days that are no more.

Still more confident in the brilliance of perceptions just out of reason's reach is Stevens' "Of Mere Being," where being is neither banal nor available to definition. What makes us happy in its company is not the endurance of objects or their solidarity, or what reason seizes: it is the equilibrium that presence and distance maintain throughout the flowing present if one focuses on just the right place in the spectrum from the near and precise to the distant and mystical. That place is at the edge of the mind where a tropical palm and a bright bird rise up. At that juncture, romantic phantomization and the need for recollection are forestalled, as are all inventories that clutter more thoroughly mapped landscapes. The bird is arresting. It allows only one acute focus. We are aware of excessive art in a line like "The bird's fire-fangled feathers dangle down," and through that excess are aware of the interplay of the fictive and the real.[41] But nothing explicitly ontological or metaphysical intrudes here any more than in Hemingway's landscape in *Farewell to Arms;* and as in "To Autumn," nothing of times not present rises up to claim our attention. Like the gifts of Ceres, the gifts of mere being are sufficient in themselves.

In his American nowness and his concern with immediate objects, Stevens is opposed to the recollective phase of romanticism in general. Though he sometimes plays with old tropes from the discard heap that the romantic overlooks from his tower (as Stevens remarks of William Carlos Williams), he is reluctant to retrieve them for his own use except as ironic contrasts. Objects without attached ideas, and mere being without myth or history, dislodge the mind from the past. Every moment is a reasonably fresh start, like awakening in the morning to a colossal sun both familiar and quite new.

However, this suggestion of a completer grammar of romantic perception carries somewhat beyond our present concern. I have suggested some of its peripheral offshoots mainly in order to frame the limitations of the phantomized past. What I want to explore next is an area of quasihistorical retrieval parallel to that past but different in several respects. In it, something assumed to be an actual past comes forward far enough to submit to detailed description, as though a cultural middle ground were after all available. *The Eve of St. Agnes* with its medieval spectacle borders on that sort of descriptively ample historicism but uses its setting mainly as a backdrop for the rites of romantic yearning, in filling out a scheme of choices within which the lovers enact their programmatic progress and their eventual escape. Arthurian materials will serve us better because they underscore a national and cultural revival having purported historical foundations.

CHAPTER 4

Ancestral Gloom and Glory

> Yet I know, where'er I go,
> That there hath past away a glory from the earth.
>
> WORDSWORTH, *Ode: Intimations of Immortality*

Literature dwindles to a mere chronicle of circumstance, or passionless fantasies, and passionless meditation, unless it is constantly flooded with the passions and beliefs of ancient times, and . . . of all the fountains of passions and beliefs of ancient times in Europe, the Slavonic, the Finnish, the Scandinavian, and the Celtic, the Celtic alone has been for centuries close to the main river of European literature. It has again and again brought 'the vivifying spirit' 'of excess' into the arts of Europe . . . The legends of Arthur and his Table, and of the Holy Grail, once, it seems, the cauldron of an Irish god, changed the literature of Europe, and, it may be, changed, as it were, the very roots of man's emotions by their influence on the spirit of chivalry and on the spirit of romance.

> YEATS, *The Celtic Element in Literature*

A S MOST OF THOSE WRITERS realized who exploited the Matter of Britain (as opposed to Greek and Roman traditions), Arthur's realm was supposedly once a center of empire: Arthur after all was said to have invaded Rome and acquired its civil powers and to have been visited by the symbol of its spiritual authority, the grail. All this has obvious implications for the transfer of empire to what had been a province: the grail's presence in England proves that the continuity that once sustained a providentially protected Rome and its satellites can carry on in a new seat of power. Poets in that new location can bind themselves to a tradition that links all Western civilization. Seeing the grail, however, also forces one to reach far enough into a purely spiritual history to suggest the weakness of any secular continuity or focus on national powers. This again urges a separation of the mythical from the historical and of poetry's visionary capacities from its chronicle duties. As Milton demonstrates as well, the onset of any Christian vision is likely to curtail one's commitment to regional matters.

For this and other reasons, the Arthurian legend confesses its own insubstantiality and capacity for continuance: it rises up seeming to offer a reinfusion of the specific past, only to falter and recede again. It always proves to be a failed retrieval, a version of lost empire. Hence the nostalgia of its revivals is a near cousin to romantic recollection and Victorian regret, as Tennyson illustrates. In it, the customs and language of the past are not actually reinstated but are part of a management of distances. By "Victorian" in this context I do not mean that Tennyson and Matthew Arnold perfected that management but that one sort of past that we can associate with the Victorians presupposes the decline of the present. The end of Arthur's reign is always a reminder of the poet's isolation: history recalls but does not revive past glory; hence the special function of elegiac commemoration so preeminent in Malory and in Tennyson's *Idylls*. The loss of paradise and the *et in Arcadia ego* theme of nostalgic pastoral are not far from that same mood; nor are tragedy, romance, and even epic at times.

The Cyclical Mythos

Although the decline of civilizations is obviously not a theme strictly for poets, it has always had special prominence in fictive versions of the past. It is one of the formative myths of commemorative and elegiac verse, and it figures prominently in epic, pastoral, romance, satire, and tragedy. When the decline moves in a little closer to the poet's own time, within the sphere of historical chronicle, it suggests an ancestral mode; it stations dynasties in the relative distance but not out of reach of detailed description, perhaps not even of memory.[1] The downward cycle from a remote, idealized golden age is also, of course, a common part of the myth, but that phase leans toward more obvious fictions and less toward verisimilitude and the pretense of factuality. Romance and epic ordinarily stand somewhere between that remote myth of beginnings and the realistic social protraiture of such historical novels as James Clavell's *Shōgun*, and *Tai-Pan*, James Michener's *Hawaii* and *Centennial*, and Patrick White's *The Tree of Man*, which concern cultural development and contain many individual rises and falls. Even where a poem's scope is not sufficient for complete development, the cycle may be there in abbreviated form, as in the personal lyric and Wordsworth's effort to recapture those "truths that wake, / To perish never" from the fugitive intimations of youth.

Of all forms, epic, when it chooses to, encompasses the downward cycle and upward turn most fully. After an initial fall, the hero must work for a heroic recovery, as Aeneas transports the household gods of a ruined Troy to a new Rome, and Christ (in Milton's version) restores his Father's image in the desert, undoing the work of Eve and Adam.

The heroic paradigm in Milton's case is repeated in subsequent types of Christ in their sore temptations: the reclaimed kingdom need not suffer other declines so long as the righteous continue to sustain it, though of course it will be lost to the vast majority, whose downward spiral knows no end. Even where the restorative cycle is absent or truncated in epic, the implication is that the monumental past of ancestors such as Roland or Beowulf deserves to survive and may do so in the poet's commemoration. Presumably no one sets out to write an epic who is not prepared to deal reverently with the past. Unable to recover that past in actuality, the poem at least puts it into a transportable heroic image: it moves from the contact with gods that heroes once had to the bard's contact with the Muses, from the former gods of war, love, sun, and moon to the mediating guardians of the recitation itself. Milton counters the downward cycle even more decisively with recurrences of the Word and Light in history, scripture, and the poem, where the Muses are variations of the same Spirit present in those other places. Although Homer and Virgil cannot trust to recurrence so confidently, they do prevent the total escape of the heroic into the dim past.

As John Coolidge has pointed out, Virgil manages a twofold movement—simultaneously backward to the golden age and forward to its renewal in the age of Augustus. He does so not only in Aeneas' transfer of Trojan civilization to Rome in epic but in the prophecy of the Fourth Eclogue and in glances at epic again in the Sixth Eclogue. These dawning times do not require a withdrawal from the active life, as pastoral often does; instead, idyllic yearning gives way to a new potency as the poem's valedictory function pulls it forward into affairs of state. As Coolidge suggests, the "Virgilian progression" can also be "assimilated into the Christian pattern of revelation."[2] Thus a similar hope for renewal turns up in the younger Milton's sense of a millenarian ending imminent in the Reformation. Similarly, in *Upon Appleton House,* Marvell makes the Fairfax family a model of active virtue, seeking with some success to restore the ideal garden state in a fallen world; in "Bermudas" his pilgrims have already arrived at such a new age. In the latter instance, the landscape of the tropical island carries them backward past all intermediary civilized ideals to an equivalent to Eden. The small epic of these pastorals (in Coolidge's notion of the great represented in small) is matched by the large pastoral of such works as *The Faerie Queene, Paradise Lost, Paradise Regained,* and Sidney's *Arcadia,* in which what a hero struggles to attain is primarily a long-lost paradise. In these versions of the attempt to reverse the downward cycle, the arduous odyssey of the hero and the resting point of the placid life are two phases of the same process: one assumes the labors of restoration and the making of civilizations; the other assumes that the realm of golden ideals is almost beyond memory and certainly beyond rebuilding; it lies mainly in the imagination. Restoration belongs not to heroes, therefore, but to poets.

The far distance of past glory is equally central to romance, but it often suggests there a different sort of remoteness, more indecipherable, less openly national and social. The details of past civilizations cannot be presented in the inventory fashion of the novel or as normalcy. The "meander of Romance" (as Geoffrey Hartman christens its remote journeys into the unspecified) tends to replace the relics, customs, and manners of realistic social portrayal with a spectrum of spirit creatures. The frequent romance theme of lost and eventually relocated children also speaks in a special way to the problem of continuity among generations. That the lost child is birthmarked in order to be found suggests an irrevocable destiny working toward deliverance and a fitting together of the generational pieces. For instance, *Daniel Deronda* returns several times to the attempt to reunite generations. Wishing his days to be bound each to each, Deronda finds in his recovered mother an affirmation of the Jewishness for which he has been spiritually preparing for some time, just as Mirah in discovering his brother Mordecai fulfills a familial urge. These restorations are obviously quite different from epic returns to a culture or pastoral returns to a golden age. Neither are they quite at the center of romance: in Eliot's novelistic mode, recognitions are not of the kind that climax romance-comedy but are full explorations of the social and contractual conditions of the generative cycle. To be rerooted requires travel among social and economic subgroups and detailed settings, and the aftermath of one's discovery of parentage takes almost as much analysis as its preparation. Meanwhile, the theme of denied kindred is a kind of antiromance or resisted upward cycle, almost a perverse willing of the Fall. Indeed, the casting away of either parents or children frustrates generational blessings and forestalls the upward cycle—as in Grandcourt's son in *Daniel Deronda*, in Mirah and her father, and Deronda's mother and her father.

A more frequent complication in romance versions of decline and restoration, however, is the burying of causes. While we can be fairly sure of the reasons for the fall of Troy in Homer, the motives of Aeneas, and the source of the fall of Milton's Adam and Eve, the causes of decline in romance are likely to be obscure and mysterious and the upward turn capricious. This inexplicability is evident in the stress on miracles and wonders and the enlarged cast of greater-than-natural beings—phantoms, archetypes, sylphs, faeries, elves, poltergeists, magicians, doubles, and creatures from beyond mountains or from forest depths. Because such creatures exist apart from the rise and fall of chronicle dynasties and civilizations, they may be looked to for healing influences as well as bewitchment. They are not destructible in the same way that Troy or Eden proves to be—merely less accessible. Thus in pastoral (which is as close to romance as it is to epic and elegy), traces of the golden age are evident not only in the general sympathy that nature feels for shepherds but in the influence of gods and goddesses. Nature's returns suggest that in basic matters one finds nothing new under the sun, and nothing very rational or controllable either.

In tragedy and elegy, the fall is more compact and catastrophic than it normally is in epic, romance, or pastoral (although any of these may be tragic or elegiac), and the restoration is less fully worked out. Ordinarily, tragedy depends less for consolation on an actual upward turn than either epic or pastoral does. As part of the ordeal of dynastic failure, a tragic son inherits a disintegrating world that cannot be repaired except by his sacrifice. Hamlet's nostalgia for the blessed time of Hamlet Senior, for instance, assumes a disastrous distance between generations. Such myths of decline are parabolic in this sense: the hero's destruction illustrates not cultural cycles, as in the fall of Troy, but the fall of great men when certain failings and the Fates coincide. As *King Lear* suggests, even when a regenerative authority passes to the younger group, it may do so without healing. To take a different case: as a figurative son to Duncan, Macbeth destroys all noble customs; and if complete ruin is finally averted, it is only because of the able sons of another line, whose victory brings about the downfall of the protagonist. Other tragedies present figures who are just now falling, in the present consummation of the tragic ordeal, which, unlike an epic ordeal, is not cast in a distant narrative past. Becaue its enactment collapses the formal distance between now and then that narration maintains, tragedy's approach to unseated ancestry is quite different in this respect from ancestral or revivalist forms, even when the setting is ancient. Unlike pious heroes such as Aeneas or Adam, protagonists such as Oedipus or Shakespeare's Roman figures overextend their powers and plunge from high place; they forestall any preference we might have for magnitude and make normality seem a relief.

In curbing the audience's desire to reenter the past, tragedy stands at one border of past-oriented modes. Elegy's insistence on the ameliorations of nature and a resigned acceptance of losses places it near an opposite extreme. It compresses decline into a single brief recognition of something lost and unrecoverable. Worked out further, as it frequently is in the pastoral elegy, that phase may give way to an upward cycle— as in the seasonal images of Bion and Moschus or the resurrection of Milton's Lycidas. The latter relocates on a personal level the same paradise that goes through loss to restoration in *Paradise Lost* and *Paradise Regained.* Like other elegies, *Lycidas* thereby assumes a tragicomic structure, following tragedy's intensified sense of waste to a point of reversal and renewal.

In elegiac modes, poets are remembering and therefore sorrowing creatures, and almost anything may trigger their sense of an irretrievable past. In this respect, several forms, including a good many lyrics, plug into the patterns of loss that shape the large-scale plots of epic and romance. The personal past, lost eras and lost nations, and specific memorable occasions become part of a calculus of loss as they escape the present and become its shadow. To remove that shadow, the visionary poet, as opposed to the remembering or historical poet, seeks a transcendental present. Thus where elegies ordinarily settle for reconstructed consolations or substitutions (as in Wordsworth's Intimations ode), *Lycidas* and *Adonais* open up avenues to timelessness. Again what Yeats's speaker asks to escape in "Sailing to Byzantium" are the limits of temporal nature, and what he requires is rescue by a combination of God's holy sages—"perning" into time to purge him of mortality—and art, in which the image of eternity appears and into which the speaker himself moves. The artifice of eternity serves a purpose similar to that of the superior pastoral realm of *Lycidas.* It is by denying such a realm and such an artifice that Stevens in "Sunday Morning" defines the elegiac limitations of the lady's naturalistic realm. There "paradise" is not unchanging but in motion; it is the earth we know in its cycles of growth and ripening:

> Deer walk upon our mountains, and the quail
> Whistle about us their spontaneous cries;
> Sweet berries ripen in the wilderness;
> And, in the isolation of the sky,
> At evening, casual flocks of pigeons make
> Ambiguous undulations as they sink,
> Downward to darkness, on extended wings.[3]

If unlike *Lycidas,* most elegies linger only on the fringes of the visionary, the same is true of Arthurian romance. But the function of the grail legend there is partly to instate a visionary level more explicitly, both to heighten the sense of loss for a passing age and to set a standard for the knight's quest beyond chivalric norms. Perhaps Milton and Sidney had the added dimensions of the grail in mind when they considered Arthurian matter for their major works. By deciding instead in favor of Eden and Arcadia respectively, they took a significant further step toward escaping ordinary history and allowing a continuous comparison between it and the golden age. The main contrast with which they work thereby became not the present and a shadowy heroic past but an incomplete and fallen temporal life and an image of perfection.

Nearly all the patterns characteristic of pastoral, tragedy, and elegy can be found in a single text in *Paradise Lost,* Milton's comprehensive myth of loss and restoration and complete calculus of higher and lower paradises. In epic, decline is ordinarily countered by a transfer of empire or the declaration of a substantial heroic mold; even Arthurian romance suggests that assertion, as an alliance of knightly powers succeeds in transferring a portion of Rome to Britain. Thus the founding of Troynovant in Spenser returns England to Troy while moving it forward in a great recapitulative spiral that replaces old empires with a new one without sacrificing all their values. Some literature, art, and philosophy is renewable. But Milton outdoes this sense of national kingdoms in the claims he makes for the renewability of man's one-time perfection. Although he too allows transfers of empire of several sorts (Satan's exodus to hell and journey to Eden, God's transfer of power to Christ, the ultimate new heaven and earth), he does so with ironic regard for military conquest, new religions, cosmopolitan institutions, chivalry, and national heroes. In effect, by universalizing the myth of decline and redefining the chosen people, he forestalls any further decline or transfer of the heroic pattern: as Christ drives home to Satan in *Paradise Regained,* once his kingdom is declared, no others will be required.[4] In diminishing Arthur and his English successors by comparison, Milton displaces Spenser as well as Homer and Virgil, the powers of renewal that he claims being attachable only to the poet as a chosen exponent of the truth and to his fit readers. With that transfer of empire from Adam's edenic kingdom to the second Adam, he renders other falls marginal and subsidiary as well: none of them really counts next to this single Fall that ruined mankind at the root. All other falls are but veiled types of the source, which makes predecessors in epic imperfect foreshadowings of the complete poem. Certain spiritual paradigms are everywhere valid; certain theological universals guarantee recurrence.

What precisely is the pattern of recurrence in Milton's cycles, and how does it compare with the Arthurian model he chose not to follow? An adequate answer must await a later chapter, but it seems clear in a preliminary way that Milton's historical logic hinges on heaven's Father-Son agreement, which is sealed in the dialogue of Book III of *Paradise Lost* and ultimately demonstrated in its earthly phase on the pinnacle of *Paradise Regained.* Unfortunately, at the Father's initial announcement of His Son's corule (in Book V), a second "son" springs forth in Satan, whose removal to separate quarters is both a primal fall and a counterparadigm for the transfer of empire—for transfer as a breaking off and as a parody of the high throne. In effect, Satan discovers history with all its ancestral joylessness, its ruptures of creature from Creator, its loss of paradise, its quarrel with the Father, and paradoxically, many of its high achievements. Satan also brings forth some of the poetic afflictions that Milton seeks to cure, among them elegiac nostalgia and guilt-ridden regret, which displace the joyful affirmation of the Father's renewed image in His generation and the hymnal response of receivers of epiphany. Satanic regret lies near the heart not only of hell's archetypal ruin but eventually of Eden's as well. Milton's several perspectives on that ruin are designed to reduplicate Satan's pattern and break it into phases. In the human phase, he limits lamentation for the lost Eden, since in view of the full myth, elegy and tragedy have only momentary functions even in the fallen world, as the poet as visionary looks past the intermediate distances to origins and conclusions.

Arthurian Revivals

The Miltonic cycle is more complicated than this, of course. It echoes and revises, for instance, its Homeric, Virgilian, and Italian precedents and constantly recollects Western traditions. But such complexities aside, Milton clearly counters the downward cycle of Arthurian materials, which in Malory and Tennyson are dominated by nostalgia. Regret and loss are especially compatible with Victorian retrospection, which is a prominent postromantic example of the dominance of historical limits. Tennyson, Morris, and Swinburne—and later in a similar spirit E. A. Robinson and at times T. H. White—are uneasy over the contrast between Arthurian chivalry and modern times. In *Merlin,* for instance, Robinson focuses on the moment of greatest disparity between Arthur's achievements and what follows from the grail. A similar hiatus between the drab present and a lost world runs through *Lancelot* and *Tristram* and tends to register most at the moment the grail passes out of view. One result of the withdrawal of those who have achieved the grail is the phantomizing of its ideals and an emphasis on the spectral matters of prophecy and long-range recollection. The poem looks from Merlin's viewpoint toward old age and the crumbling of empire:

> "Tomorrow I shall go away again
> To Camelot; and I shall see the King
> Once more; and I may come to you again
> Once more; and I shall go away again
> For ever."[5]

Although Merlin's previsions of disaster look like stage fictions, they illustrate a real enough anxiety about the elusiveness of glory. Evening tones deepen into night in *Lancelot* as well.

A similar melancholy runs through Tennyson's *Idylls.* In "The Lady of Shalott," the heroine floats down to Camelot on a barge to "mournful, holy" chants. On similar barges we find eventually the fair Elaine and finally Arthur himself. The image suggests appropriately the gentle passing of a period and the quiet end of its turmoil. Like Robinson, Tennyson is aware of the vast interval between us and the Arthurian ideal; past glory recedes slowly and tantalizingly, as Arthur himself does in Sir Bedivere's last view of him:

> Long stood Sir Bedivere
> Revolving many memories, till the hull
> Look'd one black dot against the verge of dawn,
> And on the mere the wailing died away.[6]

As Sir Bedivere's moment hovers between past and present, it takes on the ghostly intangibility of marginal things. He is understandably reluctant to throw Excalibur away and thereby disallow the memory that clings to relics:

> "If indeed I cast the brand away,
> Surely a precious thing, one worthy note,
> Should thus be lost forever from the earth . . .
> What record, or what relic of my lord
> Should be to aftertime, but empty breath
> And rumors of a doubt?"
>   (139–151)

A tangible memento has advantages that poetic legends and historical records lack, carrying as it does a convincing image of splendor in its "myriads of topaz lights, and jacinth-work / Of subtlest jewellery."

Unlike Milton's visitations of the same Spirit that descended to Moses, such a repossession of Arthurian glory through mementos "stored in some treasure-house of mighty kings" maintains a distance between us and our ancestral sources. The grail does not descend anew to us, nor is the poet privileged in reciting its history. Tennyson doubts the validity of the poet's attempt to reclaim even this much of the past. The original setting of *Morte d'Arthur* is a banquet at which the poet Evard Hall reads a poem he has saved from the fire to which he has already consigned the rest of an Arthurian epic. Although one may dream of Arthur's return, one must live without such things. Arthur himself challenges Sir Bedivere's nostalgia accordingly: " 'The old order changeth, yielding place to new' " (291).

Despite such attempts to root out the bereavement around which he constructed so many of his better lyrics, Tennyson did not take the backward view lightly, as the length and ambition of the *Idylls* testifies. The grail especially extracts a deep veneration for the past from the present, even as it undermines the secular worth of modern civilizations. Such an exceptional gift is required to achieve it that, as it turns out, only three knights have any success; and two of them, Percivale and Lancelot, have very little by comparison to Galahad. In the company of the grail, all ordinary accomplishments become mere vanity. In pursuing it, Percivale finds everywhere a recurrent diminution of the ordinary; everything he reaches for turns to ashes. Certainly Arthur is correct to foresee the ruin of the court so long as it insists on pursuing ideals beyond its capacity. Like the objects in "Tears, Idle Tears" that disclose their essences just as they disappear, the grail signals the vanishing of the real past just as it fulfills itself. Imagination and reality pass each other going in opposite directions. Thus whereas Milton loses only history in discovering the reinstated image of the father in the wilderness, both history and the grail escape in Tennyson's downward cycle. The poet's retrieving symbolism and narrative capacity are dedicated to the task of disclosing what they cannot seize upon or bring back alive.

In neither Milton's restoration of the Word nor in Tennyson's nostalgia have we considered the recurrence of the achievement of other poets; yet the intervention of a line of poets dealing with the same ancestors puts another light on the downward cycle. From the perspective of a T. H. White, for instance, the way to Spenser and Malory is blocked by Tennyson and perhaps a little by James Russell Lowell, Swinburne, Arnold, and Charles Williams. As each recounting of the legend faces that accumulated past, it implicitly takes stock of its own location. From another perspective, however, that inheritance may be not a burden but an uplifting. Even a revivalist who feels nostalgia for a lost past may find a haven in the collaborative fable that tradition gives him. As long as he dwells in the realm of the imagination—until he emerges from his recollective trance into an unchivalric present—he finds a workable compromise between the glittering past and what he sees about him.

White in *The Once and Future King* handles the collision between now and then somewhat differently from his predecessors, however, and generally disapproves of their idealizing of Arthur and his court. Like Tennyson and Robinson, he has few illusions about the present; but unlike them, he also clings to very few about the past. He entertains a complex sense of recurrence, the Arthurian literary precedents he must unseat if his Arthur is to find a place, and intertwined historical phases and intervals. On one hand, he suggests the developmental course of France, Wales, and England from medieval to modern periods; and his particularity about castles, armor, hunting, fighting, building, and training make that past both foreign and reverential. On the other hand, he also reminds us constantly that our station in the twentieth century is very similar to Arthur's in certain basic things: although we are perched on the edge of world wars among advanced technologies, we find the same motives operating now as always. Along with the familiar cycle of the seasons and the age-old processes of learning and maturation, these elements of recurrence restore much of the past to us.

By describing the outmoded surfaces of a historical society in detail, White exposes the fictitious idealizing of rival Arthurians; but the gap between moderns and ancients, and again between White and Tennyson, comes less from realism than from the presence of a narrator whose seasoned judgment provides counterchecks for other views of the Round Table. The art of storytelling is governed by his personality and by his awareness that he is too far into the twentieth century not to feel ironic about magic, the grail, and the marvels of Merlin. White thus displays the operations of the imagination in such as way as to make them self-consciously part of the bond between writer and reader; in the surface of the telling he dramatizes an awareness of the quaint, the bizarre, and the lyric as these enter the fable.

In back of Arthur lies an even deeper past—prehistoric and even prehuman—which only a modern narrator versed in archaeology could know. By stressing racial similarities and diminishing the differences among social systems and customs, White allows that past to have an effect on the distancing of the primary story. Merlin uses his magic not merely to enforce the destiny that Arthurian convention guarantees but also to open up a set of contrasts for the impressionable mind of Wart: the object of Wart's metamorphoses is to make him sufficiently removed from human habit to suggest quite different alternatives from those that the social context suggests. Besides the larger cycle of animal kinships to which Arthur gains access through metamorphoses, White outlines several smaller steps forward in social institutions. These movements are not totally progressive, however: after a first failure at social reform, Arthur encourages the grail quests, seeking to siphon off excess energy and derail the possessive and fighting instincts indefinitely. But the quests too fail—for somewhat the same reasons that they fail in Malory and Tennyson: they divide the Round Table into those who (in their purity) leave the secular realm altogether and those who return to it no better than when they left. The second downward turn is not curable; but in converting trials by arms into carefully weighed, reasoned argument under abstract law and institutional justice, Arthur introduces a third movement. Ironically, it is the law itself in the final relapse that destroys the Round Table, when under its due processes Guenever is convicted of adultery. Thus each reform judges those who introduce it: the grail quest that was to have perfected the chivalric quest ends by exposing Lancelot's version of it as inadequate and obsolete; the abstract justice that was to render peace among contending parties undermines the fragile structure they have learned to maintain under less ideal rules.

In White's view of the historical process as a series of ups and downs, it does not particularly matter where he establishes his examples historically; the rhythm of social orders and collapses will presumably go on and on. Whatever has been may be at any other time, in another costume. Also, any of us may return to the quasisanctuary of the childlike

without searching out a racial golden age in a distant mythos. Thus
White mixes indiscriminately elements from nearly every period from
the sixth century to the fourteenth and discovers common denomina-
tors in animal and childlike kinships for all of them. Even in his concern for the mechanics of tilting, horsemanship, rabbit and boar hunting, and archery and for what the drink, food, clothing, habits, and
emotional patterns of Arthurian life were (or might be imagined to have
been), he does not allow much scope for laments for lost times. Instead,
he exploits many of the satiric elements of the antichivalric tradition in
Chaucer, Cervantes, and Samuel Butler to prevent the overenlargement
of knighthood. Certainly the imagination does not seek to establish its
ideals only in a kingdom of long ago; it finds the lowest as well as the
highest common features in the Arthurian material.

This is true also of the grail quests, which White finds not transcendent but of a piece with other human projects. Whereas E. A. Robinson
and Tennyson propose the grail quests as models of spiritual idealism
and withdrawal from historical entanglements, White thinks of them
(for all but Galahad) as an intensification of motives at work elsewhere
and subjects them to the crossfire of several conflicting points of view.
(In that respect he does not really pursue a myth of decline at all.) Even
Galahad is subjected to a number of perspectives from which Tennyson's Galahad is immune, all of them hostile except for Lancelot's.
White departs from Malory as well in his view of the evils of fighting
and the origins and purposes of the quests. The tension between secular and religious fellowship is less central to his account of the quest,
and Lancelot's love for Guenever is not the same transgression it is in
most of his predecessors. Nor is the grail related to modern society as
exalted myth to mere history. Instead, several levels of idealism and
human limitations are present simultaneously (though in different
mixes) in each of the heroes and each of the periods. Where White follows Malory in granting visions of the grail according to degrees of purity in the knights, he does not appear to do so in order to verify the
rightness of what each discovers but to measure the egoism that underlies the pursuit even of ideals. From several perspectives, Galahad is
socially obtuse, priggish, and immensely self-centered. In the service of
the wrong cause, untranscended, his egoism might easily become the
destructive force of holy wars or world wars; armed with a self-right-
eousness sufficient to wreck lesser ideas, it might suggest the Hitlerism
that haunts White's view of the modernist "fort Mayne." But White
finds short-comings in Galahad's critics as well. As we see from Lancelot's more favorable assessment, the pursuit of holiness is countered in
Galahad by humility and the sacrifice one makes to higher goals. Galahad's rigor in putting down inferiors is part of an uncompromising spiritual search for truths beyond the ordinary. If he is blind to the sof-

tening decorum of chivalry, it is because he finds that decorum to be too concerned with trivia.

At this view of Galahad suggests, beyond the antiquarianism and the strategic usefulness that White finds in lessons from the book of conduct, he locates a mythopoeic realm that allows the imagination to expand its horizons. In this he seems indebted more to romantic recollection than specifically to Arthurian predecessors. Certainly more things than the grail quests sustain worthy ideals in the work. Like Stevens in such poems as "Disillusionment of Ten O'Clock" and "The Emperor of Ice Cream," White takes a child's view of unusual perceptions and such things as kindness, tolerance, and avuncular wisdom. Merlin's wizardry and its kingdom of animals are part of that view. Much of Wart's research among animal forms in the realms of water, earth, and air suggest that behind the metamorphoses of romance is an escape from normative human rule. After such an education, Arthur cannot be satisfied with the faulty political and social institutions he inherits, which trap him in a combination of Orkeney perversities, past mistakes of his own, and the technology of medieval castles, agriculture, and war making. The imagination constantly measures such things against the magic, the animal kinships, and the ennobling possibilities that boyhood entertains so openly. Although nothing quite comes round as Arthur wishes, White's realism is not disillusioned. His version of Arthur's story ends in disaster, as all versions do, but it does not follow a one-way, downward cycle. It manages a complex attunement of older to newer societies and of nature to the marvelous in a mode that is partly a book of manners and partly a Bildungsroman in a historical setting.

One index to that combination of modes and its compromises between realism and hope is the relationship of tutor to pupil and of father to son. The text is filled with ceremonies, rituals, the proper ways of doing things, and thus with the rites by which elders indoctrinate and shape the impressionable minds of their students. These methods of training provide an alternative to naked power for the continuance of ruling authority. However, I want to reserve until later the implications of specific father-son relationships and cite here only one example. As the narrator stations Arthur in the respectful distance as a figure about to disappear into myth, Arthur offers hope for a new start to a page boy who becomes his sole inheritor. The implication is that if Arthur is to return, it must be in the imagination of someone who carries his image hopefully, just as Wart in his training period has received the knowledge that Merlin finds suitable. Arthur's gift to the page boy fulfills the drift of the final book as a minimal novelistic demonstration of character and an expanding book of conduct and wisdom. Arthur can exist, if nowhere else, in such a book as a counselor and advice giver. As a knowledgeable mediator between the past and the reader, the narrator brings Arthur's secrets for survival into a new climate and thus strikes a final bargain with the audience, the key to which is Arthur's legacy to the page boy. The distance between then and now is not totally without elegiac regrets, but White makes a gesture toward the continuity of a durable spirit.

Spenser and the View from Eumnestes' Chamber

In his narration to the page boy, White's Arthur leaves the fields of action and joins historians, lecturers, and poets in committing the past to renewable records and their teaching. He points up the fact that every version of the Arthurian cycle works simultaneously with the perpetuation of legend and a historical hiatus. The Arthurian revivalist knows that he is a long way from the historical base he honors, which he sees through a tradition of interpreters. Even from Spenser's much nearer distance, the historical Arthur exists primarily as a bookish convention; he does not live in the presumed accuracies of William of Malmesbury, Gildas, or Nennius but in the reduplicating imagination.[7] To both Malory and Spenser, in fact, not only Arthur but medieval chivalry is largely legendary: if Arthur is a millennium away from Spenser, the best of chivalry is nearly half that, despite Elizabethan attempts to revive it. Yet since chronicle materials presumably lie behind the legend, the suspicion that Arthur once served as an English captain imposes certain conditions on the poet's handling of the materials— conditions that do not necessarily obtain for Greek and Roman materials, as William Caxton's preface to his edition of Malory attests. The lessons of Arthur are parabolic and applicable to the English present. As Spenser's chief national predecessor, Malory does not, of course, make any use of fairyland's free play with temporal sequence and anachronism in establishing those lessons; instead he frames the Arthurian story as a social and religious model distant enough to be manipulated but real enough to seem historical. *Morte Darthur* offers models of conduct in the manner of *The Mirror for Magistrates* in ethical matters that Malory undoubtedly believed to be still at issue.[8] In this respect, he sets a precedent that White's book of advice can exploit.

However, as an anatomy of the founding, rise, and decay of an extraordinary civilization, *Morte Darthur* also comes closer than White's version to a general myth of decline without renewal. Whereas Spenser's history has recurrent Christian and Platonist types to reinforce its claims for renewal and for a destined historical movement climaxing in the Tudors, Malory's is largely periodized and nonrecurrent. The tone of *Morte Darthur* falls accordingly much nearer to Victorian nostalgia. For instance, like Tennyson's cleavage between lesser affairs and the grail quests, Malory's introduction of the grail spells the end of the secular dynasty. Realizing that competition from the grail dooms the Round Table, Arthur utters the first of several dirges to lost glory:

> "Alas!" said King Arthur unto Sir Gawain, "ye have nigh slain me for the vow that ye have made, for through you ye have bereft me the fairest and truest of knighthood that ever was seen together in any realm of the world. For when they depart from hence I am sure they all shall never meet more together in this world, for they shall die many in the quest. And so it forthinketh not me a little, for I have loved them as well as my life. Wherefore it shall grieve me right sore, the departing of this fellowship."[9]

Like Tennyson's Arthur, he is correct about the grail, not only because the secular reign is belittled by it but because in revealing individuals to each other in a different light, the grail raises a new inward potential in them. "Then began every knight to behold other, and either saw other, by their seeming, fairer than ever they were before . . . There was no knight that might speak one word a great while, and so they looked every man on other as they had been doom" (p. 634). The best fulfillment of individuals is no longer a concerted social action but individual, otherworldly visions. As the timeless realm of religious ideals pulls them away from institutional and historical achievement, it also requires a reliance on allegory, and in that respect too brings about a discrepancy between social chronicle and spiritual achievement.

In contrast with Malory's lament for passing greatness, the Tudor view of the Arthurian past, at least in Spenser's version, is more optimistic about blending history, fiction, and religious myth and thus about renewing past ideals not merely in the poem but in society. Recurrent Christian and Platonist archetypes can be reinstated in different courtly centers and descend into the glory of monarchs wherever the social order is prepared to receive them. But it is also true that history leads through temporal deflections and militancy on its way to an ideal court, and one cannot construct the earthly city of Cleopolis quite in the image of New Jerusalem.

The concept of revival is thus complex and troubled. It includes the possibility of the poem's replacing other epics in the celebration of a complete civilization; it includes (in St. George) a specifically English reform of the religious establishment (which Spenser viewed not as an innovation but as a revival of the original church); it includes the recollecting of Arthur's model of chivalry and kingship in the new monarch; and it includes the best of Aristotle and Plato in the poet's image of the complete knight. Indeed, with all its allusions, its network of repeated imagery from previous romances, its reuse of structural shapes from epic journeys and ideas from Plato and Aristotle, its allegorical devices from Prudentius, its historical references from English chronicle, and descriptive topics such as the bower, the labyrinth, and the forest, the poem is obviously a great repository of the past. The reader's frequent impression that he has encountered something before is reinforced by the text's own habits of reduplication, as analogous episodes repeat Spenser repeating Virgil or Ariosto. As Stephen Barney remarks, the text is an "edifice of planned repetition."[10]

In all these respects, and in the typological reliving of the old and new Adam in Everyman, the contemporary court should be a focal climax of a long historical development. It is also true that the mix of fictional realms, historical reference, and contemporary matters is assisted by the fact that history for Spenser includes Greek ancestry, the legend of England's founding by Brutus, and oblique references to Eden and other Old Testament matters. In these greater distances and in the concept of typological recurrence, fact readily blends with legend and its paradigmatic models, which are applicable anywhere. Hence for most purposes, the poem has no real need to sort these things out; it may take for granted not only our common human origins in Adam and Eve but the bridge between Eden, Christ, and, as in other ambitious Renaissance world histories, all subsequent empires. As the latest flower in the course of civilizations, England embodies the same types that once took Greek or Hebrew specification. The courses of the City of God and Cleopolis (the city of earthly fame) can obviously be parallel and mutually supportive.

Granted this blend of the fictive and the historical, it may seem capricious to question the applicability of Arthurian legend to contemporary matters. But in episodes such as Red Cross's vision of New Jerusalem and the breaking up of Colin Clout's vision on Mount Acidale, Spenser nonetheless suggests that different levels of a scattered and mutilated One tend to draw apart in history's strung-out episodes. The removal of the poem to a faery realm to begin with underscores the fictive nature of the Arthurian materials (as Michael Murrin aptly remarks, "The Muses do not preside over the Public Record Office"[11])— especially if by "faery," as Northrop Frye suggests, Spenser means partly antique, Edenic nature.[12] Whether its geographical location is India, America, or the Middle East, faery ideality transcends its contemporary materials, even if, as Frank Kermode argues, the poem's celebration of Elizabeth Tudor and other contemporaries can be quite specific.[13] The relationship between fictive models and chronicle events is often problematic at best, and never more so than in the expressly historical sections of the poem. On one level of allegory, materials from different eras can be combined in the way Red Cross returns to Eden to rescue Adam and Eve while remaining St. George and serves a queen who is the narrator's contemporary while encountering King Arthur from the fifth century. But a chronicle of nations demands continuity of another kind and does not fit smoothly into a program of spiritual and moral definitions.

Where then do the ideals that Spenser calls Arthurian actually exist: in an irretrievable real past or in floating universals that descend into this or that national manifestation of glory? Do they reappear in cycles? Or in a linear and spiral course of national empires that have moved from old to new Troys, perhaps from greater to lesser examples? Or do they exist only in the poet's fictions, which project them as more or less perfect, while their embodiment in history is postponed until New Jerusalem materializes outside its visionary projections?

The main passages in which Spenser takes up the collaboration of actual past moments and universal patterns of ideal or exemplary conduct are the recitation of Red Cross's biography (I.10), the history that Guyon and Arthur read in the House of Alma (II.10), Merlin's chronicle of kings (III.4), and more obliquely, the Mutability Cantos. I want to take these up in turn and explore the degree to which Spenser manages to yoke together his floating models of chivalry, the Arthurian past, Christian and Platonist master models, and contemporary reality. In a capsule, the first of these seems to me to leave us with an unresolvable tension between religious vision and historical duty. The second swings to the other extreme and subordinates the mythos of the eternal city to the chronicle of earthly cities and drops something in the process. The third, Merlin's education of Britomart, strikes a workable compromise between several elements of the poem—myth, nature, providence, philosophic precept, and history—and is probably Spenser's most successful blend of these. The fourth destroys that blend, or at least renders it relatively unimportant by withdrawing from historical incident to philosophical precept and myth.

Among these passages the one that most puts historical matters under visionary scrutiny is the hermit's explanation of Red Cross's heritage and destiny. In linking Cleopolis to New Jerusalem by its capacity to "eternize" in a lasting "book of fame" those who serve the queen, the hermit establishes not so much a chronology of events as a hierarchy of places and types. The problem is to bring down into any historical place an image of glory that has only one true, lasting fulfillment. Unlike glory in *Paradise Regained*, the hermit's secular realm does catch substantial reflections of that source, as the queen distributes glory through the realm by the authority her own greatness gives her. The hermit also hints at correspondences among the biographical record of St. George, certain allegorical equivalents to the Old Jerusalem in England's destiny, and the celestial origins of all images of blessedness. Moreover, concerned as it is with modeling a typical soul in search of holiness, Book I as a whole uses historical allegory to draw certain illustrative figures into its program of abstract qualities. The hermit's vision might be said to seal the definition of holiness historically (Red Cross as St. George), morally (Red Cross as the soul in pilgrimage), and anagogically (Red Cross as a figure of Christ). Unfortunately, the glory of human achievements is also quite different in kind from eternity's, and those who aim for one kind are obliged to postpone aiming for the other. The efficacy of the earthly city as an expressive analogy to New Jerusalem is not beyond debate. As Red Cross finds to his disappointment, he must perform the obligations he has undertaken before he can put aside his militant phase and seek the peace of sainthood in "painful pilgrimage." Like Colin Clout on Mount Acidale, he finds his career breaking into two phases—one contemplative, removed from action, and attuned to idealizing vision; the other bound to moral projects. The center of the latter is Everyman's conquering of sins, which must be accomplished in temporal contexts.

The narration becomes more perplexed with specific historical reference in Book II, as Guyon and Arthur read their respective chronicles in Eumnestes' chamber (II.9). Before he brings them to that point, Spenser anticipates objections to the mixture of history and allegory he is about to offer and steps forward to address the queen on the topic of fairyland fictions generally:

> Right well I wote, most mighty Soveraine,
> That all this famous antique history
> Of some th' aboundance of an ydle braine
> Will judged be, and painted forgery,
> Rather then matter of just memory;
> Sith none that breatheth living aire does know,
> Where is that happy land of Faery,
> Which I so much doe vaunt, yet no where show,
> But vouch antiquities, which no body can know.
>   (II.1)

His reply to such critics is that the land of faery exists in the same way Indian Peru, the Amazon, or Virginia did before explorers found their exact azimuths—that is, by rumor and in imagination. Unfortunately, if no one knows the antiquities that are the poet's sources and no one has actually sailed to fairyland, no one can vouch for either. Peru and Virginia may exist on the same plane as Devonshire or London, but no Columbus with a flotilla of well-stocked ships could reach fairyland.

The central matter is not the claim that fables touch upon the literal truth, however, but the assumption that putting proper names in a fabled world establishes a definite relationship between fairyland and history. The narrator has no hesitancy in mixing the two, as he proceeds to do in considering poetry analogous to a mirror:

> And thou, O fayrest Princesse under sky,
> In this fayre mirrhour maist behold thy face,
> And thine owne realmes in lond of Faery,
> And in this antique ymage thy great auncestry.
>   (II.4)

Is Elizabeth's inheritance an ancestral ideal that comes from specific Arthurian distances or a projection that can be posited of several places? The two sorts of ancestry yoked together here—the ancestry of types in the Creator's image and the ancestry of real historical primogenitors—presuppose quite different powers of recollection. One gives the poet a primary shaping role; the other requires him to serve specific national interests through documented narration.

The chamber of Eumnestes offers a different proposal about the mixture of history and fable and in fact turns the issue around: what matters is not how representatives of temporal glory are bound to figurative analogues but what faculties we employ in seeking the truth in past records and in a proliferation of fantastic images. Spenser's concern is the seat of imagination, judgment, and memory, which (in handling prophecy, the present, and the past) dominate youth, maturity, and age:

> The first of them could things to come foresee;
> The next could of thinges present best advize;
> The third things past could keepe in memoree.
>   (II.9.49)

Though Spenser does not insist upon it, these faculties might presumably be exemplified in the poet as seer, the governor, and the historian. This would make a complicated three-way equation that set fictions across from contemporary reality and historical chronicle as something roughly equivalent to the imagination in its systematic relation to judgment and memory. In this arrangement, which Arthur or which Jerusalem one sees would depend on the faculty with which one scrutinizes the evidence: under imagination, Arthur predicts a not yet reigning magnificence; under judgment, he is a perfect governor; under memory, he is a distant figure in a more or less true chronicle.

The difficulty with this elaborate equation (besides its stretching farther than Spenser apparently intended) is that it does not coincide with the poem's portraits of these mental faculties. Although as one of a line of kings, Arthur is the historian's business, that observation does not clarify his connection with magnificence in the moral allegory. Next to the structure of virtues in our minds, as James Nohrnberg suggests, Arthur on horseback "becomes a somewhat out-of-touch factotum."[14] Nor is Phantastes an exemplary figure for the poet constructing his fables. Both memory and fantasy fall into such confusion that they cast doubt on the mind's capacity to maintain order among its impressions. If from the outside the House of Alma is besieged by something like T. S. Eliot's "undisciplined squads of emotion" and "the general mess of imprecision of feeling," inside, its chamber of imagination is chaotic:

> And all the chamber filled was with flyes,
> Which buzzed all about, and made such sound,
> That they encombred all mens eares and eyes,
> Like many swarmes of bees assembled round,
> After their hives with honny do abound:
> All those were idle thoughtes and fantasies,
> Devices, dreames, opinions unsound,
> Shewes, visions, sooth-sayes, and prophesies;
> And all that fained is, as leasings, tales, and lies.
>   (II.9.51)

Whether or not the land of faery and the present poem are included under those tales and lies, Spenser clearly distrusts undisciplined image projection, as he does in other parts of the poem as well. With falsehood so rampant in the world, the poet as a professional liar is especially vulnerable, particularly in modes as freely imaginative and prolific as fairyland romance. His very profession requires him to sit daily in Phantastes' chamber, where the walls are "dispainted all with in / With sondry colours," with creatures of fantasy, "infernall hags, centaurs, feendes, hoppodames, / Apes, lyons, aegles, owles, fooles, lovers, children, dames."

Although the poet need not rely on fantasy alone to lead the way out of this fertile residue of impressions, he finds no real help from memory, which perhaps should be but is not a storehouse of wisdom and judgment. The chamber of Eumnestes is as cluttered as that of Phantastes and even more riddled by paradoxes. It is "ruinous and old," yet durable and sturdy; Eumnestes himself has infinite remembrance, yet is half blind to the world and relies upon worm-eaten scrolls and parchments full of canker holes; he is lively in mind but feeble in body. That he "tosses and turns" his source materials "withouten end" suggests the dissatisfactions of research: though the past is full of a number of things, none of them is self-defining. Whatever the prizes of Platonic recollection (where those sparks of divine life reside that kindle genius in Augustine), memory here has no scintillating lights or privileged moments. Whereas Phantastes multiplies visions of potential happenings and sensory impressions, Eumnestes proliferates facts. Both are without a principle of redemption or selective discard. Even with the help of books and records, then, Eumnestes' chamber is a place of disintegration; like the ground under the wheels of Brueghel's wagon of time, it is strewn with the impediments of wrecked achievements, arts, and sciences.

The difficulty with the faculty psychology that Spenser sketches here, even under the control of a judgment that fixes these prolific materials of mind and record in categories (presumably under such disciplines as the law, the arts, and philosophy), is that Phantastes and Eumnestes are reduced to suppliers of source materials. They do not function as vital elements of perception or retain their natures as imaginative and remembering forces in acts of judgment themselves. Hence one finds little guidance for determining what the relations might be between the imagination, which produces fairylands, and the records that house almost all survivals of history.[15]

Presumably both Guyon and Arthur learn something about their respective lineages from the books Eumnestes hands them. But ordinarily a lineage in allegory is not what it is in chronicle history: it is a fictive anatomy of ingredients in the offspring—or a linear way of classifying components of an abstract quality. In contrast, the succession of kings about which Arthur reads in *Briton's Moniments* makes no particular revelations about England's general movement toward centrality and away from a divisive provincialism. The succession itself it not complete. (After Uther's reign, we expect Arthur's, but the narrative breaks off and is replaced by Guyon's roll of elfin emperors.) The translation of the Tudor dynasty into elfin terms has several advantages (besides shielding the reader's eyes from Tudor brilliance): since some seven hundred elfin emperors have succeeded one another in order and "due descent," elfland suggests the ideality of the Tudor heritage to which it leads.[16] It also avoids the genealogical arguments that Hardynge attempts to make, for example, when he establishes a single line from Adam to Edward IV. The break between the two kinds of chronicle also makes possible a joining of Arthur and Gloriana as though they were of the same period. Among other things, this strategy sets aside the "ruins of the times" and puts off the elegiac tone that so often accompanies Arthurian revivals; by asserting the actuality of Arthur's predecessors, who are remote, and the elfin ancestry of Elizabeth, who is near, Spenser mingles the mythic and the historic in both of them. All times become marvelously copresent in the freedom of the fiction.

Although in this instance Spenser bypasses the opportunity to blend the ideal and the actual in Elizabeth herself, he clearly has such a convergence in mind elsewhere.[17] In Book III, in returning to chronicle narration once more and adding Britomart and Artegal to the design, he draws historical materials farther into the allegorical scheme. The proposition here is that whatever ideal continuity history manages and whatever contact it has with shaping molds and patterns derive from the nature of love and justice. Since love in the Platonic ambience is the urge to pursue ideal forms, a historical sequence may be governed by the mind's advancement toward its constitutive images. What the imagistic faculty proposes, the memory holds and the judgment follows up. For instance, Artegal (whose name means "equal to Arthur," as Joanne Craig remarks[18]) substitutes the pursuit of justice for Arthur's actual reign. In a sense, the book of conduct again serves as an intermediate level between first principles and applied—or multiplied—actions. Insofar as Britomart and Artegal may be historical on one level (as facets of Elizabeth and an ideal suitor, let us say), they propose both a specific and an ideal monarch. This notion is not identical to the blurred idea that Spenser defends at the outset of Book II, but it goes some way toward justifying the mirror image proposed there. The central theme of Merlin's narration is accordingly the destiny of England, which Spenser holds out for the guidance of his readers:

> "For so must all things excellent begin,
> And eke enroutted deepe must be that tree,
> Whose big embodied braunches shall not lin,
> Till they to hevens hight forth stretched bee.
> For from thy wombe a famous progenee
> Shall spring, out of the auncient Trojan blood,
> Which shall revive the sleeping memoree
> Of those same antique peres, the hevens brood,
> Which Greeke and Asian rivers stayned with their blood."
> (III.3.22)

Thus, Merlin tells Britomart, "Renowned kings and sacred emperours, / Thy fruitfull offspring, shall from thee descend" (III.3.23). Through the partly mortal, partly divine inheritance that Merlin outlines for Britomart, broken and scattered Britons shall be brought together and their "decayed kingdomes shall amend" (III.3.23)—this by the decrees of the same "Eternall Providence" that at the outset caused her to see the image of Artegal in the mirror and instantly fall in love with it.

Love thereby initiates a guided and meaningful historical search. It shapes the course of achievement to the ideal forms the mind instinctively seeks and joins the earthly city to the heavenly one. It reorders the clutter of plots and the mind's impedimenta into disciplined pursuits, unites the past to the future, action to contemplation, and the inner or private man to the public man. As long as love so rules, the memory has no room for ancestral gloom: all times and places rise to a plane on which ideal forms transcend time even while one pursues them within time. Rather than establishing a literal chronology of descendents all the way back to origins, Spenser can allow a reinfusion of originating vision in the midst, among others by the poet himself in his proposing of images. The descent of an ideal into an exemplar makes a new beginning; the materializing of one's dream makes a completion. In part, what is at work in this process is a kind of reduction in which the personal actions of heroes and heroines serve as analogies to the larger historical processes. As Fate's instrument, love draws its victims into an unbreakable mechanism, takes over their wills, and subjects them to certain laws of allegiance and collective action. When in Book IV Britomart sees Artegal in person, both her warrior's arm and her tongue are put under a spell that resembles the enchantment of poetry. Seeing the same "lovely face of Artegall" that she remembers from the "enchaunted glass" in her father's hall, her "enhaunced hand she downe can soft withdraw":

> Yet she it forst to have againe upheld,
> As fayning choler, which was turn'd to cold:
> But ever when his visage she beheld,
> Her hand fell downe, and would no longer hold
> The wrathfull weapon gainst his countnance bold:
> But when in vaine to fight she oft assayd,
> She arm'd her tongue, and thought at him to scold;
> Nathlesse her tongue not to her will obayd,
> But brought forth speeches myld, when she would have missayd.
> (IV.6.27)

Although Spenser contributes this scene to English history without the blessing of chronicle sources, it is apparently not intended to be merely a fairy legend. The portrait of the willful virgin is applicable to anyone who might be tempted to preempt justice. The poet as an ethical philosopher advances that portrait as a general policy under the ruling analogy between fairyland and England. Whether he works through fables or actual incidents is a matter of indifference for the moment.

The view of the past that Spenser proposes in Books III and IV is representative of more than his own opinions. It draws upon Renaissance interpretations of temporal logic and its proper consummation. Both Spenser's neo-Platonism and his assumptions concerning poetry's ability to reform readers—not merely reflecting but helping to bring about a golden age—are evident, for instance, in the romance traditions in Tasso and Ariosto and in the Florentine Academy. They are perhaps most fully explicated by Sidney, whose neo-Platonism in *Astrophel and Stella*, *Arcadia*, and *An Apology for Poetry* is similar to Spenser's. The implication of these texts, and of Spenser's *Hymns* and *Amoretti* as well, is that neither philosophy nor history suffices by itself to conduct us toward the visionary imagination. In Sidney's familiar view, philosophy leaves those ideals too remotely abstract and unexampled, whereas history, which is all specificity and example, has little grasp of defining principles except what it borrows from the poet or philosopher. Fairyland, in contrast, enables the poet to blend past and present, form and illustration, to concretize philosophy while idealizing history, and thereby gain a clear ascendance over strict truthfulness. By comparison, the historian, in Sidney's version, is to be condemned for scarcely giving "leisure to the moralist to say so much, but that he, loaden with old mouse-eaten records, authorising himself (for the most part) upon other histories, whose greatest authorities are built upon the notable foundation of hearsay; having much ado to accord differing writers and to pick truth out of partiality; . . . curious for antiquities and inquisitive of novelties . . . denieth, in a great chafe, that any man for teaching of virtue, and virtuous actions is comparable to him." "Being captived to the truth of a foolish world," he is "many times a terror from well-doing, and an encouragement to unbridled wickedness."[19] (In that he bears some resemblance to Eumnestes.) The philosopher is no better. "Setting down with thorny argument the bare rule" (pp. 106–107), he presents a danger opposite to confusion: he teaches so crabbedly that no one can digest his offerings.

In contrast to both of these, the poet reinforces precepts with examples and recollects the golden world that has been missing in history since the Fall. His invented ideals are not really fictions at all but restorations of essence. In fact, the reality of ideas and essences must be perceived in feigned images. Sidney makes that point also at the expense of the historian: "So then the best of the historian is subject to the poet; for whatsoever action, or faction, whatsoever counsel, policy, or war strategem the historian is bound to recite, that may the poet (if he list) with his imitation make his own, beautifying it both for further teaching, and more delighting, as it pleaseth him: having all, from Dante's heaven to his hell, under the authority of his pen" (p. 111).

Such a view suggests that on one level neither Sidney nor Spenser bothered unduly about mixtures such as Merlin's blend of actual kings and allegorized concepts. Both what the poet takes from history and what he feigns offer improved images of virtue that guide us, in Sidney's words, to "as high a perfection as our degenerate souls, made worse by their clayey lodgings, can be capable of" (p. 104). In a theoretical way, this answer to reservations about a mingling of fairyland and historical chronicle is perfectly sufficient. But Spenser does more with Merlin's recitation and with other periods from the Hebrew, Greek, and Roman past than gather images for the guidance of the reader. He claims an interior logic in historical succession itself, conforming to the same teleological thrust that the imagination establishes in fables. That the ultimate order is "out there" and not merely in the mind's gathering of materials or the poet's pursuit of ideal forms claims more for the historian's contribution to the poet than Sidney suggests.

It also encourages a closer identity between moral allegory and historical reference than the poem can sustain. The temporal logic of *The Faerie Queene*, in fact, must inhere finally not in the providential unfolding of history but in the structure of the entire poem as an aesthetic and didactic contrivance. The books on public virtues that were to have completed the design presumably might have filled out the connections between political life and the interior man that already exist. But as it is, the most important context for the reading of any particular passage is much less that of historical information than the poem's overall chart of virtues and, of course, its form, which dictates the terms under which the history of ideas, the book of conduct, and the chronicle materials may enter when they do come forward. Hence, as Edwin Greenlaw demonstrates, certain passages may gather up and drop their historicity and even their philosophic precepts as they need them; but the story must go on. Queen Gloriana is meaningful not primarily as a paraphrase of Queen Elizabeth but as a hub of all plots. When we come down to it, not much specific history or social custom could be held to have survived if *The Faerie Queene* were our sole record of it. Nor is the poem particularly fortunate in the chronicle materials it does incorporate explicitly. For long stretches in listing the British kings in Book III, Spenser suspends nearly every principle of development except the forms of stanzas and the music of proper names. In contemporary references, too, he may have exhausted the possibilities of topical allegory without needing additional books and without demonstrating any decisive teleological principle in the historical process.

In any event, Northrop Frye suggests plausibly enough that Spenser went about as far as he could in flattering Elizabeth, worked in most of the evils and goods he needed, and "may well have ended his sixth book realizing that he might not write any more."[20] Finally, in the Mutability Cantos he abandons references to contemporary events in the interests of philosophic myth, which can now dominate without the nagging sense of truancy that intrudes in earlier escapes like Calidore's to the land of Pastorella. We cannot assume too readily that Spenser made this retreat to myth positively, however.[21] Despite the optimism of Merlin's lengthy prophecy in Book III and the projected union of Arthurian and Elizabethan periods, he appears less hopeful about the evolving of a better kingdom as early as Book V, where he adopts a more or less straightforward version of the myth of decline that is hard to reconcile with the transfer of empire to Troynovant (V.1). It is also true that the Blatant Beast cannot be contained in Book VI, where robbers and brigands ravage Pastorella's land, Colin Clout comes down from his hill, and brute force threatens to triumph everywhere. Nor is the tone of the Mutability Cantos themselves hopeful until the end. All of this may seem to argue that faery ideality has withdrawn from historical England; certainly Spenser is not entirely immune here to the ancestral gloom that so often accompanies Arthurian revivals.

However, the change in later books in less drastic than it may seem at first. At various times Spenser can be found voicing nearly all the major views of historical change—degenerative, progressive, and cyclical. Though the intermittent intrusions of Providence are capable of modifying any of these, degeneration from the golden age is in keeping with the Christian Fall, an idea that is emphatic already in Book I of *The Faerie Queene* and also in earlier poems—as, for instance, in the pessimism that begins and ends *The Shepheardes Calender* and dominates the ruin poems. Moreover, both Books V and VI place much of the blame for lawlessness and crudeness not on a totally degenerating state of affairs but on the masses, for whom Spenser never entertained great enthusiasm (any more than Sidney and Shakespeare did). All told, it is difficult to prove that he ended his career much more darkly than he began it or sustained it, despite the millenarian hope for a new empire that momentarily bolsters the account of Britomart and her search for Artegal.

As to the mood of the Mutability Cantos themselves, it is admittedly mixed and curious.[22] All change is bad by comparison to "the pillars of eternity," and Spenser makes it an especially aggressive force. He follows the custom of allotting different historical and natural provinces to more or less independent gods and goddesses in the phantheon, none of whom can prevent Mutability from claiming vast territories. Yet two things qualify this basic otherworldliness: Ireland's landscape is as pleasant as that of older pastoral places and as logical as an abode of the gods; and the pageant of the seasons is orderly, beautiful, and beyond the fall of civilizations.

The central theme is not degeneration and spreading mutability but recurrence of the kind that poetry so often commemorates in its resignation to natural forces. The mood is not unlike that of *The Tempest*, Keats's "To Autumn," or Stevens' "Sunday Morning," in which the poetic harvest is both a garnering and a recognition of allotted cycles. Actually three realms—natural forms, ideas, and the distilled, referential garden of words—come together in this final dimension of fairyland. Whereas the greatest historical ambition is to transfer empire to the Anglican church and the Tudors in other passages, Spenser here looks beyond that conclusion to a greater one: " 'But time shall come that all shall changed be, / And from thenceforth none no more change shall see' " (VII.7). Though it may be only a temporary swing of the pendulum, the eschatological movement here sounds like the triumph of Red Cross's paradisal yearning over the secular service required of him by the welfare of Cleopolis and the militant church. Progressive historical labors, for which the great past of Arthur's Britain supplies models, give way to another kind of recurrence. The historical image of Arthur is not discredited by that return to the myths of beginning and ending, but all intermediate phases are clearly contained and reduced by it—as are all inclinations to lament their passing or honor their memorial histories and poems.

Kinships

Not merely Arthurian romance in particular but romance in general is concerned with ancestral revival. Rome's ancient authority in *The Marble Faun*, to take an arbitrary but obvious case, weighs heavily upon the new generation, as do the ancient houses and mansions of other Hawthorne novels and the inherited guilt that initiates undertake in "Young Goodman Brown." What such texts suggest is the potentially ominous side of a heritage that will neither stay in the past nor come all the way forward to instruct the present freely and openly. Wherever romance borders on the gothic, the past returns accusingly like this, as again in the diffused authority of Kafka's *The Castle* and *The Trial*, where an indecipherable past sits in judgment, enforcing a book of conduct that has gone awry. Because the ruling authorities have retreated out of sight, the protagonist cannot find what is demanded of him; he does not know whom to revisit or to petition.

If Arthurian precedents are less oppressive than this, it may be because they are more visible. But one aspect of any such reused materials is the heft of temporal echoes and the ambivalent feelings of latecomers. No doubt the urge both to lament and to return to the past draws some of its power from that ambivalence, as Harold Bloom suggests in *The Anxiety of Influence*. Because a given Arthurian poet or novelist offers variations of plots that his predecessors have already developed, he cannot escape his secondary place. However, this does not necessarily limit him to two alternatives: slavish replication or treasonous revision. In its conservative aspect, a revival can also offer support for one to launch an exodus from a distasteful present.

Whatever swerve a text takes from either its current circumstances or its leading forerunners, its own internal kinship patterns are likely to offer clues to the writer's sense of continuity and his own place in the tradition. It may be, for instance, that the reason for T. H. White's surprising ranking of Malory as the greatest British writer next to Shakespeare is hinted in the several family relations and surrogate fathers he builds into the text of *The Once and Future King*. Certainly, those relationships are numerous and central enough to suggest that White pursued renewal and revision consciously. From one angle, Malory is to White as Merlin is to Wart—a substitute father, a bringer of information and wisdom, and a guide to the transfer of a heritage. And just as Merlin retreats to give Arthur room to mature—thereby leaving a number of issues up in the air—so Malory carries only so far in solving problems for a modern redactor and casts White on his own for the rest. Also, Lancelot's adultery is an almost permissible or good theft, implicitly tolerable even to Arthur.

Transfers of authority and possession would go smoothly enough if these were the only relationships in question. However, the farther one looks, the more problematic White's kinships appear. The anatomy of political and social affairs begins in sublimated and indirect parental images, and accompanying the transfer of political power from generation to generation is always the complicating matter of territorial rights, taboos, and guilt. Arthur as a father betrays Mordred, whom he has tried to have murdered for fear of his future influence; and in return Mordred betrays and overthrows his father. The filial worship that Lancelot bestows on Arthur not only finds a poisoned opposite in Mordred's sickly, inturned hatred but is itself quasi-Oedipal (insofar as Guenever is a kind of disguised younger stepmother). Agravaine's love-hate feeling for Morgause (also Arthur's paramour momentarily) is an unqualified evil in White's view, like Mordred's desire to marry Guenever in the final eruption of semi-incest. Moreover, in slaying his adopted son, Gareth, Lancelot himself is responsible for turning brother against brother among the Orkeneys and is thus also responsible for the final war. His own son, Galahad, usurps his position as the best knight in the world, transcending the old regime of knighthood and casting the entire world of his father into shadow, unceremoniously unhorsing Lancelot in the process. Galahad thus initiates a new period in a succession of historical phases that is one violation of tradition, one unseating after another. If this version of the son's overthrow of the father stood up, it would guarantee a pattern of transcendence and lift the new generations into a mythic realm of grail epiphanies while canceling all normal family bonds. But it would do so, as Gawain realizes, at the expense of secular continuity, since purity is a lonely and destructive virtue. In any case, Galahad is too much outside social history to have an influence or a son of his own. He represents an unattainable ideal that defines the lowliness of common humanity and the usual social contract (with all its uninspired displacements and power struggles) but without offering anything in their place.

The final father-son relationship—the healing one between Arthur and the messenger boy—returns to a middle plane. It preserves the concept of a kingdom of the future and suggests that a peaceful transmission of wisdom from one generation to another is possible where no real transfer of authority is in question. Arthur bequeaths to his surrogate son images and ideas of a kind similar to those of Malory. *The Once and Future King* suggests that where kinships of such a kind exist, they create a different sort of brotherhood from the fellowship of the Round Table's military order, honorable though that fellowship may be. The transmission of wisdom—as opposed to the transmission of authority—is truly chivalric. Arthur's heritage depends on his own exemplary conduct and on imaginative models passed from him to others. Or to look at it another way, normal history has its active, militant successions, in relation to which poetic fables, as we noted earlier, are wayward digressions. In White's view, because ruptures from the past are due in part to active territorial battles in which one generation usurps the space and power of another, public history will continue to be strident. But within that general warfare, poets and visionaries may establish their own cults of writer and reader, teacher and pupil. These too may compete for attention, but the models that Arthur and Malory set for White and the page boy are not destructively competitive: both are helpful and generative without being stifling.

The style of fifteenth-century romance left ample room for development without forcing White to rebel pointedly against it. Much of that development came from another heritage of course: the novel between the time of Malory and White had rendered certain details of courtship, the realities of political and social management, interior thought, the founding of adult behavior on childhood development, depth psychology, an articulated sense of historical periods, the adaptation of marvels and magic to children's literature, and a self-conscious, ironic interplay of realism and chivalric heroics (from Cervantes)—none of which were part of Malory's stock in trade. In return, taking Malory as a primary antecedent enabled White to collect Dickens, Thackeray, Eliot, and Fielding effortlessly. Tennyson as an obstructing figure was also relatively easy to deal with, thanks partly perhaps to Evelyn Waugh and P. G. Wodehouse, since assuming a comic stance toward many of the things the *Idylls* had held sacred gave White all the distance he needed. As White illustrates, then, even such a formulaic mode as Arthurian literature can pick its way through a series of revisions. It is capable of numerous turns, or "tropes," along the way. New efforts in an old literary form, as in the dictionary definition of behavioristic tropism, may contain some "involuntary responses of an organism to external stimuli" (namely predecessors); but they also inevitably coin new variants and divert the tradition in unpredictable ways.

In establishing connections across chronological gaps, the poet sometimes discovers a new access to his own times (as White finds in Malory's anatomy of power insights into Hitlerism); or he may discover access to remote things, crossing the temporal distance by means of vividly imagined concrete detail (as when the sight of some domestic item from an ancient Egyptian regime makes a household servant of three thousand years ago instantly familiar to us). But paradoxically, descriptive details also remind us of that distance, so that we cross it and pay heed to it at the same time, moving back and forth across the temporal hiatus as point of view and style direct us.

White's handling of the medieval setting suggests another aspect of that paradox as well, since romance can either set us at great distances from its subject or provide an alternative avenue to immediacy. Pentangles, quests, and holy grails can bridge past and present as effectively as the familiar touch of concretion; but clearly the surface of romance objects establishes a different presence from that of an inventory of household items, customs, and ordinary actions. Such objects have a heightened significance of the kind that Yeats assigns to Byzantium and its mosaics or that Charles Williams assigns to his version of the grail myth. As Stephen argues to Lynch in Joyce's *Portrait of the Artist,* "The esthetic image in the dramatic form is life purified in and reprojected from the human imagination." When it is first conceived, the mind "in that mysterious instant" is like Shelley's fading coal: "The instant wherein that supreme quality of beauty, the clear radiance of the esthetic image, is apprehended luminously by the mind which has been arrested by its wholeness and fascinated by its harmony is the luminous silent stasis of esthetic pleasure."[23]

Stephen of course puts the power of the symbol in the most romantic terms, but the arrest and the quality of epiphany in the artist's perceptions do place the symbol in a special category of its own, lifting it from history as Sir Bedivere would liberate Excalibur. Around such ancestors as Yeats, too, presupposes in his version of the Celtic revival, an aesthetic or cultic group may form, or even a political group, as Yeats speculates in "The Statues" in finding Cuchulain beside Pearse in the Dublin Post Office. In any case, the recurrent notion of art as an enduring memorial is based partly on such a renewal of the past not in the scattered remains of memory or ordinary discourse but in the recreation of perceptions through symbolic fictions. Thus in the hands of writers like Yeats and Charles Williams (or even Mary Stewart), the Arthurian material is assembled as an assortment of glittering images and legends. Actually, whenever a poet arranges events in order and confirms the rightness of what happens as a series of revelations, he moves toward that "clear radiance" of which Stephen speaks, simply in seating images in a certain intelligibility. In this respect, Arthurian works like *Sir Gawain and the Green Knight,* Crestien's, the Vulgate Cycle, and other sources on which Malory drew share with Spenser's fairyland the quality of intrigue in their avoidance of matter-of-factness and their courting of wonder: they ascribe to incidents and surfaces the significance of hieroglyphs. Chivalry in them often takes the form of visual splendor not merely as the surface of a lost way of life but as clues in the reader's journey toward an aesthetic location of relics and objects.

One cure for anxieties about literary predecessors and perhaps cultural degeneration as well lies in the writer's coming upon such perceptions of a real or imagined way of life at a distance, either through concrete detail or the centralizing authority of key symbols. While his attention is held by those images and expressive details, the successful fabler presumably does not linger over the downward cycle of his own civilization. Literary predecessors who help kindle an upsurge of workable materials are not necessarily barriers to his imaginative excursion, provided that they stand aside when the time comes. Hence it is by no means inevitable that a Malory or a Spenser will inhibit a T. H. White; quite the contrary, predecessors may provide the leverage that lifts into view what a work needs in order to get under way. Without the tradition, White would not have invented anything like *The Once and Future King*, which at once both proves his indebtedness and clears the debt. The reader too, on balance, must find allusions to such predecessors part of a text's complex charm, as the fictive work conjures for him not a real geography or set of actions but a mixture of the potentially real, the conventional, and the imaginative.

One could easily overstate the collapsing of distances that concrete symbols and images bring about, however, since they always contain an element of estrangement. Perhaps it would be more accurate to say that they fasten the reader's attention to the text and its art, as the eye is fastened to a Byzantine mosaic rather than to some reality glimpsed through it. If some genuine past is present in the surface, it is perplexed there. The medium through which we see is not clear but intricate; time is not cleanly layered or rendered in distinct calendar accuracies but both reduplicative and alterable. Finally, it cannot be freed from the surface of the images themselves in their divided presence, both contemporary and ancient. Also, fictions are contemporary only for a reader who goes to meet the text and joins it on its own terms, and sooner or later he must return. Another phase of awareness always asserts itself, whether what has triggered the reader's identification with the past has been realistic detail or romantic symbol. As he withdraws from his fixed attention on the imagined life of the fiction, that life retreats and the layers of time once fused in its objects pull apart.

The nostalgia of lost ancestry is compounded by the nostalgia of the finished and closed fiction, which may already have been encouraged by the elegiac tone or the dramatized distance of the narrator from his materials throughout. Thus even as a revivalist stages a luminous return of a pretended past, he is likely to find the present a wasting of the heritage whenever it stands far enough apart to be compared: making one thing especially memorable makes others just the opposite. If Tennyson and Robinson emphasize the fall of the present recurrently (by implication), they are merely letting into our ongoing reception of Arthur an outside perspective that becomes inevitable in the imagination's plunge into and retraction from its digression. They do no more in that respect than Malory and Spenser come to do, at least implicitly. (Yeats too of course, was not especially keen on his portion of the twentieth century and sought access to the artifice of eternity through Byzantium and other localities, dramatizing the act of "sailing" there as a withdrawal from the present.) In this gray area of ancestral gloom, the revivalist touches romantic disillusionment, of which Keats has given us such impressive parables in the knight's exile from fairyland in "La Belle Dame sans Merci," in the escaped lovers of *The Eve of St. Agnes*, and in the painful approach of the poet to the gods in *The Fall of Hyperion*.

More comprehensive than these figures as a systematic reviewer of the past is Milton, who despaired not merely of the present but of virtually the entire secular enterprise. I want to circle back to him again in order to explore more fully the limits of reusable forms and a Renaissance version of something akin to Stephen's "radiance." The one true source of both the primary world and its secondary images that Milton recognizes is the Father, who is not only both ancient and current but a living force identifiable continuously in historical actions. The aesthetic image for Milton thus coincides with the Father's image imprinted in material forms as well as in sacred books—indeed, in all privileged versions of the Word. Although the poet cannot deny the legacy of Adam and the events that follow from him, he seeks to undo the Fall by retrieving the image implanted within Adam's original clay. He is therefore responsible not to a specific past civilization, as an Arthurian revival is, but to an ideal form that poetry and theology collaborate in recovering.

III

DISCONTINUITY

CHAPTER 5

Milton's Siege of Contraries: Universal Waste and Redemption

L IKE ROMANCE, epic is revivalist when it acknowledges that an older heroic action is still of importance to the poet and his audience. What Milton recovers from the past is basically the image of paradise and the one greater man who restores it. This recovery is the vocational fulfillment of the poet who, without assistance from the highest Muse, would find sacred truths concealed by the letter of history, as Michael warns Adam they will be for most people after the apostles have left "their story written." Others will seize upon those truths only to convert them into mere doctrines; they will seek to capitalize on the "mysteries of Heav'n," leaving truth to "those written Records pure, / Though not but by the Spirit understood" (*Paradise Lost*, XII.110–111). When the Spirit accompanies the interpretation of history's letter, however, the surface of events—and the texts that tell of them—come alive again.

Perhaps more noteworthy in Milton than the poet's reconstruction of recurrent sacred truths, however, are initiating moments triggered by disconnection from those truths and the abrupt interventions of Providence. Before those interventions, the hero and the poet are often isolated, stalled in an apparently meaningless duration that leaves them without calling. The extreme type of that extended, restless isolation is Satan, whose decision to separate from his source initiates Milton's chronological story. At the other end of things, Christ in *Paradise Regained* goes immediately into isolation in the desert, breaking with one phase of his development in order to find entry into the next. Samson and Adam are less extreme types whose isolation is extended but not endless.

Whether or not the present is charged with the recurring Spirit, it often demands a long, passive wait as preparation, as Christ's perform-

ance in the desert and on the pinnacle consists chiefly of a patient re-
fusal to act. (As Hugh Richmond points out, Milton in the pinnacle
passage comes to a full recognition of what serving by waiting means.[1])
Paradise Lost might also be regarded as preparation for the "last things"
of Michael's vision, when Christ will dissolve

> *Satan* with his perverted World, then raise
> From the conflagrant mass, purg'd and refin'd,
> New Heav'ns, new Earth, Ages of endless date.
> (XII.545-549)

At that point, "this transient World, the Race of time," as Adam appreciates, will yield to a fixed time that "is all abyss, / Eternity, whose end
no eye can reach" (XII.555-556). Only in that eternity can one discover
the quiet of mind that unveiled knowledge delivers. Until then, Adam
and Eve, although not stalled as Satan is in endless futility, cannot proceed to conclusions. Among Milton's later figures, only Samson actually finishes his work and arrives; and even in his case, what fills the
protracted middle of the play is a probing of the disconnection between
the hero and God and between the future he has glimpsed in prophecy
and his present uselessness. But eventually in all these instances, a moment of clarification arrives in which even the interim ordeal, in retrospect, makes sense. In contrast to Yeats's protagonists, caught in the incessant turmoil of history's gyres, Milton's Adam, the reclaimed
Samson, and the redeeming Christ take part in a succession of events
that points toward a meaningful culmination.

The prominence of ruptures in Milton is nonetheless not easy to explain. Even for a poet whose recurrent subject is war (as Charles Williams observes[2]) violence and disconnection are unusually central to
the major works. Abruptness crops up in dialogues, in transitions between passages, and in the way in which new directions come into the
historical process. The conflict between Milton's heroes and their an-
tagonists is especially abrasive, as in Samson's husbandly remark to
Dalila, "Out, out Hyaena," or in Christ's deportment toward Satan, or
again in the lady's replies to Comus. Even Adam's responses to Eve in
their post-Fall moments are full of "mutual accusation" and "vain contest." Disruption in these conversions is not merely a matter of style or
some inherent divorce temperament: it springs forth so readily—as antagonism does also in heaven when Christ is announced to the host as
God's only begotten son—that it seems almost inevitable and necessary
to the nature of things.

We should not be surprised to find so pervasive an embattled spirit
in history as well. Nor is Milton's readiness to dispose of most of the
human past limited to later works, although we tend to think of *Samson*
and *Paradise Regained* as his most renunciatory works. The tone of the

youthful poems is milder, but almost from the outset it reveals a root-and-branch propensity for cleaning house.[3] Usually the pivotal moments of history spring out of moral contests and dramatic reversals that confirm some injunction that descends from a higher level. The turning points are surprising and ironic. Where one might expect Christ's kingdom to be civilized, military, and splendid, it turns out to be devoid of human glory in the usual senses and is of course revolutionary. It is obscurely consigned to the desert to begin with and is subsequently denied connection with all the established institutions of empire. Where Samson expects to serve as God's champion and athlete, he must serve first as fool and victim, and again his service is destructive. We recognize such moments as divinely guided precisely by their upsetting of normal expectations and their reversal of the momentum history has generated. It is the task of narrative, dramatic, and lyric explorations of the historical labyrinth to probe for points of conversion in which dark will turn to light, confusion to enlightenment, the letter to the Spirit. All salvageable creatures in whatever station must locate such points if they are to break through the obscurity of history.

Paradoxically, Milton's idyllic imagination contributes to the ferocity his protagonists display in fending off the interfering world. If God is beyond all stir on an unshakable throne and Christ comes from that high peace, the saint and the poet might be thought to share in the calm of the Father with him. But human seekers of repose proceed by agitation, dramatic ordeal, and lyric meditation. The speaker of *Lycidas* is the more disturbed at nature and injustice because they stand between him and the sort of calm that Lycidas discovers in his apotheosis. Christ and Samson are all the harsher with human failings because of the ideals they have implanted within them.

The primal eruption that makes all delay necessary to begin with is the war in heaven, which creates the militant Christ in answer to Satan and sets the style of subsequent wreckage.[4] In a lower key, the human Fall initiates a similar militancy in Adam, although something very close to abruptness has already surfaced before that in Eve's dream and again in her decision to alter the work routine the morning of the Fall. The latter incident leads uncomfortably close to abrasive dialogue before its time, as Adam, after a mild answer and then healing words, begins a fervent reply: "O Woman." Even the comparatively narrow gap between man and woman begins to appear unbridgeable. Beyond these preparatory steps toward the Fall are other signs of abruptness. Adam and Eve are subject to puzzlement of a sort and thus to discrepancies between appearances and ultimate causes. Since earthly knowledge is to remain only that and nothing more, Adam cannot keep learning forever: he must stall at a certain point and turn back. He must remain in history while his instinct wishes him safely within God's unchanging presence. His spirit requires the gift of a total mythos, while his edenic condition requires a cyclical, quasihistorical succession of days and new dialogues.

A partial answer to this difficulty is evident in Adam's reception of evidence. As an interpreter of signs, he is perceptive, modest, and intuitive in sensing the limitations of induction. As a hymnodist, he does not require muses and invocations and has no deficiencies in perception to overcome comparable to the narrator's. His language gives no evidence of a battle against obstructions on its way toward a blameless expression of holy light.[5] Nor does he envy higher beings or experience puzzlement over threshholds he cannot cross and mysteries he cannot solve. How long he could have maintained that balance had he not fallen may be open to question, but the Fall prevents our having to ask. History henceforth has its genuine surprises, and Milton can proceed with the combative mode that the desire for ultimate peace creates. Adam too may then take up the past as something problematic and possessed of enigmatic turns—which leads in part to his developing the techniques of meditation, self-scrutiny, and prophecy.

The Poet's Coming Forth

How does Milton fit the poet's calling into this scheme of instrusive revelations? What does his historical station portend for his own functions as a complementary herald—as a bringer of perspectives from outside the chain of historical events? Pursuing a career as Milton did through lesser poetic forms (pastoral, the masque, and lyric) and on to longer and more ambitious forms required him to bring within compass an increasing sweep of Western history and tradition. He understood classical forms—not only pastoral, epic, and tragedy but oratory and historiography.[6] One of the functions of *ingenium*, or poetic genius, is to perceive likenesses and, insofar as the poet can be guided by the philosopher, to perceive them systematically. Hence, unlike the lyric poet or maker of masques, the epic poet, in Milton's encyclopedic view, cannot offer merely a series of self-contained moments; he must gather materials from study and assimilation.

Yet the poet's coming forth also means his emergence as a new historical force and the discarding of much of the past. If one counts vicarious as well as explicit examples, Milton stages his emergence in the Nativity ode, "L'Allegro" and "Il Penseroso," *Comus*, in *Lycidas* in the disguise of the reluctant swain, in the invocations and analogous emergences in *Paradise Lost*, in *Paradise Regained*, and finally in Samson's emergence from prison to search for his lost mission. Each new emergence is complicated by former ones, so that by the time the poet comes to *Lycidas*, for instance, he has his former commitment to pastoral in *Arcades, Comus, L'Allegro,* and *Il Penseroso* to consider. When he returns to pastoral in *Paradise Lost*, he has *Lycidas;* and by *Paradise Regained*, he has a long career indeed behind him. The new does not necessarily reject the old in these instances. The new pastoral of the epics emerges from the earlier pastorals as organic growth, as though establishing an enlarged, transformed whole. *Paradise Regained* and *Samson* both have much of the résumé about them, with long introspective and retrospective passages and an accumulation of prophetic signs to be interpreted. The poet's emergence in *Paradise Regained* has other implications as well:

> I who erewhile the happy Garden sung,
> By one man's disobedience lost, now sing
> Recover'd Paradise to all mankind,
> By one man's firm obedience fully tried
> Through all temptation, and the Tempter foil'd
> In all his wiles, defeated and repuls't,
> And Eden rais'd in the waste Wilderness.
> (I.1-7)

As Arnold Stein has suggested, the echoes of Virgil here constitute "an amazing . . . literary joke of unprecedented dimension"[7]: as Milton moves from pastoral to epic and makes *Paradise Regained* his real epic, he appears to reduce *Paradise Lost* to a preliminary pastoral. At the same time, he claims to have no real predecessors in his special access to a heroic history so far left "unrecorded . . . through many an Age."

Ordinarily when the poet emerges, he does so with some awareness of the limitations of his vision and his need to await the Muse's help. The result is a paradoxical coming forth and hanging back. But both that point and the general theme of the poet's calling are perhaps better illustrated by the sonnets than by the larger works—not merely by sonnets concerned with the poet's stalled unproductivity ("How Soon Hath Time," "When I Consider") but in a special way by "Me Thought I Saw." This poem's concern with the aftermath of vision and its reflection indirectly of the sonnet tradition are telling,[8] especially when we place the poem beside the sonnet of Sir Walter Raleigh that it echoes:

> Me thought I saw the grave, where *Laura* lay
> Within that Temple, where the vestal flame
> Was wont to burn, and passing by that way,
> To see that buried dust of living fame,
> Whose tomb fair love, and fairer virtue kept,
> All suddenly I saw the Faery Queen:
> At whose approach the soul of *Petrark* wept,

> And from thenceforth those graces were not seen.
> For they this Queen attended, in whose stead
> Oblivion laid him down on Laura's hearse:
> Hereat the hardest stones were seen to bleed,
> And groans of buried ghosts the heavens did pierce.
>   Where Homer's spright did tremble all for grief,
>   And cursed th'access of that celestial thief.

Raleigh's sonnet is in commendation of *The Faerie Queene* and its rival predecessors. Milton's sonnet, of course concerns the return of a spouse to her blind husband in a dream:

> Methought I saw my late espoused Saint
>   Brought to me like *Alcestis* from the grave,
>   Whom *Jove's* great Son to her glad Husband gave,
>   Rescu'd from death by force though pale and faint.
> Mine as whom washt from spot of child-bed taint,
>   Purification in the old Law did save,
>   And such, as yet once more I trust to have
>   Full sight of her in Heaven without restraint,
> Came vested all in white, pure as her mind:
>   Her face was veil'd, yet to my fancied sight,
>   Love, sweetness, goodness, in her person shin'd
> So clear, as in no face with more delight.
>   But O, as to embrace me she inclin'd
>   I wak'd, she fled, and day brought back my night.

Both poems—Raleigh's explicitly and Milton's implicitly—set aside previous visions on behalf of a new one. Raleigh's view is that Spenser has outdone his predecessors in a new version of living grace: the beauty of the fairy queen so effectively displaces that of Petrarch's Laura that the tradition is undone—not only Petrarch's portion of it but Homer's and perhaps more as well. Whereas love and virtue can do no more than attend Laura's tomb as a kind of memorial, Spenser's poetic miracle saves his queen from effacing time.

Milton does not say anything directly about rival poets, and the visitation he receives, although genuine, offers only a fleeting glimpse of a future. But with regard to the tradition of the *donna angelicata*, both poets subvert it, or to borrow George Kubler's word, cause its original message to pass through a "relay" point that reforms it.[9] When the poet's vision comes forth, two things happen: through the gift of that vision, the poet momentarily returns to paradise in imagination; his native darkness then reaches out again to reclaim its victim and plunges him back into deprivation. Such visitations establish landmarks both in the sonnet tradition they interrupt and in the implicit stages of the speaker's own biography. Milton's possession of his spouse goes through several stages: first a kind of edenic pre-Fall in which she is alive and present, then death's separation, and finally an imagined consummation both of her being and his sight of her. This eventual reunion will put all former possessions in the shadow, since earthly visions are lesser and have restraints. Each new vision diminishes the value of lesser moments; each coming forth of the Muse is disruptive. Normal historical processes are transcended and poetic traditions along with them. Thus although Milton's sonnet does not offer an explicit critique of the pursuit of the beloved in Petrarch or in Spenser, it does not have to; it presents a rival version of marital love in a Protestant context and reconceives the valedictory function of the sonnet.

Despite the redundancy of the repeated sonnet form and its images, then, such a new moment brings a crisis in transmission similar to that of the abrupt Miltonic hero in his moment of privilege: the succession of events up to that point gives way to a new force that enters from elsewhere, although in this case the familiar dark descends again for what we imagine to be an extended interim. New revelations and the poet's coming forth to proclaim them are not only forms of disruption but synapses by which the turns of history are transmitted to succeeding parties. The poet serves as conduit for eternity's recharging of time; his secondary creations repeat in a local time and place the primary act of creation; his words share in the Word, as the spouse shares ultimately in the state of blessedness and helps constitute its concretion even now, in the momentary dream.

Abrupt Bushes with Frizzl'd Hair Implicit: Placement and Transition in the Creation

Let us assume, then, that special visions are responsible for at least some of the abruptness that Milton's heroes display, the adversary nature of his dialogues, reversals of plot, and breaks with tradition. In terms of narrative and dramatic movement, when the time comes for an emergence or enunciation at the doorway, all preparatory stages prove inadequate, and the logic of development is broken: the stages of interrogation in *Lycidas* fall short of predicting the "weep no more" movement; Samson's self-scrutiny and his trials are incapable of providing a dénouement; Christ's triumph on the pinnacle, however one chooses to interpret it, is sudden. Nor do hierarchy and levels of abstraction adequately bridge the gap between parties in any of these poems, any more than narrative cause and effect or dramatic gestures do. In one respect, the hierarchical aspect of the problem is the same as the one that Johnson identified in the Great Chain generally: although a gradual series of creatures binds the plenitude of creation together, reason cannot ascend it by stages to the top, because the distance between the most high and the next most high remains infinite.

Milton's version of cosmic order complicates that built-in difficulty in mediation with Satan's parody of all phases of hierarchical obedience, manifestation, and command. The order of heaven itself is barely imaginable, even to the privileged poet, and is so complicated that it seems irregular:

> That day, as other solemn days, they spent
> In song and dance about the sacred Hill,
> Mystical dance, which yonder starry Sphere
> Of Planets and of fixt in all her Wheels
> Resembles nearest, mazes intricate,
> Eccentric, intervolv'd, yet regular
> Then most, when most irregular they seem.
> (V.618-624)

In the unfallen universe, below that intricate design, the Creator's descent to his creation is not always harmonious and accommodated, at least from the standpoint of the creature: it is sometimes sudden and arbitrary. After the Fall, of course, the imperfect reflection of the Creator's image in the book of creatures makes the gulf between them even more drastic, until no easy conceptual passage from lower to higher is imaginable.

When translated into dramatic and narrative terms, these gaps in the hierarchy are revealed as problems in transition, dialogue, and continuity. The siege of contraries that satanic warfare generates, for instance, is basically a sequence of actions and reactions, theses and rebuttals without resolution. Whenever satanic inversions assume control, syntax (within sentences), logic within passages, and the placement of episodes and larger units within the narrative whole illustrate a similar abruptness. For the poet himself, as "Methought I Saw," the outbreaks of *Lycidas*, and the invocations of *Paradise Lost* reveal, lyric moments can become isolated interludes. As angels and men pause to attitudinize in those stalled moments, they do not necessarily find themselves disconnected from an ongoing action. The function of invocations *is* basically to connect—to link the speaker to the rest of the fable and inner to outer worlds. But the intensity of the lyric petition acknowledges the threat of isolation, just as the dream of the spouse intensifies the husband's habitual dark.

Every gap is a partial version of chaos, a partial return to the pure abrupt, which is primal matter before the Spirit and the Word command it into regulated place. As the temporal universe is beset by wreckage, so the physical universe has its litter and its uncontrolled profusion. These lie everywhere, not merely in chaos and hell. We can see an index of their antagonism to the mind's predisposition to order in various hailings of landscape, especially Satan's awakening, but also in Adam's, where intelligence comes upon an existence that is foreign to it and seeks to find the decipherable signs of order in it. To some extent, *Paradise Lost* and *Paradise Regained* are poems of placement and setting in which exteriors mirror internal states and require that the mind labor to discover its correpondences, its ways of crossing the gap and finding its source in divine reason. The beginning, middle, and end of human temporality are defined by their greater or lesser proximity to paradise—immediate and satisfying; lost and nostalgically distanced; foreshadowed, recollected, or restored, and doubly satisfying after absence. Certainly paradise as a set of traces of the divine haunts the mind in its search for clear exponents of God. That a landscape can also be a form of history is clear the moment we see that all fragmented and imperfect forms in the brazen world are retrospective; they summon their origins, if only by contrast. They are resourceful in ways totally unlike Wordsworth's recollections at Tintern Abbey or elsewhere.

The distance from paradise of some of the points where the search begins is nonetheless insurmountable. In the limbo of fools, for instance, misled philosophers whose brand of illogic has rushed them to the wrong conclusions are pushed hither and yon by capricious winds, their expectations dashed just as they seem about to be fulfilled:

> All th' unaccomplisht works of Nature's hand,
> Abortive, monstrous, or unkindly mixt,
> Dissolv'd on Earth, flee hither, and in vain,
> Till final dissolution, wander here.
>   (III.455-458)

Though the creation does not, strictly speaking, require such a place, the limbo (together with chaos, hell, and the wilderness) is a logical contrast to paradise in its scattering of litter and things "unkindly mixt." Milton stations it close by heaven's threshold probably because false philosophy and miscreation are peculiarly threshold matters: as a continuous train of reason seems about to deliver a revelation, even admission to paradise itself, the philosopher's expectations disappear in the emptiness of mere words, just as in eating the apple Adam and Eve soar on wings of divinity only to discover that their exaltation is no more than inebriation; they are drunk with prospects, not intellectual power. Similarly, trying to cross chaos and land in paradise, Satan falls into ultimate confusion, where the bridging Word has not yet called fire, water, air, and earth to their stations and all things stand and wait, or move in no particular direction. Conglomerates are without character, consistency, or definition there, and each moment is an abrupt denial of the momentum of other moments; nothing recollects the divine Word.

In parody of the spanning of gaps and making of connections, Sin and Death counter the stairway to heaven with an avenue to hell that is peculiarly deadly in that it will allow the lost to transport themselves to their final extremity. The bridge connects only as a chute to bottom-lessness:

> The aggregated Soil
> Death with his Mace petrific, cold and dry,
> As with a Trident smote, and fix't as firm
> As *Delos* floating once; the rest his look
> Bound with *Gorgonian* rigor not to move,
> And with *Asphaltic* slime; broad as the Gate,
> Deep to the Roots of Hell the gathr'd beach
> They fasten'd, and the Mole immense wrought on
> Over the foaming deep high Archt, a Bridge
> Of length prodgious joining to the Wall
> Immoveable of this now fenceless World
> Forfeit to Death; from hence a passage broad,
> Smooth, easy, inoffensive down to Hell.
> (X.293-305)

As opposed to the floating, indecipherable image that Death presents to Satan initially, Death now commands a semblance of solidity. He has quite literally gained footing in a defenseless world. The irony of that acquisition is that Death lacks the inspiriting life and organic vigor of the creative Word and only by subtracting the moving Spirit from the elements freezes them with the "Mace petrific." Unlike the arduous, abrupt leap the saved must make to move upward, this bridging, "smooth, easy, inoffensive," requires no apparent discontinuity from what the sinner has chosen to be.

Satan's own destiny, of course, is not chaos but the landscape of hell, which keeps his contradictions astir. Whereas Eden's landscape (before the Fall) offers Adam a set of discrete, complementary items that bridge the gap between him and the Creator, hell's landscape impresses on the shocked sensibility of the fallen an indecipherable "Universe of death," of "Rocks, Caves, Lakes, Fens, Bogs, Dens" (II.621). The problem of continuity in hell is not Satan's alone; it is also the narrator's and reader's. Scenes as different as hell and Eden are not available in the same way to the bridge of language by which the narrator seeks to bring them to us. The implicit norm in our perception of all landscapes is the human scale, but neither hell's jumble nor the ideality of heaven has the limits, the metaphysical or physical laws, or the mixed texture of reality as we know it. Seemingly, we can recognize as familiar only the wilderness, which is half paradisal and half hellish. But Milton seems to endorse a position that Northrop Frye has put best; namely, that only an archetype, in this case paradise, has the full, undisplaced reality of primal myth and hence a total knowability beyond confusion. Only there is the mind really home and free of disconnection. The trees and creatures that Adam observes lack both hell's absurdity and heaven's ineffability.

In contrast, the lack of particularity in Satan's survey of hell's topography stems from its unrealizable qualities. Milton cannot portray an absurdist setting in any of the ranges of precise, enumerative language that belong to Eden's "sweet interchange," where connection is constant and flowing. Thus, although we can know darkness and visiblity, we cannot know "darkness visible" or imagine a source for it; we can imagine hideous ruin and combustion, but only as decomposition or gradual ruin, not as permanent states. We cannot know chaos at all; it is anti-intellectual, antiverbal. We can say about such contradictory places that they are inversions of celestial reality and encompassed creation; but that does not deliver them completely to poetic imagery or logic. As the roll call of devils also indicates, the ruin that is thus perfected in hell spreads throughout the later historical world and becomes the confusion of Babel and of history's false gods. All these scenes interpose surfaces between mankind and the image of glory that is its only satisfying sight. All ruin is ultimately meaningless and absurd. Its completion must be hastened, until the "conflagrant mass" is "purged and refin'd" for the "New Heav'ns, new Earth" that in foresight give Adam all his mental vessel can contain.

Although the imagery of hell's abrupt landscape is not articulate and precise, it serves a purpose: it leads the reader part way toward a realization of the absolute gap between nothingness and the intelligible Word. Nothingness, paradoxically, enhances or stands behind the poem's sense of created blessings in their gradual series. Satan awakens not to a chain of surmises leading to a call or to a conviction of light implanted miraculously within but to a fixed siege. His hymn to hell— his version of the lyric address to scene—predicts the strange reciprocity of the fallen self and its scene after the human Fall as well:

> Farewell happy Fields
> Where Joy for ever dwells: Hail horrors, hail
> Infernal world, and thou profoundest Hell
> Receive thy new Possessor: One who brings
> A mind not to be chang'd by Place or Time.
> (I.249-253)

In place of the lyric response that other landscapes attract, hell extracts a challenge. Surrounded by evidence of deterioration and the impossibility of stability, Satan asserts his own changeless permanence. But ironically, that unchangeable mind is grounded in constant change: asserting the calm of fixed being, Satan paradoxically confirms the unavoidability of restlessness. Narratively, hell's antagonistic jumble arises from war and its aftermath, which includes not only the making of hell but the making of the universe. Hence as in approaching hell we must bear in mind the order it parodies so in understanding the Creation and its verbal accounting we must bear in mind this threat of disconnection, unlikeness, and the "vast abrupt."

I suggested earlier that there are equivalent startling elements in the Creation before the second, human Fall as well. Almost from the outset Eden has problems in transition and even of discard and waste (if we take Adam and Eve's pruning and trimming seriously).[10] Moreover, the perspective from which the narrator sees Eden includes an awareness of other paradises that have fallen by the way, which intensifies his and our awareness of waste, just as the "simplicity and spotless innocence" of Adam and Eve drive home the corruption of courtly heroes and heroines. Also, Milton's selection of Eden as a paradigm of the perfect life sacrifices most of what civilization has produced, including clothing, food, social amenities, music, painting, philosophy, architecture. This extreme discarding of what we might expect to constitute epic splendor has no direct bearing on whether or not Eden is itself abrupt, although the gap we must cross to arrive there is not trivial. But beyond that, it has its own eruptive energy. A certain edginess shows in Adam's use of the word "evil," in Raphael's importing into Eden a detailed account of rebellion and warfare, in Satan's implanting of an anxiety-ridden dream of high flight in Eve's mind, and in the arguments of guardian angels with the intruder over relative strength and merit.

In addition to these elements of narrative and dramatic unease is the riotous life of the Creation itself. The abundance of Eden prepares in some ways for nature's bursting of forms after the Fall, just as Eve's headstrong independence prepares for her attempt to negotiate at one leap the vast distance from Eden to godhead. From most angles, this energy of nature's is not particularly problematic; it is merely evidence of the generosity of the Creator. Proceeding from Christ's pronouncements, which raise the classifications of gradual being from idea to material kinds, paradise suffers no Platonist separation from its source. In imitation of the creative Word and its harmonious intervals and connections, the language by which Adam renders what he sees about him has concretion, amplitude, ritual control, and immediate intelligibility. Each particular fits into its system without difficulty, just as each moment joins the synchronic diagram of the Creation in its dancelike ritual. As the common Renaissance metaphor expresses it, the universe is a musical instrument: its different parts contribute to a symphonic whole. Seemingly, then, nothing runs out of control; nothing is in danger of breaking loose or being wasted. Each tier in the constructed universe from single objects to universals is attached firmly to those above

and beneath, and the entire edifice finds an answerable mental consti-
tution to understand and celebrate it.

Yet the same distance from the source that gives Adam freedom to
fall is also perceptible in the individuality of things. The Creation
springs forth with more than a hint of combativeness, as in the "corny
Reed / Embattl'd in her field." The line between objects possessed of a
dangerous abruptness and objects possessed merely of a legitimate
power and self-direction is obviously a fine one. The ranges of being in
Book VII command attention in somewhat outlandish, if still basically
peaceful ways:

> He scarce had said, when the bare Earth, till then
> Desert and bare, unsightly, unadorn'd,
> Brought forth the tender Grass, whose verdure clad
> Her Universal Face with pleasant green,
> Then Herbs of every leaf, that sudden flow'r'd
> Op'ning thir various colors, and made gay
> Her bosom smelling sweet: and these scarce blown
> Forth flourish'd thick the clust'ring Vine, forth crept
> The smelling Gourd, up stood the corny Reed
> Embattl'd in her field: and th' humble Shrub,
> And Bush with frizz'd hair implicit: last
> Rose as in Dance the stately Trees, and spread
> Thir branches hung with copious Fruit: or gemm'd
> Thir Blossoms.
>   (VII.313-326)

The frizzled bush and the dancing trees make a strong impression.
Satan is properly more startled upon awakening in fiery perdition than
Adam is in awakening in Eden and finding such things before him; but
the fierce individualism that greets Adam does declare the wit and invention of a Creator who opts for sensory impact, variety, and wonder
over pastoral peace and otium. This Eden is clearly not a tame paradise
of classical valleys and streams. Without declaring a potential enmity
or disrupting the creative ritual, the frizzled bush assumes a vigorous
place in the dance of things.

Milton seldom lets the commanding idea of God's order deprive him
of the evidence of his senses; and certain vagaries of mind among nature's forms, which flower so brightly in *Arcades, Comus, L'Allegro,* and
Lycidas, come on strongly here and even continue to put in appearances
in *Paradise Regained,* albeit more sparsely. As though in answer to the
restless and destructive power of hell, Milton pursues the energy of the
Creation in all its baroque plenty:

> The Earth obey'd, and straight
> Op'ning her fertile Womb teem'd at a Birth
> Innumerous living Creatures, perfect forms,

> Limb'd and full grown: out of the ground up rose
> As from his Lair the wild Beast where he wons
> In Forest wild, in Thicket, Brake, or Den;
> Among the Trees in Pairs they rose, they walk'd; . . .
> The Tawny Lion, pawing to get free
> His hinder parts, then springs as broke from Bonds,
> And Rampant shakes his Brinded mane; the Ounce,
> The Libbard, and the Tiger, as the Mole
> Rising, the crumbl'd Earth above them threw
> In Hillocks; the swift Stag from under ground
> Bore up his branching head: scarce from his mould
> *Behemoth* biggest born of Earth upheav'd
> His vastness: Fleec't the Flocks and bleating rose
> As Plants.
>   (VII.453-469)

At the same time, although the rhythm and the numerous plosives suggest a galloping abundance, the ritual of the divine pronouncements and the initial image of the golden compasses maintain discipline. Adam's reason and poise quickly master the potential terror of the big cats, the subtleties of the serpent, and the confusion of sheer numbers. The birth of each of the species provides an occasion for the mind's new marriage to specific forms and punctual lyric responses, as Milton imagines Ideas springing into material shape in categories that the mind readily seizes. Unlike the violent noisiness and incessant movement of Sin's offspring in the main satanic parody of generation, then, the activity of creation has processional showmanship as well as sustained energy. That this generation of things in turn guides the poet's generation of images—that the Garden of Eden is a source for the poet's garden of words—gives recollection and the career of the poet mythic roots: part of the poet still dwells in adamic time, which is measured by the cycle of days and the tasks of georgic labor.

Nonetheless, Eden is after all the scene in which the human breakdown occurs. In advancing Satan there and observing his reactions to Adam and Eve, Milton explores the sharpest of differences among the characters of the epic. The narrator's perspective from outside and the reader's from centuries hence never let us forget the abruptness with which our world and Eden's come together. At the same time, the great gap between the highest and the low, and between good and evil, is broken into smaller gaps and transits in Eden, as Satan's and God's primary contest becomes a sequence of lesser ones. Eve's decision to leave Adam momentarily, for instance, brings the unfallen a step closer to the Fall. Paradise begins to assume for her some of the competitive opposition that it has for Satan, only scaled down. Likewise, the gap between Adam as he is created and Adam as he becomes Milton fills with other "gestures" (in Arnold Stein's apt word). Both his excessive attraction to

Eve and his decision to let her roam on the morning of the Fall are narrative stages in the gathering momentum of the actual conversion from paradise to wilderness.

After the Fall, Eve changes her style of speech and assumes a new enmity between herself, the spies around her, and the rest of Creation. God himself suddenly becomes "Our great Forbidder." Nature unleashes the war of beasts that the original individualism has hinted. Where kinds and universals had earlier provided upward bridges and kept particulars from slipping out of place, objects now become declassified by their metamorphoses; one thing perishes into another or is consumed by it. But Milton also capitalizes on the broader hiatus that stems from the Fall and allows a new freedom of surmise and exploration.

One of the compromises in the human wilderness between a closed, ceremonial order and chaos is the meandering of Adam and Eve after their Fall. In that wandering, epiphanies and reversals become more startling than they have been. In Michael's teaching, for instance, indirection replaces immediate and accurate intuitions of truth, and Adam must suffer new knowledge as an ordeal giving way at key points to ecstasy. Actually, Adam's original poetry has already possessed a certain waywardness, arising as it has in moments aside from Eden's labor. But such moments are devoted to praise of the Creator and to reaffirmations of the order that all things comprise. Adam's hymns amount to an exact linguistic placement, equivalent to other labors of trimming and ordering, so that poetry, domestic tasks, science, and even lovemaking are enactments, each in its own way, of a continous self-fulfillment and placement. Eve is wrong to assume that the distance of Eden from its source makes her invisible to divine vision or allows her latitude to stray from one category to another. Wandering is more serious when one can actually go astray from the connecting order. But even in postlapsarian temporality, it has its limits, and sooner or later Adam and Eve are meant to see through or beyond the gaps that history presents; they are intended to progress through the wilderness toward the destiny Michael holds out to them. History as a serial careening—as a succession of veiled prophecies, laborious readings of signs, stalled moments, and wandering—has a kind of harmony composed of antiphonal good and evil parts, especially in the visionary experience of saints and seers.

Meanwhile, Milton grants the poet too a definitive emergence as an integral member of that number for whom the ultimate "siege of contraries" is music—a measured use of gaps and intervals, most regular when most irregular it seems. Even in the desert, one may repair the damaged hymnody that stems from Satan's separation from his source. The hymn that completes *Paradise Regained* returns Milton to the beginning of his own career, to the Nativity ode, "Ad Patrem," "At a Solemn Music," and *Il Penseroso*, which proleptically reach toward the greater harmony that Christ's victory enters into the historical record.

Choral Response

For all his emphasis on discontinuity in the way of actions and dialogues and for all his breaks with tradition, Milton is not by choice a poet of jagged edges. He limits the areas within which it is necessary to contend, wander, and mourn the exile from paradise. Ancestral gloom and romantic phantomization are not his way, nor is a modern view of the present and its objects. Typical of his arresting of nostalgia, for instance (nostalgia as the emotion of severance without revival), is the brevity of Eve's reaction to exile:

> O unexpected stroke, worse than of Death!
> Must I leave thee Paradise? thus leave
> Thee Native Soil, these happy Walks and Shades
> Fit haunt of Gods? where I had hope to spend,
> Quiet though sad, the respite of that day
> That must be mortal to us both. O flow'rs,
> That never will in other Climate grow,
> My early visitation, and my last
> At Ev'n, which I bred up with tender hand
> From the first op'ning bud, and gave ye Names,
> Who now shall rear ye to the Sun, or rank
> Your Tribes, and water from th' ambrosial Fount?
> Thee lastly nuptial Bower, by mee adorn'd
> With what to sight or smell was sweet; from thee
> How shall I part, and whither wander down
> Into a lower World, to this obscure
> And wild, how shall we breathe in other Air
> Less pure, accustom'd to immortal Fruits?
> (XI.268–285)

This passage gathers up the tone of the poet's own earlier lament for his blindness and reveals the heavy weight of bardic ambition in embracing the Fall. But Michael does not allow it to continue. Paradoxically, by plunging into the deadened landscape of the post-Edenic world, the poet completes the itinerary of reclamation: from the dark, God is visible in a new way. Eve is given her vision of reconnection and her own historical task. In this revised mathematics of evil (reminiscent of "So much the rather thou Celestial Light / Shine inward"), Michael admonishes Adam and Eve to seek for what cannot be lost in time or place—in effect, to carry within them the plan of the historical labyrinth and the way out, which happens to be the chart of the very poem before us, historical in only one phase. Michael does not proceed immediately to the paradise within but coaches Adam with respect to the ways and means of God's presence in the lower world:

> Doubt not but in Valley and in Plain
> God is as here, and will be found alike
> Present, and of his presence many a sign
> Still following thee, still compassing thee round
> With goodness and paternal Love, his Face
> Express, and of his steps the track Divine.
>   (XI.345–354)

The doctrine of special signs is one answer to the dislocation that the first parents and all their offspring suffer; it enables the informed reader to rediscover images of the Creator and evidence of His reinstalling of good in remote regions.

As the retrospective lament for loss and ruin is allowed its moment and then converted into this balancing hope of recurrence, Milton limits the effects of the three new earthly personifications of the broken logos: Discord, Sin, and Death. But the final step in restoring paradise is more radical. When Christ justifies the return of the choral celebration in *Paradise Regained*, he simultaneously displaces or subordinates other kinds of divine figuration. A choral hymn does not deny that other styles and genres have their due place, as tragedy, pastoral, elegy, and sonnet, and epic all do. But like other last things, the truly responsive hymn is merely predicted by incomplete and negative versions. The total narrative cycle of decline and restoration includes pauses such as Adam's morning orison and the poet's invocations that in effect transpose divine celebrations into a lower key. Taken together, these moments of hailing and response point toward a transcendence that celebrants discover in glimpses of the concealed father.

Once we think of Milton's place descriptions and salutations in this way, a curious turnabout takes place in our sense of what constitutes the primary action of the poem; not the dramatic plot, history in its various phases, or the poet's occasional emergences but the still apprehension of a totality becomes the poem's true spiritual center. Events and partial perceptions that hold the stage at given moments prove to be betrayals as well as proleptic hints of that totality. Another way of putting it is to say that enthroned as the witnessing center of the poem beyond narrative process, God and Christ draw all actions away from specific localities, and they complete the poet's career—or supersede it—as a superior broadcasting or manifesting principle. What is truly heroic is defined by its responsiveness to them. As participants in the epic struggle to finish their ordeals and cross the line into the framing tableau, they retrace the movement of Christ, who descends from the upper

realm to the lower region and ascends back again as the true paradigm
of the bridging agent and thus the ultimate cure of abrupt transitions.

The poet's lyrics and the salutations of angel witnesses bring into serial history special moments of enlightenment that transcend local
cause and effect. Adam's realization of such a moment himself, as Michael's presentation of the future nears completion, leads him to rejoice
in a mode that once again approaches the hosanna:

> O goodness infinite, goodness immense!
> That all this good of evil shall produce,
> And evil turn to good; more wonderful
> Than that which by creation first brought forth
> Light out of darkness!
> (XII.469–473)

He regards Michael's instruction as a complete and accurate account of
the change the Fall has wrought and wonders if one need repent of sin
when more glory, good will, and grace come from it:

> How soon hath thy prediction, Seer blest,
> Measur'd this transient World, the Race of time,
> Till time stand fixt: beyond is all abyss,
> Eternity, whose end no eye can reach.
> Greatly instructed I shall hence depart,
> Greatly in peace of thought, and have my fill
> Of knowledge, what this Vessel can contain.
> (XII.552–559)

The final anthem of *Paradise Regained*, the consummation of Milton's
two epics, reaches a still higher tone. There the verbs can at last be cast
in the present tense: "A fairer Paradise is founded now / For *Adam* and
his chosen Sons" (IV.613–614). Because the heroic paradigm is henceforth set and available, it leaves no ground for nostalgia. At least a selected portion of humankind can now come full circle to what *Paradise
Lost* has promised from the greater man who set out to "Restore us, and
regain the blissful Seat." The return of the divine image to the most
parched of earthly places—where history seems to have reached a dead
end—counters the historical waste that follows from Eve's choice. To
repeat, however: in undoing Eve's work, Christ also undoes most other
human achievements as well. In place of the works of poets, philosophers, engineers, military leaders, and statesmen, Milton installs a single image of glory at the center of the visionary consciousness. Replacing the desire to recapture past moments with the desire to obliterate
them on behalf of that image, he joins an extreme poetic conservatism
to a radical spirit of reform. With one and the same stroke, he establishes the true record of the greater man and clears from that record—
or reduces to erring prediction—all predecessors and poetic rivals.

Because the totality of that epic retrieval, like its wreckage of everything else, is ideally extreme, it gives us a certain leverage in gauging other compromises between higher tiers (on the level of mythos), intermediate or recurrent institutions, and the flow of unique occasions. Despite its reliance on the most ancient of traditions (namely God's use of instruments as His expressive means), Milton's rejection of the past and of secular empire is predictive of modernism (even as his confidence in God's efficient power makes him one of the last medievalists). As a general rule, modernism too emphasizes the gap between realms and the incapacity of ordinary language, memory, or imagination to reach ultimate sources; and with the exception of Eliot, it rejects the dominance of the Latin tradition. It differs from Milton, of course, in that his skepticism does not extend all the way to the "upright heart and pure"; and it differs from its transcendental and romantic predecessors in scaling down its ambitions to begin with. It also substitutes for Milton's transcendent God a hope merely for immanent worth in the object and in the moment. In Wallace Stevens, it recognizes the fictive nature of what the poet proposes in his lyric moments, isolated from connecting plots and overall logic, in notes toward a supreme fiction.

Which returns us to the notion that I sketched earlier concerning the development of the professional fiction maker (as opposed to the mimetic recorder or rearranger of an assumed natural and historical order). Milton naturally supposes the supreme mythos to be not a fiction but a prophesied and yet startling reintroduction of the divine image into history, where the poet as chronicler can represent it and measure rival images of glory and empire against it. For most modernists, an image of paradise is only one of several poetic myths and experiments in perspective.

CHAPTER 6

Questers in an Icy Elysée: Moderns without Ancestry

What word have you, interpreters, of men
Who in the tomb of heaven walk by night,
The darkened ghosts of our old comedy?

WALLACE STEVENS, *"Of Heaven Considered as a Tomb"*

I F MILTON REJECTED all national legacies in the interests of a single inheritance from Adam and the second Adam, romanticism, especially Wordworthian recollection, followed him in casting aside certain intervening historical institutions and social systems. The difference is that for Wordsworth, paradise as a common legacy is also disallowed, although as M. H. Abrams has demonstrated, both Wordsworth and other romantics seek for equivalents to such traditional concepts.[1] Keats in the Hyperion poems works out his own set of evolutionary terms in the succession of gods, but his setting lies beyond recorded documents and the newly specialized discipline of archaelogy.

This disengagement of poetry from the documented past is not the invention of the romantics, but they illustrate it usefully. They look both toward a cherished past, now phantomized, and toward a present of privileged landscapes and objects. The dramatic tension of Keat's "Ode on a Grecian Urn" derives from that bifurcated vision. The Grecian past still matters as it did to Keats's contemporaries in their scholarly explication of the Elgin marbles; but art also rises above chronicle time, where truth and beauty are frozen and identical. As the urn suggests, the work of art provides access both to sylvan histories and to a realm of fixed forms. What is missing is some equivalent to Milton's deliverer archetype and the cylical restoration of paradise. Or to change the terms to a favorite Keatsian speculation: when Milton's Adam awakens from his swoon, a Creator has made Eve for him in the flesh; Keats's Eden remains a dream locatable in the imagination. Even fallen humankind in Milton finds a reinstatement of the father's image:

> True Image of the Father, whether thron'd
> In the bosom of bliss, and light of light
> Conceiving, or remote from Heaven, enshrin'd
> In fleshly Tabernacle, and human form
> Wand'ring the Wilderness, whatever place,
> Habit, or state, or motion, still expressing
> The son of God, with Godlike force endu'd
> Against th' Attempter of thy Father's Throne,
> And Thief of Paradise.
> (*Paradise Regained*, IV.596–604)

In contrast, Keats relies on art to materialize truth and beauty and takes a significant step toward an externalist, or descriptive, poetics of Marianne Moore's and William Carlos Williams' kind.[2] Romantic revelations tend to hinge on privileged objects like Keats's nightingale or Wordsworth's cuckoo and to be virtual as opposed to actual. Some transcendental principle is not quite stable in them yet is thought to be there and is unknowable otherwise. Thus Keats's nightingale brings with it a certain consciousness of supernatural realms but at the same time reminds the poet of an oppressively historical world:

> Thou was not born for death, immortal Bird!
>   No hungry generations tread thee down;
> The voice I hear this passing night was heard
>   In ancient days by emperor and clown:
> Perhaps the self-same song that found a path
>   Through the sad heart of Ruth, when, sick for home,
>   She stood in tears amid the alien corn;
>   The same that oft-times hath
> Charm'd magic casements, opening on the foam
> Of perilous seas, in faery lands forlorn.

Although the poet is intensely aware of time, the bird is free to ignore what passes in each generation. Like Shelley's skylark, it has never known "the weariness, the fever, and the fret / Here, where men sit and hear each other groan." It is precisely the longevity of the nightingale and the ideality of its faery realm that occasion the intensified sense of history in the speaker and hence, paradoxically, the object nature of the bird, which finally draws off as something enigmatic and distant:

> Adieu! Adieu! thy plaintive anthem fades
>   Past the near meadows, over the still stream,
>   Up the hill-side; and now 'tis buried deep
>   In the next valley-glades.

Other changes that occur in the grammar of objects between Milton and modernism need not detain us. But we should perhaps recall at least that the battle between moderns and ancients gained momentum

in the later seventeenth century, when a surviving respect for the imitation of classical models fought a rear-guard action against an increasing sense of distance between those models and the present. As Dryden
complains in *Mac Fleckno*, even Christian typology appears to have
slipped into the mere tautology of Dulness. It is precisely such a "burden of the past," as W. J. Bate calls it in its eighteenth-century circumstances—rather than the reinstatement of relivable forms—that most
poets felt after Milton, whichever side of the ancient-modern quarrel
they happened to take. The real beginnings of the modernist attitude in
the romantics gained some impetus from a rejection of that burden as
well as from the transcendentalizing of objects in the present. When the
modernist attitude emerged in such poets as Stevens, Williams, and
Moore, it was free to fasten on contemporary objects with little need to
pay deference to commonplace topics, myths, or received ideas. As
Harry Berger, Jr., has observed, the traditionalist attitude toward the
created world assumes that it exists intact outside human making, and
the prevailing modern notion (which of course has older advocates, just
as traditionalists have some currency still) insists that, as Marx says,
"Men make their own history."[3] Thus, in modernism generally, men
are collectively responsible for what was once presumed to have its
own ontological status and momentum.

An object that holds to its uniqueness also maintains its foreignness
to categories and rationality.[4] It refuses systematic definition. It does
not readily volunteer to serve either history or higher realms as a messenger. For instance, a good deal of Stevens' *Harmonium*, with its snow-
man, its emperor of ice cream, and its drunken sailors catching tigers in
red weather suggests Lewis Carroll and the arbitrariness that children
know before they become trained in commonplaces. Even glittering
and beautiful creatures such as the bird in the palm in "Of Mere Being"
are at the end of mind, where mere being unites estrangement and
beauty:

> A gold-feathered bird
> Sings in the palm, without human meaning,
> Without human feeling, a foreign song.[5]

As Stevens advises the neophyte poet in "Notes toward a Supreme Fiction," Phoebus as a name for the sun is dead; we must return to "the
truth itself," as the ignorant man sees the sun "with an ignorant eye"
(*Collected Poems*, pp. 380–381). And so the sun itself, the most familiar of
objects, also becomes estranged, without human associations. Only
when it reaches that novelty of perception can it come forth again as a
thing without ideas, "Surrounded by its choral rings, / Still far way" (p.
534).

Saving and Throwing Away: Dealing in Antiques and New-Made Things

Although no small group of figures will serve as spokesmen for either the traditionalist or the modernist attitude toward objects, George Herbert and Donne at one end, and Stevens, Williams, and Richard Wilbur at the other end (or at various points near it) illustrate the difference with sufficient typicality to be useful—especially if we recall several others whom we have already consulted in other regards, such as Wordsworth, Keats, Eliot, Spenser, Milton, and Yeats.

Herbert is perhaps foremost among those who make objects into recurrent exemplars and hieroglyphs under the auspices of Christian dogma and Renaissance commonplaces. On the nature of history, the way the poet serves as a secondary creator, and the infiltration of the present by types and archetypes, he agrees basically with Milton. *The Temple* might be regarded as a set of "notes toward a supreme fiction" were it not that the figure of the temple itself, with its architecture, furniture, and rituals is a privileged, central place. The volume as a whole portrays the spiritual itinerary of the poet and of Everyman among personal and historical phases. Its several coordinated and interlocked progressions include the movement from genesis to doomsday, the reader's introduction to the church and movement toward the mystical repast of "Love III," and the speaker's descent into spiritual trials, some of them serialized in groups of poems. As "The H. Scriptures II" says of the Bible, "This verse marks that, and both do make a motion / Unto a third, that ten leaves off doth lie." All lights combine in "the configurations . . . of glorie" that those verses make, and each reader's destiny is summed up therein.

On several occasions, Herbert writes on both sides of the issues that change raises—for instance, on what one loses and salvages at a personal level from a world destined eventually to be consumed not article by article but all at once. Kinds naturally survive longer, in the interim before doomsday, than do individual things, but only the soul survives everything. Although it dwells in the company of daily objects, it must learn to extricate itself from them. Thus in "Vertue," Herbert concludes:

> Sweet spring, full of sweet dayes and roses,
> A box where sweets compacted lie;
> My musick shows ye have your closes,
>   And all must die.
>
> Onely a sweet and vertuous soul,
> Like season'd timber, never gives;
> But though the whole world turn to coal,
>   Then chiefly lives.

The word "closes" points up the ritual control that rules over the world's procession of sweet things. The verse itself is a music of closes and formal phrases, rounded off in end-stopped rhyme and ruled by a meter with a minimum of irregularities. Such closes represent a triumph of the human scale over vast times and spaces and yet are responsive to those greater measures also. Even as the burning world shrinks to a coal at time's end, the soul's continuity will prevail and, to judge by the tone and diction here, will do so on comfortable moral grounds. Though everything has its season, the world as a whole until its close is upheld by a sustaining power that all perpetuity requires. Meanwhile, the soul does not invent its destiny but inherits it, and the rules for doing so are within its command. If sinners have ups and downs, periods of absence from God, intensities and slackness, it is because of their own changes, not because of flaws in the Creation. Hence, although Herbert concedes the inevitable scattering of the material world in historical time, as again in "Death" and "Dooms-day," he has some confidence in the tested and reaffirmed beliefs that guide one's journey.

Equally important in placing all times and places under the control of the poet's closes are abstractions. As "Temper I" concludes:

> Yet take thy way; for sure thy way is best:
> Stretch or contract me, thy poore debter:
> This is but tuning of my breast,
> To make the musick better.

> Whether I flie with angels, fall with dust,
> Thy hands made both, and I am there:
> Thy power and love, my love and trust
> Make one place ev'ry where.

If one place *is* everywhere, one time must also be all times; travel is an illusion. Love, power, and trust are systematic abstractions that bring the world under command. The music that names them surpasses its own measure because it is attuned not to prescribed things in themselves but to an infiltration into all particles of God's characteristics. If God is visible in a mote of dust, whatever floats up before us becomes uniform and permeated with significance. In "Death," for instance, the Resurrection puts the natural world under the soul's control and enables it to confront death with equanimity:

> For we do now behold thee gay and glad,
>   As at dooms-day;
> When souls shall wear their new aray,
> And all thy bones with beautie shall be clad.

Time is again reduced to human scale, as doomsday falls into place among the celebrations of the yearly calendar with the familiarity of

Easter festivities. The final day recalls the creation and typical rejoic-
ings in calendric time. "Dooms-day" is similar in imagining the final
awakening to be a reacquaintance of intimate part with part and a recovery from temporal dispersal and apparent waste:

> Come away
> Make no delay.
> Summon all the dust to rise,
> Till it stirre, and rubbe the eyes;
> While this member jogs the other,
> Each one whispring, *Live you brother?*

Those objects that are newly stirred by the soul resume their existence
in due time. They must return to coherence if paradise is to be outfit-
ted.

However, Herbert does not overlook the stress the soul experiences
in seeking its itinerary through local circumstances. Its victories over
time and difference are often hard earned and require miracles of divine intervention. Thus in "Dooms-day," the appeal for a final ending
grows more urgent as the world's particles scatter. Elsewhere too, Herbert's meditations on the past stress the need for a miraculous reconsti-
tution of the world's body and the handicaps with which the poet
begins all dealings with it. The poet on his own is incapable of rescuing
either objects or himself. In "Heaven," he stages the poet's effort to
penetrate the language of objects as an inadequate series of surmises,
collected and saved by a power rebounding from heaven itself. In his
error-prone method, the poet cites things that are not salvageable, at
least not in his terms, although he does so in a way that sets in motion
an ironic reversal, as what is faulty and perishable on one level points
toward something less vulnerable on another level:

> O Who will show me those delights on high?
> > *Echo.*   I.
> Thou Echo, thou art mortall, all men know.
> > *Echo.*   No.
> Wert thou not born among the trees and leaves?
> > *Echo.*   Leaves.
> And are there any leaves, that still abide?
> > *Echo.*   Bide.
> What leaves are they? impart the matter wholly.
> > *Echo.*   Holy.
> Are holy leaves the Echo then of bliss?
> > *Echo.*   Yes.

The pun on "leaves" both equates with scripture and devalues nature's
book. That heaven is not an echo of earth but earth that of heaven
points up the crucial difference between traditionalist and modern tendencies. Herbert's redefinitions of a world that periodically fails—the

world as a dying echo—stems from the way in which the final substance of an image descends from beyond human guessing and is discovered, not invented. It is fully actual, not virtual.

Poets do not extend significance to things either by the conventions
of language or by their own imaginations but seek to discover how
earth and heaven reinforce each other. From the human perspective,
the historical process is a series of gestures toward a validation of
heaven's echoes, a back-and-forth movement in which the human time
scheme serves as an introduction to another arena that constantly replaces and completes it. The external shape of the poem itself participates in both realms, as rhyme—the punctual reminder of the poem's
progress—marks the transition from one level to the other and dissolves the surmise of a first word in the realization of a second. Herbert
here experiences few if any of the conflicts between the fixed, eternal
realm of art and temporal process that plague Keats in "Ode on a Grecian Urn" and Yeats in "Sailing to Byzantium." Nor does he subordinate art to historical change, as Yeats does in "Lapis Lazuli" and as Stevens so frequently does. Poetry is neither a record of change nor a
counterproposal from a realm of permanence; in this case at least, it is
a process of interrogation and discovery, a dialectical drama in which a
quester is introduced to a sense of heaven by slightly incongruent analogies. In the same way, social bargaining in "Love III" is a vehicle by
which divine communion is finally approached. Indeed, it is possible
for almost any metaphor to serve as an opening to the discovery of sac-
ramental essences: any of the variety of spiritual occasions, concrete
social and natural settings, or specifying words that the poet selects
may pry open the same door; any word may be polysemous and
layered.

How typical is Herbert in this use of objects? Can one locate something like a Renaissance index of divine retrieval in *The Temple's* arrangement of them? We should first acknowledge the multiplicity of
versions of past making in any period. Certainly we would have difficulty packaging poets as diverse as Spenser, Herbert, Shakespeare,
Donne, Greville, Jonson, and Marvell together under any but the
broadest of labels. Yet these and other figures do have in common a
combined sense of classical heritage and beginnings and endings. They
also share a certain hierarchy of natural and social forms and the hegemony of some concepts over others. To put it the other way around,
even many of those Renaissance thinkers and poets in whom Chris-
tian-Platonist orthodoxy is more drastically challenged than it is in
Herbert do not illustrate anything like modern skepticism about the
external order. If we think of Donne's version of the decay of general
order in *The Anniversaries*, for instance, it is less an anticipation of modernism than a roundabout endorsement of beliefs essentially like Her-

bert's. Donne assumes a realm of incorruptibility to which the soul escapes. He also assumes the possibility of the poet's hearkening after it and returning with answers. Despite its present condition, the senseless, degenerate world has not always been what it is, "All in pieces, all coherence gone; / All just supply, and all relation" (211–213). It is true that what is left "is crumbled out again to his atomies":

> As mankind, so is the world's whole frame
> Quite out of joint, almost created lame:
> For, before God had made up all the rest,
> Corruption entered, and deprav'd the best.
> (Donne, *The First Anniversary*, 191–194)

But none of this crumbling destroys the poet's capacity to gather particulars into types, the chief of which is Elizabeth Drury herself, the "best, the first original / Of all fair copies" (227–228).

The poem becomes for Donne not merely an anatomy of ruin, then, but a harbinger, the function of which is to awaken men and save memorable things from oblivion: as the divine voice once spoke to Moses and commanded a song for his people, so the poet now undertakes a "great Office," which is to bring news from a realm of permanence and establish a name in an enduring human record. Like Herbert, Donne thereby makes the cosmic and the human scales adjustable to each other:

> Nor could incomprehensibleness deter
> Me, from thus trying to emprison her.
> Which when I saw that a strict grave could do,
> I saw not why verse might not do so too.
> Verse hath a middle nature: heaven keeps souls,
> The grave keeps bodies, verse the fame enrolls.
> (*The First Anniversary*, 469–474)

In his more positive seeking of reclaimable images of paradise in *The Second Anniversary*, Donne is less concerned with the loss of God's image and more encouraged by the progress of the soul. The periods of the world's history, now in its last stage, are superseded by the soul's stages of ascent and ultimate arrival.

The modernist difference in both the status of objects and their contexts is suggested by Stevens' use of the phrases "supreme fiction" and "parts of a world," which suggest that although he did not abandon the attempt to conceive of a totalized world, he found it fragmented in the poet's inventions. "The Sail of Ulysses" concedes that "there is no map of paradise" and that if "the great Omnium" does descend, we will discover it to be a divination of "a life beyond this present knowing" in which the "litter of truths" becomes a whole. Individual poems spring not from facets of a perceived whole but from isolated occasions that are more or less fortunate and often pinned to the suggestiveness that objects generate. History itself assumes no particular storied shape. Lacking a teleological principle, the poet cannot think of it as progress. What surfaces now belongs exclusively to now, and the order the poet applies he must invent: "Everything needs expounding all the time."

The chief differences between Milton's or Herbert's version of the past and Stevens' stem from that central assumption about the need constantly to recompose a world. When Stevens remarks in *Adagia* that poetry replaces God as the projection of order, he apparently means that within the duration of a given poem, poetry has the function that gods were once assigned in the cosmos; but it works strictly within its own confines. As Stevens perceives in "Two or Three Ideas," "All of the noble images of all the gods have been profound and most of them have been forgotten. To speak of the origin and end of gods is not a light matter. It is to speak of the origin and end of eras of human belief" (*Opus Posthumous*, p. 205). Religious belief is symptomatic of a belief in reality itself. To forget such figures as the gods is to forget eras and their special reality and thus to discard the sensibility of former times. At moments (though it is somewhat out of character), Stevens suggests Victorian regret over that loss, when the disappearance of the gods leaves a vacancy that no modern idea of nobility has so far replaced:

> To see the gods dispelled in mid-air and dissolve like clouds is one of the great human experiences. It is not as if they had gone over the horizon to disappear for a time; nor as if they had been overcome by other gods of greater power and profounder knowledge. It is simply that they came to nothing. Since we have always shared all things with them and have always had a part of their strength and, certainly, all of their knowledge, we shared likewise this experience of annihilation. It was their annihilation, not ours, and yet it left us feeling that in a measure, we, too, had been annihilated (*OP*, pp. 206–207).

If the Hyperion poems come to the edge of that perception in dwelling on the wreckage of the gods, Stevens finishes an incomplete Keatsian plot in the realization that all transcendence has come to nothing. The poet has awakened from his dream and reentered the present. He is not disillusioned, however, and does not particularly need the past that the gods filled; there can be "no crying out for their return." They left behind no mementos, thrones, or mystic rings (p. 207). The poet must not turn evangelist and seek to reinstate them: "After all, he shares the disbelief of his time. He does not turn to Paris or Rome for relief from the monotony of reality" (p. 213). He discovers that the "only possible resistance to the pressure of the contemporaneous is a matter of herrings and apples or, to be less definite, the contemporaneous itself" (p. 225). Indeed, "All history is modern history" (p. 166).

Equally typical of the differences between Stevens and a traditionalist poetic is the interrogation of heaven's interpreters in "Heaven Considered as a Tomb." Unlike Herbert's speaker in "Heaven," Stevens' speaker calls out to exegetes who in turn question wanderers at great remoteness:

> What word have you, interpreters of men
> Who in the tomb of heaven walk by night,
> The darkened ghosts of our old comedy? . . .
> Halloo them in the topmot distances
> For answer from their icy Elysée.
> (*CP*, p. 56)

The wasteful cosmos allows neither echoes nor harbingers to return from the abode of the dead. If the poet's scanning of the skies foretells anything, it is merely the long night of the spent universe when even the stars will cease to wander.

Stevens' skepticism, unlike Donne's or Montaigne's, does not presume prevalent, entrenched beliefs to be dislodged. The lack of these has its drawbacks, but it also permits a certain pagan liveliness to have its day. In "A High-Toned Old Christian Woman," for instance, poetry is the source of whatever projections of order one manages: "Poetry is the supreme fiction"; and "the conscience" of Christians "is converted into palms, / Like windy citherns hankering for hymns." Heaven is thus replaced by a fanciful masque "beyond the planets":

> Thus, our bawdiness,
> Unpurged by epitaph, indulged at last,
> Is equally convereted into palms,
> Squiggling like saxophones.

Unlike the icy Elysée, this version of heaven has no ghosts, but rings with a noise that cures self-punishing monks and ascetics of their spiritual ailments:

> Allow,
> Therefore, that in the planetary scene
> Your disaffected flagellants, well-stuffed,
> Smacking their muzzy bellies in parade,
> Proud of such novelties of the sublime,
> Such tink and tank and tunk-a-tunk-tunk,
> May, merely may, madam, whip from themselves
> A jovial hullabaloo among the spheres.
> This will make widows wince. But fictive things
> Wink as they will. Wink most when widows wince.

If Herbert's apocalyptic festivity in "Death" compresses end things in a domestic, social metaphor that makes no one wince, Stevens' holiday in contrast is a circus novelty that lets imagination run riot. Behind its shattering of propriety is an assumption that if heaven can be imagined as this or that, why not as an Elks' convention or Fourth of July parade? All metaphors for it are useful only for their provocation and their interpretive suggestions. The masque exists in a world not of probabilities but of ideas and of discourse, as a proposition in a dramatized argument, or a dance of symbolic attitudes. "Beyond" is entertained for the light it enables the skeptical wit to shed on belief "here." This is not to say that Stevens has Herbert or any other specific poet in mind; but the effect of his proposition about heaven is to reconceive such texts as the *Divine Comedy*, *The Temple*, and *Paradise Lost* as imaginative ventures rather than reflections of truth. Intellectual history for Stevens becomes a series of myths, each phase of which unfolds a newly problematic relationship between imagination and reality, which is composed of the statements we made about it.

Neither "Heaven Considered as a Tomb" nor "A High-Toned Old Christian Woman," however, indicates the complexity of Stevens' view of the past as a series of inventions. Though they make clear that he thinks of that past as a reliquary of systems and images, they offer no real sense of the countermyths he proposes. His more explicit assessments of the past are reserved for the essays. Some of these complement Eliot and Yeats, though they are much more skeptical about the retrievability of the past. In "The Noble Rider and the Sound of Words," for intance, in taking up Coleridge's remark that Plato's pure poetry was "dear, gorgeous nonsense," Stevens suggests that a reader of older images such as Plato's horseman-soul may enter into the spirit of their myths and images, but when a sense of history reasserts itself as it must, "Suddenly we remember . . . that the soul no longer exists and we droop in our flight and at last settle on the solid ground." The winged horse then seems antiquated.[6] Why does it shrink to a mere "rustic memorial"? Stevens' answer is not particularly original and appears to owe something to the sociologist's association of art with general epochs. It is simply that our reaction is inhibited not by the unreality of the figure itself or lack of confidence in Plato but by the progressive mental states of the race, which have carried us away from our starting points. That antiquation does not necessarily take a long time in all instances. Stevens finds even some of his own previous moments deplorably faded, as in his youthful journals he remarks about an earlier entry, "What silly affected schoolgirl drivel this seems to me now." (In rejecting Plato in "The Noble Rider," too, he is actually turning against a former self that not long before made Jowett's translation a constant companion.)

Stevens' rejection of ancestors and former selves is not always this decisive, however. As Merle Brown observes, his "unhistorical reality is haunted and shadowed by the historical imagining which it denies."[7] The possible poet, Stevens remarks,

Will have thought that Virgil, Dante, Shakespeare, Milton placed themselves in remote lands and in remote ages; that their men and women were the dead—and not the dead lying in the earth, but the dead still living in their remote lands and in their remote ages, and living in the earth or under it, or in the heavens—and he will wonder at those huge imaginations, in which what is remote becomes near, and what is dead lives with an intensity beyond any experience of life (p. 23).

As he adds succinctly elsewhere, poetry is "a cemetery of nobilities." The difficulty is that although collectively the noble figures of the past define possibilities that have existed for poets, it is not clear how they can reenter a modern style honorably, without parody; or how, for the poet specifically, they remain alive as predecessors "with an intensity beyond any experience of life."

One answer is that even an extreme modernist cannot avoid certain aspects of recurrence. As George Kubler points out in assessing the pervasiveness of copies, the available combinations of matter are limited, and the replications of energy and form are staggering in total. Mere duration without repetition would be a timeless chaos: "Without change there is no history; without regularity there is no time." Hence "time and history are related as rule and variation: time is the regular setting for the vagaries of history. The replica and the invention are related in the same way: a series of true inventions excluding all intervening replicas would approach chaos, and an all-embracing infinity of replicates without variation would approach formlessness."[8] In a different context, Buckminister Fuller has remarked that even scrap is not waste but merely one step in a progressively more efficient use of forms. Hence where we do not reduplicate, we dismantle and reassemble. Or as Lévi-Strauss suggests:

> Man has never—save only when he reproduces himself—done other than cheerfully dismantle million upon million of structures and reduce their elements to a state in which they can no longer be integrated . . . Taken as a whole, therefore, civilization can be described as a prodigiously complicated mechanism: tempting as it would be to regard it as our universe's best hope of survival, its true function is to produce what physicists call entropy: . . . 'Entropology,' not anthropology, would be the word for that discipline that devotes itself to the study of this process of disintegration in its most highly evolved forms.[9]

The verbal conventions, ideas, and genres that a writer has at his disposal are no exception. Creations are made not from chaos or the miscellaneous seeds of things but from salvageable forms, which, when they are recycled, look something like their previous selves. As Stevens admits in "The Auroras of Autumn" (a more sober meditation on time and change than "A High-Toned Old Christian Woman"), "The cancellings, / The negations are never final." The father who sits in space "measures the velocities of change" without himself disappearing like the gods. Given this inevitability of recycled forms, is not the avowed modernist less successful in his break with the past than he hopes to be? Is he not, in Bloom's word, always "belated"? Do not all his presumably discrete objects drag a burden of recollections with them?

Certainly we discover in Stevens not a simple contrast between traditionalist and modernist tendencies but several complexes that include recurrence and cyclical renewal. On the one hand, the modernist *is* likely to agree with Williams' remark that "to refine, to clarify, to intensify that eternal moment in which we alone live" is the primary task of the imagination. On the other hand, as Williams again says not many pages later: "Every step once taken in the first advance of the human race, from the amoeba to the highest type of intelligence, has been duplicated, every step exactly paralleling the one that preceded in the dead ages gone by. A perfect plagarism results."[10] the seeming contradiction is compressable into a paradox that *Spring and All* puts succinctly:

> The decay of cathedrals
> is efflorescent
> through the phenomenal
> growth of movie houses
>
> whose catholicity is
> progress since
> destruction and creation
> are simultaneous.
>   (p. 127)

A concept of innovation depends on an eruption, a violation of normality in the cycle of sameness.[11] Thus for Stevens too, composition is a complex matter in which the balance between invention and replication is struck anew at every turn. It is a struggle with received words and images, a growing realization of perceptions, a glance over the shoulder at the past, a following of genres previously mapped out, yet a displacement of them and a quest for greater permanence than they possess. Every choice the poet makes discards something; thereafter, standing amidst all that it does *not* contain, the work affirms itself as a positive, always present entity. It may allude to its layered past but cannot contain it. It may parallel it, but in a different style.

By the time a poet has a lifetime of composing behind him, one of the layers that the past presents him is his own personal accomplishment, which is also subject to disintegration and recycling. But unlike that accomplishment in Milton's case, the personal is largely debris for Stevens. It does not accumulate as the additive interpretation of a single order increasingly understood and rendered. In Stevens' late poems, when the present writer and his previous selves meet in the meditative quiet of composition, the meeting is a challenge to the preexistent self. In "The Planet on the Table" and "The Poem that Took the Place of a Mountain," for instance, Stevens suggests a present qualified by the past that it must unravel and remake. Even so, as "The Planet on the Table" indicates, one cannot rid oneself entirely of the satisfaction of accomplished work:

> Ariel was glad he had written his poems.
> They were of a remembered time
> Or of something seen that he liked.
>
> Other makings of the sun
> Were waste and welter
> And the ripe shrub writhed.
>
> His self and the sun were one
> And his poems, although makings of his self,
> Were no less makings of the sun.
>
> It is not important that they survive.
> What mattered was that they should bear
> Some lineament or character,
>
> Some affluence, if only half-perceived,
> In the poverty of their words,
> Of the planet of which they were part.
>   (CP, p. 532)

The reality to be composed is somewhat hugely the world itself; yet the composition itself is a mere poem, a piece on the table before the poet. The past self returns and reenters the act of appreciation now; the planet endures; the mountain repeats itself. No other precedents are needed, as other makings fade and become "waste and welter." Certainly whatever is to be reused must be recomposed or it cannot be re-cited (or resighted). If the personal past is to be restorable, it must be broken down into elements and recombined as the imagination now dictates. Such a past will be so thoroughly reintegrated into the present, as something represented in a new class of objects, that it may not even appear as the past—certainly not as a romantic or a Wordsworthian past. The present object, the current mountain or planet, is ever emergent, and perhaps without completion, as "July Mountain" is a "constellation / of patches and of pitches," not a planet entirely on the table but "a page of poetry" in an "always incipient cosmos" (OP, pp. 114–115).

Richard Wilbur and Others: What to Do with Junk

The belief of Williams and Stevens is that only when a poet has severed connections with the common heritage can he concentrate on the world of free objects before him. In poems such as "The Planet on the Table" and "The Poem that Took the Place of a Mountain," Stevens stands somewhere between Eliot and Williams in the completeness of that severance. Williams, of course chastised Eliot specifically, and all history writing in general, for looking backward rather that outward. As he proposes in his own odd version of history writing, *In the American Grain*, history "portrays us in generic patterns, like effigies or the carvings on sarcophagi, which say nothing save, of such and such a man, that he is dead. That's history. It is concerned only with the one thing: to say everything is dead. Then it fixes up the effigy." An important difference exists between objects like the sheet of paper in "The Term" and effigies—one surrendering to the blowing wind, the other standing in mockery of what lies inside the tomb. Rather than pursue what is irretrievable, the poet (for Williams) must immerse himself in what flows through the visible space before the senses. An effigy is merely a substitute or portable reproduction. It requires its viewer to decipher a distant intent that can never be seized with confidence. Only if history "could be that which annihilated all memory of past things from our minds" could it "be a useful tyranny."[12] Almost as acidly, Williams remarks after the burning of the library in *Paterson:*

> There is no recurrence.
> The past is dead. Women are
> legalists, they want to rescue
> a framework of laws, a skeleton of
> practices, a calcined reticulum
> of the past which, bees, they will
> fill with honey.
>
> It is not to be done.[13]

However, as Stevens realizes in his view of Williams as the man on the dump—and thus a true exponent of universal discard—even Williams never entirely rids himself of a vestige of romanticism; and in his romanticism is a style of cherishing that embraces some moments of the past, like the interwoven historical anecdotes of *Paterson*. Hence, though Williams rejects romanticism in principle, Stevens finds that to be a peculiar and partial sort of rejection: "The man has spent his life in rejecting the accepted sense of things. In that, most of all, his romantic temperament appears. But is is not enough merely to reject: what matters is the reason for rejection. The reason is that Williams has a romantic of his own." It is because the romantic is a special creature, rebelling against traditions while seated among their remains, that Stevens imagines Williams beating his tin can on a dump filled with both old and current items:

> What, then, is a romantic poet now-a-days? He happens to be one who still dwells in an ivory tower, but who insists that life would be intolerable except for the fact that one has, from the top, such an exceptional view of the public dump and the advertising signs of Snider's Catsup, Ivory Soap and Chevrolet Cars; he is the hermit who dwells alone with the sun and moon, but insists on taking a rotten newspaper.[14]

What Stevens sorts out here and in "The Man on the Dump" is not so much past from present as the recurrent and natural from the cheap and vulgar—and therefore timely. As tired old metaphors in "Man on the Dump" intrude upon the moon and sun and obliterate them with their tawdriness, so the advertising sign and the newspaper render reality not as accurate epitomes but as exaggerations: in its attempt to catch the eye with some stellar feature of the product (at the expense of its other properties), an advertisement becomes a monstrous aberration. Although the romanticism that Stevens finds in Williams encourages discontinuity, then, Stevens recognizes that a thoroughly ruthless discarding of older things delivers the poet over to the domination of the present. Once the poet sacrifices the reflective, preserving, sifting, evaluating, and judgmental functions of mind, he surrenders the present moment to the next—and so on in a ceaseless turnover. Declaring history to be unrepresentable and finding all language subject to the discard heap makes now, too, intangible and uncherishable.

Still more moderate than Stevens in such considerations is Richard Wilbur. He too honors the object in its vivid present; but he also traces complex acts of mind by which we assess and assimilate it. Like Williams, he toys with rejections of the past and its stockpile of formulas and conventions; and like Stevens, he makes composition a recurrent concern, concentrating on perception and language in their interplay with objects, in the act of matching words and things. The matter of selection is often at issue: given a world of objects demanding more or less equal attention, the line between detritus and heritage takes a discerning eye to discover.[15] Unlike either the romantics or Walt Whitman, Wilbur is not a poet of avatars or inventories. Unlike the imagists too, he seeks to balance an exact pictorialism with the skeptical approach of thought to the object, in what he labels the "great straddle."[16] To write Williams' kind of visual poem, the poet has to have great confidence in the self-composition of single items or landscapes and in the capacity of words to catch the world's shining bits and pieces with precision. In contrast, even in Wilbur's most exact pictorial passages, the pace tends to be set by associative consciousness. Objects may be collected at the poet's elbow, like puzzle pieces, but his goal is to place them in a designed assemblage.

Yet no such assemblage automatically works agains the scattered nature of the world's moving parts. Typical of Wilbur's poems in this way is "Statues," which concerns a variety of postures unlike the fixed memorials that normally go under the name "statues." His statues are quite different from Stevens' succession of obsolete forms in "The Noble Rider" or Yeats's lasting, repeatable Phidian sculpture. The latter is a replication of the past that provides moderns with meditational objects. It assists their realization of once-dominant forms as a stimulant to a revolution that turns backward:

> When Perse summoned Cuchulain to his side,
> What stalked through the Post Office? What intellect,
> What calculation, number, measurement, replied?
> We Irish, born into that ancient sect
> But thrown upon this filthy modern tide
> And by its formless spawning fury wrecked,
> Climb to our proper dark, that we may trace
> The lineaments of a plummet-measured face.[17]

For solitary boys and girls (who press "live lips" upon that "plummet-measured face"), the essence of the revisited past consists not of its style or even its human image (the human face is reduced to characterless calculation and measure) but of a passionate sense of perfection. If the present is to be overthrown, let it be on behalf of something not new but salvaged in mosaic, architecture, in mementos like Sato's sword or depictions like those of "Lapis Lazuli."

Stevens' statues diverge as sharply from Yeats's as they do from Wilbur's. In "Dance of the Macabre Mice," Stevens belittles heroes frozen in statuesque poses:

> In the land of turkeys in turkey weather
> At the base of the statue, we go round and round.
> What a beautiful history, beautiful surprise!
> Monsieur is on horseback. The horse is covered with mice . . .
>
> The founder of the State. Whoever founded
> A state that was free, in the dead of winter, from mice?
> What a beautiful tableau tinted and towering,
> The arm of bronze outstretched against all evil!
> (*CP*, p. 123)

What Yeats takes to be the strength of art—its reapplication of ideal forms in widely separated moments—Stevens finds at best problematic. The tableau to be sure, is beautiful; it is well shaded and imposing. But the gestures of military figures seem melodramatic once the war is over (as "The American Sublime" also suggests). Unlike Yeats's Cuchulain, a George Washington or an Andrew Jackson has nothing to say to modern revolutionaries. His fixed state and the "lordly language" of his inscription are inflexible and pompous. All accomplished, finished art, whether music or sculpture, is left behind in the turning seasons. Insofar as the American sublime attempts to fix itself in memorial shapes, it grows stuffy and grotesque.

The statue maker of "The Old Woman and the Statue" in *Owls Clover* has more success in coping with change, at least initially; although cast in marble, his horses leap "in storms of light":

> White forelegs taut
> To the muscles' very tip for the vivid plunge . . .
> Arranged for phantasy to form an edge
> Of crisping light along the statue's rim.
> More than his muddy hand was in the manes,
> More than his mind in the wings. The rotten leaves
> Swirled round them in immense autumnal sounds.
> (*OP*, p. 43)

But his view of the group is only one of several: after sampling others, Stevens eventually cancels the liveliness of the horses. Setting manmade objects against nature, he sees both of them in the context of universal waste:

> At some gigantic, solitary urn,
> A trash can at the end of the world, the dead
> Give up dead things and the living turn away.
> There buzzards pile their sticks upon the bones
> Of buzzards and eat the bellies of the rich,
> Fat with a thousand butters, and the crows
> Sip the wild honey of the poor man's life,
> The blood of his bitter brain; and there the sun
> Shines without fire on columns intercrossed,
> White slapped on white, majestic, marble heads,
> Severed and tumbled into seedless grass,
> Motionless, knowing neither dew nor frost.
> There lies the head of the sculptor in which the thought
> Of lizards, in its eye, is more acute
> Than the thought that once was native to the skull;
> And there are the white-maned horses' heads, beyond
> The help of any wind or any sky:
> Parts of the immense detritus of a world
> That is completely waste, that moves from waste
> To waste, out of the hopeless waste of the past
> Into a hopeful waste to come.
> (*OP*, p. 49)

In an image that he considered an essential summary of the poem, Stevens salvages some consolation simply in the recurrences of nature: "For a little time, again, rose-breasted birds / Sing rose-beliefs." But such birds obviously do not manage a return of lost forms and values; they reassert a rebirth that nature orchestrates among the general ruins. Only what moves recurs, and by definition memorials do not do that.

If Stevens' and Yeats's statues suggest extremes in the usability and recurrence of the past, Wilbur's statues fall somewhere in between. They are living or mimelike art rather than memorials. In an experimental way, the children who enact them strike poses in gargoyle shapes and pretended monstrosities:

> These children playing at statues fill
> The gardens with their shrillness; in a planned
> And planted grove they fling from the swinger's hand
> Across the giddy grass and then hold still
>
> In gargoyle attitudes,—as if
> All definition were outrageous. Then
> They melt in giggles and begin again.
> Above their heads the maples with a stiff
>
> Compliance entertain the air
> In abrupt gusts, losing the look of trees
> In rushed and cloudy metamorphoses,
> Their shadows all a brilliant disrepair,
>
> A wash of dodging stars, through which
> The children weave and then again undo
> Their fickle zodiacs. It is a view
> Lively as Ovid's Chaos, and its rich
>
> Uncertainty compels the crowd:
> Two nuns regard it with habitual love,
> Moving along a path as mountains move
> Or seem to move when traversed by a cloud;
>
> The soldier breaks his iron pace;
> Linked lovers pause to gaze; and every rôle
> Relents,—until the feet begin to stroll
> Or stride again. But settled in disgrace
>
> Upon his bench, one aging bum,
> Brought by his long evasion and distress
> Into an adamantine shapelessness,
> Stares at the image of his kingdom come.[18]

The interplay of sameness and difference, settled form and fleeting image, reaches a balance in the arrested pause at the end of each pendulum swing. Like action on a stage under a strobe light, what we see is paradoxically a study of shapes that move and pose, move and pose. In the background, the universe continues to turn. The poem's figures are etched against the movements of tree and shadow, and the zodiac is a shadowy "wash of dodging stars," a distorted constellation created by the play of light. Thus, whereas Stevens' statue stands against the "rotten leaves" that swirl around it, Wilbur's children assume their postures within a visual field that shifts with every new fixation of the eye. None of this posturing prevents each party from seeking the stability of habitual role playing. While those who observe the children are content with the roles they have learned, the children themselves, unformed and restless, experiment with several postures. Meanwhile, the hapless derelict in his oxymoronic "adamantine shapelessness" (at the opposite end of the life cycle from them) illustrates the results of drifting: An example of human waste and passive evasion, he is seized by uncertainties and finds his fixity only in destroyed form.

As the children freeze at the top of each swing before their next fall, their recurrent rhythm gives them neither a definitive state nor complete turbulence. They perform not amid a chaos or a wilderness but in a garden: the maple grove is planned and the scene set up for the poet's composing eye. In other ways as well, the poem is full of definitions, even as the children make definition seem outrageous. We recognize clear and distinct types in a parade of class names, nuns following their customs like mountains, formal maples, the ageless games of children, the clinching certainty of the apocalyptic in its most reassuring title, the "kingdom come." Uncertainty itself is so rich in possibility that the poem is not discouraged by the absence of lasting statuary. Nor does uncertainty mock the idea of fixed form, as Stevens' macabre mice do; the poem merely insists on the fluidity of living processes—natural, social, and psychological.

With its acceptance of ages and its balancing of change and stability, "Statues" suggests an occupation for the poet somewhere beneath the bardic office and short of the elegist's view of universal detritus. The impulse for fixed poses is universal. In moments of uncertainty, the mind locates its defining entry, its arrest; at the same time, invention and free play are part of what it discovers and what it attempts. Given the world of balanced change and recurrent form, new invention is as inevitable as children's play, which of course also repeats mostly what other generations of children have done, each thinking itself original, each merely reaffirming the likeness of all members of the species. The trick is to catch just the kind of definition one's individual pause allows while taking in an impression of the general swirl of things.

How does the poet determine which objects will be fixable in a common heritage? What formulates youth if not the plummet-measured standards of the past impressed upon the passions and the mind? Is every connection made by chance and every role capricious? Or can one evaluate, justify, and organize a display of forms more permanent than the children's postures? Wilbur gives us not definitive but variable answers to such questions. In "Junk," for instance, he finds momentary consolation for civilization's abundant gimcrackery in things that have kept their composure. Far from being works of art, the items of "Junk" have returned to the materials they were before men tampered with them. Sand extricates itself from glass, and wood grain emerges once more from ill-made ax handles:

> Yet the things in themselves
> > in thoughtless honor
> Have kept composure,
> > like captives who would not
> Talk under torture.
> > Tossed from a tailgate
> Where the dump displays
> > its random dolmens,
> Its black barrows
> > and blazing valleys,
> They shall waste in the weather
> > toward what they were.
>   (*Poems*, p. 9)

Deep down in nature's unmaking factory, diamond forms out of destroyed matter. If the pressure that poetry applies to its objects is in any way akin, poets might hope to apply its transforming intentions to stubborn objects, not to tame them but to press out what they have within. But Wilbur does not often deal in images of transfiguration or of permanent beauty. Moreover, part of the cost of converting junk into diamond is an emptying of all differentiation: the objects in "Junk" are denaturalized in the deep work chambers of the legendary smith Wayland and "halt Hephaestus." One diamond is much like another; all transcend history, time, place, and can be no more humanized than a star can be.

Poems are called forth by another kind of making, more human in scale. In another sort of recycling in "For a New Railway Station in Rome," for instance, the signatures of past greatness in Roman ruins do not make for either excessive veneration or unconsolable regret:

> Those who said God is praised
> By hurt pillars, who loved to see our brazen lust
> Lie down in rubble, and our vaunting arches
> > Conduce to dust;
>
> Those who with short shadows
> Poked through the stubbled forum pondering on decline,
> And would not take the sun standing at noon
> > For a good sign

those "pilgrims of defeat" are advised to look closely at the new structure of "reinforced concrete" set in "cantilevered swoop." Rising above
the "broken profile of these stones" the roof of the booking hall issues
"such a sudden chord"

> as raised the town of Troy,
> To where the least shard of the world sings out
> In stubborn joy.
>   (*Poems*, p. 109)

The world of change is as hard on statuesque poses here as it is in "Statues" and as destructive of man-made things as it is in "Junk"; but like
Yeats, the poet has homo faber to celebrate, carrying his perfection in
"blue unbroken reveries" of the past. These recollections are printed
within the mind, to be recast again and again. To salvage the past is not
to renovate its crumbling structures but to make something new.

"For a New Railway Station" brings Wilbur in contact with a vener-
able city and simultaneously with innovation and in the process says
something about an American in Europe. Its view of wreckage is in
keeping with that of the Stevensian modernist, though more vigorously
and less meditatively than Stevens' old philosopher in Rome, for instance (and less gloomily than Hawthorne's and James's visitors there).
At moments it is also surprisingly less decisive in its dealings with the
past than Yeats, for whom the razing of ancient cities brings a reckless
joy. In that respect, Wilbur and Yeats are capable of exchanging positions: Wilbur may ponder past eons nostalgically, while Yeats is less
convinced at some times than others that recycling is a good idea. In
"The Circus Animals' Desertion," for instance, Yeats finds within the
heart not a residue of ideal forms from old myths and images but a discard heap. For a moment he seems more like Stevens or Williams, a
man on the dump, or like Wilbur's poet of junk than like the poet of
Celtic mythology and artifices of eternity.

> Those masterful images because complete
> Grew in pure mind, but out of what began?
> A mound of refuse or the sweepings of a street,
> Old kettles, old bottles, and a broken can,
> Old iron, old bones, old rags, that raving slut
> Who keeps the till. Now that my ladder's gone,
> I must lie down where all the ladders start,
> In the foul rag-and-bone shop of the heart.
>   (*CP*, p. 336)

In such a shop, if one relocates the images of Greece or ancient Ireland,
they must be miracles of restoration indeed, given what has happened
to master forms of the past.

For Wilbur, the new station neither returns a specific ancestral form nor arises out of rubbish. It breaks with the past that surrounds it and adds another layer to history. Its materials are not marble, whose thrust is vertical, but concrete, shaped in a defiance of gravity that no previous builder could have achieved. A Frank Lloyd Wright does not return to an older geometry but imposes undreamed of swoops on pliable new materials. In that respect, "For a New Railway Station" is not entirely typical of Wilbur, nor is "Junk"; neither poem reflects his concern with individual objects and the preservation that he looks for in things made or found. Aesthetic value and salvageability more often depend on the object's inherent property or swerve from commonness—its twist from straightness away from geometrical regularity. In "Driftwood," the main threat to such a particularity comes not from transience but from a devouring generality or indefiniteness—not from gimcrack manufacture or the fleeting nature of time but from some metaphysical oblivion of sameness. The universality of that sameness threatens the balance of change and stability:

> Then on the great generality of waters
> Floated their singleness,
> And in all that deep subsumption they were
> Never dissolved;
>
> But shaped and flowingly fretted by the waves'
> Ever surpassing stress,
> With the gnarled swerve and tangle of tides
> Finely involved.
> (*Poems*, p. 153)

In this case, rather than seizing and dissolving the pieces of wood as it might have, the sea actually sets off their inner qualities and brings them to the visual surface. The sea-fretted gnarl and tangle heighten the singularity of each piece. As nature's inborn patterns yield what art requires, the poet's making is limited to the collaboration of reason and observation, which locate and then put forward these more or less found aesthetic objects; what they conduct the eye toward is not a sense of transcendental radiance somewhere behind nature but a set of distinctions and aesthetic perceptions embodied within them.

Whatever his concern for the discovery of preservable objects, however, Wilbur does not usually look as microscopically at them as Williams and Marianne Moore do. Williams, for instance, observes that locating differences between objects is more important than finding similitudes for them. If things exist strictly on their own, they do not have classes, and they draw nothing forth from memory or records. "Poetry should strive for nothing else, this vividness alone, *per se*, for itself. The realization of this has its own internal fire that is 'like' nothing. Therefore the bastardy of the simile . . . There is no need to explain or compare."[19] For Wilbur, in contrast, similitude counts for a good deal. It prevents the object's escape from classification into willful anarchy. Despite the high value he places on the spotlighted objet d'art, he is unwilling to leave poetic images at the mercy of an unintegrated miscellany.

But Wilbur encompasses too wide a range of views on objects for any single formula to be entirely representative. Some poems, for instance, are more boldly anti-imagistic than antiromantic in their stress on defining acts of perception. "Poplar, Sycamore" is an instructive example to set beside "Statues" and "Junk" inasmuch as it too seeks a compromise between the fixations of language and thought and the fleeting panorama of objects passing before the senses. It is typical both in doing without the assistance of classical and romantic landscapes and in allowing the trees to suggest their own value before the perceiver adds his comment. What Wilbur notices about the poplar is its balance of change and stability, its interplay of definition and elusiveness. The eye may be praised for its discriminating perception, since objects do not automatically grant access to themselves, and their surfaces evade definition even as they attract the eye to the finest details. A descriptive poetics therefore does not move quickly toward thematic statement and clairvoyant symbol making. The tree insists upon its own quicksilver movement, which the poet must somehow match despite the ponderousness of words:

> Poplar, absolute danseuse,
> Wind-wed and faithless to wind, troweling air
> Tinily everywhere faster than air can fill,
> Here whitely rising, there
> Winding, there
> Feinting to earth with a greener spill,
> Never be still, whose pure mobility
> Can hold up crowding heaven with a tree.
> (*Poems*, p. 216)

Such a pure objectivity holds off the ego's investment; the poet makes no appeal to an internal paramour or to muses as transcendental projections of his local genius. However, the tree on its own terms does catch more than the eye. It quickens our interest and therefore our sense of pertinence. Our observation is not dry or scientific but has the quickened beat of discovered beauty.

Of course the tree also stays put for definition so that the mind is exercised even as the eye is. A tree that was merely wind wed and not faithless to wind would be no solider than air; but because the poplar holds its place and returns to its shape, it is subject to this careful measurement. Its balance of change and stability allows the synchronized movement of eye and word. (The quickness of "tinily everywhere," for instance, is as though interest inhered equally in the sounds of syllables and the movements that the eye catches.) The imprint of the poet shows in this cleverness, in the studied accuracy, the curve of implicit feeling, and the form and shape of the whole. The precise focus closes down a considerable range of romantic speculations, however. Such Yeatsian questions as how one knows dancer from dance are not pertinent, nor is nature, even in such light-glancing form, merely "a spume that plays / Upon a ghostly paradigm of things." The tree as incarnate beauty in motion requires no justification and urges no abstract speculation. Language, object, eye, and thought fall into a natural collusion that raises no traumatic assertions of the self and its positions, remembrances, or feelings.

The description of the sycamore pries word, thing, and perception farther apart and opens the way for a limited amount of skepticism over one's capacity to formulate what exactly the object is. Through a crack which that skepticism opens, the self rises into view, not exactly disturbed but willing to accept and even to celebrate a certain degree of mystery:

> Sycamore, trawled by the tilt sun,
> Still scrawl your trunk with tattered lights, and keep
> The spotted toad upon your patchy bark,
> Baffle the sight to sleep,
> Be such a deep
> Rapids of lacing light and dark,
> My eye will never know the dry disease
> Of thinking things no more than what he sees.

Where the mobility of the poplar asks for wakefulness and the noting of fine, quick differences, the sycamore, with its tattered lights and shadows, defeats clear perception. In the poplar, the eye *is* tempted by the dry disease of prescriptiveness, perhaps too proud of its own accuracy; the sycamore counters that precision, again not with transcendental speculations but with the suggestiveness of half-vision, as words take on muffled, oblique, indecipherable kinships with an object that is more than what the eye sees. The mind is not thereby called upon to raise explicit issues, merely to offer an axiomatic principle and closure; its work is entangled implicitly in the innuendos of bafflement, as the eye is in lacing light and dark.

As these poems suggest, in Wilbur the eye and the mind at times collaborate and at times struggle. Their collaboration is assisted by a number of order-making devices. In "The Eye," for instance, the observer imagines binoculars framing the scene before him, their "lunging focus" creating a "sense of the import of a thing surrounded." To some extent, such instruments, which could be taken as analogous to the formal closure of poems themselves, dominate the order and quality of the things they present; yet a free play of speculation accompanies them whenever the observer does not merely absorb what he sees passively but discovers a "sudden premise of a frame" and perhaps wants, in addition, to be an "unseen genius" of middle distances. His latent romanticism emerges in that desire, not with a great eruption but as a reserved assertion of difference. Vision through focused binoculars is after all precise, whatever role the additional meditations of observers contribute. It is a different matter when nature itself is so in motion that it refuses to be framed. In "March," for instance, its migrations give fits and starts to both vision and meditation. The light that shines on beech leaves that wind gusts have torn loose is only half certain. Even to prophetic sight, the leaves are "bodies of gold shadow / Pecking at sparks of light." Nothing is more fleeting than sparks of light, but then few things are more suddenly accurate than birds who have taken aim and pecked a seed: the escaping spark and the grasp of the observer are well matched. If shadows and light alternate on such surfaces, as they do also in "Statues" and "Sycamore," it is partly because nothing settles into place permanently in some lexicon of common emblems. In "A Sketch," a more emphatic example, the speaker is visited by a goldfinch that shines a moment from the branch of a pine before settling deeper within. Recollecting that change in its presence, the speaker finds the quickly contrasting moments significant:

> Briefly, as fresh drafts stirred
> The tree, he dulled and gleamed
> And seemed
> > more coal than bird.
> (*The Mind-Reader*, p. 16)

Under such circumstances, even the strongest visual impression is like a glance at rough "sketches tacked on a wall," in which everything is "so less than enough." We offer posterity not a permanent museum or gallery of portraits but fleeting insights, unfinished and hung up in the most makeshift way.

To some extent, these later concessions to the opposition of fixed vision and change (from the recent volume *The Mind-Reader*) return full circle to Wilbur's earlier lyrics and maintain the epistemological wavering of *The Beautiful Changes*, where eye-dominated vignettes are subject to the removals and shifts of the subject. The result in *The Mind-Reader* is a seating of the poem amidst an alternation, a surmise of surfaces. Wilbur's goldfinch seemingly has little more ancestry than Stevens' bird in "Of Mere Being," which sits at the edge of the mind in some incipient mythologizing region. But it is after all a goldfinch, however much it resembles a coal. Seeing it as a coal merely reinforces our seeing it as a very bright, insistent bird. Wilbur wishes no total disintegration or combustion of surfaces, and indeed most objects do manage to claim a clear identity in his poetry. Like the old birch of "A Black Birch in Winter," an object may "grow, stretch, crack, and not yet come apart."

Even if the subject plunges out of sight, some sense beyond eyesight, hearing, and feeling may still retrieve it. When Wilbur shifts once again from the receding object to the powers of observation and recording that respond to it, he discovers a mind-reading capacity ready and able to trace its course. Again mind and object collaborate well enough to subdue the romantic trauma of time. Given the same sort of vista that "The Eye" describes, "The Mind-Reader" follows the descent of a sun hat from a high parapet as it cartwheels down over escarpments "through mica shimmer" into distant pines. Its disappearance is as complete as that of a book "whose reader is asleep, garbling the story" when it glides from the deck of a ship and yields "its flurried pages to the printless sea." Without navigational fixes on such points of disappearance, we might conceivably settle for an elegiac view of their irretrievability. But Wilbur proposes a cure, a "fixative of thought" (or fixing up of thought), to counter the eye's losses; and by analogy to his powers, the mind reader ponders the possibility of some "huge attention" that marks the fall of every sparrow. Whether or not such divine omniscience exists, his own intense vision recalls from hiding places what it most wants; he seizes falling objects in thought and word, as though the mind were in fact an ocean "where each kind / Does straight its own resemblance find"—though the sea itself retains no imprintings.

In such commemorations of objects as "Driftwood," "Junk," and "Poplar, Sycamore," and in such relocations of lost or metamorphosed objects as "The Mind-Reader," we find reiterated one of the sources of Wilbur's appeal. It is an appeal shared by a number of American poets whose faith in real things is declared and open without demanding the salvage of all objects indiscriminately in an encyclopedic or Whitmanesque way. That it is a peculiarly American focus on "things" is suggested by Wilbur's recalling Brooks Adams' comments on the "incoherence of American democracy" and thinking himself that America is a "very thingy country, a very practical country," of an inventing, manufacturing sort. Whereas Europe has a "long and coherent, relatively unmixed tradition," American poets live "close to the wilds"—not literally in the West or Alaska, of course, but in their exposure to untamed plenitude. Because that plenitude includes tools and mass-produced articles as well as nature's plenty, poets are enjoined to assimilate the machine, as Hart Crane advised. "Junk" indicates that this assimilation presents certain problems when it comes to the rubbish that civilizations make and cast off. But remembering Crane's admonition, Wilbur confesses that he felt special pleasure in putting the phrase "reinforced concrete" to use in a poem. Insofar as the modern poet has anything by way of a tradition behind him, he has only "the solid and homely and concrete words" of writers like Emerson, Thoreau, and Whitman.[20]

In following that tradition, Marianne Moore, the Williams of "no ideas but in things," and the Stevens of "Not Ideas about the Thing but the Thing Itself" likewise practice descriptive fineness and loyalty to fact.[21] But for Wilbur, as we have seen, no dry diligence to reality is sufficient for poetry. What he requires is a mixture of sharpness and distance, the plain and simple on one hand and an echoing or retreating surface on the other. The balanced perception that the poplar and sycamore urge is not easily acieved where dark overpowers clarity or where the publicity of certain realities comes down the street like Stevens' fatal, dominant x (in "Motive for Metaphor"). Wilbur's poetic space is not centered in a quiet vacuum but jangles with a multitude of objects, not all of which are as cooperative in backing away as the sycamore is.

To remind us of that aggressive fullness, Wilbur jars the mind out of its casual interplay with things on several occasions, perhaps most explicitly in "A Fire-Truck," where we glimpse the advantages of distance to a poet in the midst of the present's untranslatable savagery:

> Right down the shocked street with a siren-blast
> That sends all else skittering to the curb,
> Redness, brass, ladders and hats hurl past,
>   Blurring to sheer verb,
>
> Shift at the corner into uproarious gear
> And make it around the turn in a squall of traction,
> The headlong bell maintaining sure and clear,
>   *Thought is degraded action!*

As sheer verbs in motion, such "thingy" objects discredit similitude and all mere play of mind. The observer gets the best of this blatancy only by letting it pass and then making the truck his own as it gradually vanishes into afterthought:

> As you howl beyond hearing I carry you into my mind,
> Ladders and brass and all, there to admire
> Your phoenix-red simplicity, enshrined
>   In that not extinguished fire.
>   (*Poems,* p. 35)

An astute observer can pull this trick on heavy realities only as time passes, as memory and imagination eclipse the object or transform it, associating it with other things in recollection so as to dissolve it. The poet's need to assert himself is satisfied by the minimal action of a spiderlike devouring of whatever falls into his web.

It is perhaps this reflective recoil as much as the fleeting surface of things that creates relics and symbols. What makes Wilbur's way with objects possible and separates him from the imaginative fixing of brilliant, stubborn objects like those of Williams and Moore is the deftness with which he catches the passage of objects into absence. His concern is the chemistry of the interaction between the phoenix-red simplicity of the fire truck and the mind's own fire. In the silence of the pause, the recollection of the noise, sensory impression fades into ideas. Indeed, one of the paradoxes that Wilbur reveals in the American emphasis on present objects is the almost instant nostalgia it produces; the fire truck is no sooner out of sight than it becomes a phantom and a metaphor. If the object either disintegrates too soon or comes forward too blatantly, it destroys the balance between presence and echoing distance, and between the thoughtful perceiver and the thing laboring to generate its temporal reverberations.

If reality is not to be fatal to metaphor and leave us "purged of nuance," neither should the spirit withdraw into its own isolated, bodiless world of ghosts and mirages. Wilbur suggests in " 'A World without Objects Is a Sensible Emptiness' " that this extreme, like the imagist extreme, is destructive of nuance. Deserts of Platonist speculation leave the "tall camels of the spirit" stranded in a deadening vacancy. Wilbur admonishes such spirits in a wry Stevensian way to turn from mirages (or sleights of sand) and look for the light that is incarnate in things. But the most exact opposite of the blatant fire truck is not spirit; it is the object that withdraws too far into imperceptibility and leaves only faded images. Wilbur is skeptical at times about the capacity of the external world to sustain itself, less because of change and transience than because of the trickiness of perception. In "Epistemology" he goes so far as to suggest that objects themselves are ultimately illusions:

I

Kick at the rock, Sam Johnson, break your bones:
But cloudy, cloudy is the stuff of stones.

II

We milk the cow of the world, and as we do
We whisper in her ear, "You are not true."
(*Poems*, p. 121)

However, the formal confidence and completeness of the couplets runs counter to their avowed distrust of perception. The playful, epigrammatic cleverness of the two statements points both to Wilbur's strength as a craftsman and to the limits he sets for himself as a philosophical poet. The fine definition of the couplets suggests that Sam Johnson and the farmer who milks the cow are really unshakable, whatever Cartesians might say about them. Neither the solid ring of "kick," "rock," and "break" nor the no-nonsense first name of Dr. Johnson is fully discredited by the softer, plangent diction of the second line. In the second couplet, the metaphor of the cow forces the world to leave its generality and become tangible. Even while the skeptic asks, "What if stones and cows are really mysteries and our senses deceive us?" the rhyme rings solidly and conclusively. Indeed, if the poem is accurate in its concluding declarations in each half, Johnson's remark that "Truth indeed is always truth, and reason is always reason" has the right spirit if a questionable metaphysics.

The patent fictiveness of the world as cow is cause not for serious doubt, then, merely for irony and humor. The poem suggests that Wilbur has no interest in pursuing his skepticism very far, and that if he did, a finely tuned, accurate verse would be the wrong instrument. The question remains: What precisely is the mind's contribution to perception in the act of composition—assuming that the object neither comes on too strongly nor evaporates entirely? Again Wilbur offers not one but a number of suggestions. Intrusions of memory, affective states, and doubts cause a number of poems to pass from descriptive statement to meditation. These poems do not represent withdrawals of spirit from the sensible world but proximate stations; the mind remains close to objects but detached from them.

"In the Elegy Season" is an impressive example of Wilbur's capacity to move in and out of contact with the natural world and interweave a variable sense of the immediate past. It reinforces two propositions: the departure of loud objects creates opportunities for reflection; and their potential evaporation generates a need for that reflection. Ideas and imagination are raised by the in-between state. Again, an instant historicity comes into our awareness of changing things.

> Haze, char, and the weather of All Souls':
> A giant absence mopes upon the trees:
> Leaves cast in casual potpourris
> Whisper their scents from pits and cellár-holes.
>
> Or brewed in gulleys, steeped in wells, they spend
> In chilly steam their last aromas, yield
> From shallow hells a revenance of field
> And orchard air. And now the envious mind
>
> Which could not hold the summer in my head
> While bounded by that blazing circumstance
> Parades these barrens in a golden trance,
> Remembering the wealthy season dead,
>
> And by an autumn inspiration makes
> A summer all its own. Green boughs arise
> Through all the boundless backward of the eyes,
> And the soul bathes in warm conceptual lakes.

Less proud than this, my body leans an ear
Past cold and colder weather after wings'
Soft commotion, the sudden race of springs,
The goddess' tread heard on the dayward stair,

Longs for the brush of the freighted air, for smells
Of grass and cordial lilac, for the sight
Of green leaves building into the light
And azure water hoisting out of wells.

(*Poems*, p. 128)

Wilbur's autumnal season is obviously unlike Keats's unrecollected processes and sensory abundance. Though it, too, brings a kind of harvest, the poem looks forward and backward and allows the interpenetration, in consciousness, of all parts of the seasonal cycle. So long as the race of spring promises the organs of hearing, touch, smell, sight, and taste the full returns of a fresh reality once again, the speaker can look past winter's deprivation and dwell secretly elsewhere. Memory and anticipation are both heightened by the mind's freedom from the tyranny of the senses. Indeed, the poem is less an elegy for real things gone than a discovery of images arising from their fading essences. In revenances tucked away in this or that sensory hint, Wilbur savors things neither too strongly present nor quite absent. The mind surmises essences partly on its own terms, converting the glaring brilliance of things into a version of the golden age, without traditional descriptive topoi. Thought does not discover in those essences some sort of transcendental ideality; even though "conceptual lakes" raise and transform to another level what at one time was merely literal, the poem has no hint of Shelley, Emerson, or Emily Dickinson and very little of the subject-object difficulty of the romantics. Let Sam Johnson's critics say what they will about such things as azure water "hoisting out of wells," it will seem no less clear and cool to the taste.

We have only to set Wilbur's poplar, grasshopper, fire truck, beacon, cigales, water walker, and toad beside the objects of the romantics and transcendentalists, or beside the symbolic furniture of Herbert's temple, to see the restrictions Wilbur places on the symbolic extension of things and also the comparative plenitude of his collection. Such objects are first of all pluralistic and present; their occasions are variable and serve as pretexts for several kinds of elegiac, lyric, or meditational acts, but never the typological recurrence of a tradition or the summoning of an autobiographical past. Poetry derives from a fortunate marriage of form, diction, imagination, and materiality. This cooperation of objects in Wilbur's verbal salvage and in self-conscious reflections on time are perhaps best illustrated by a poem that I will take as a final example, "Year's End." This elegant poem concerns other themes and issues as well, such as the salvaging of relics, the weaving of a tapestry that combines memory and perception, and a sense of changing configurations that they form. But its central tension is between the stir of present life and a gripping, quieting permanence that descends like death but without either decomposition or an object-sacrificing ideality.

A sense of formal periods gives Wilbur his initial occasion: the year's end closes one door and opens another, as though one could cross a threshold and enter a period of calm from which to look backward. In that small yearly turn is modeled the play of eras and the special perspective one gets from the act of boundary making and definition. The present maintains its dominance, but it is framed by consciousness of its placement and its cyclical recollection of similar moments. The fixation of the moment is reinforced by snow and ice, which not only muffle but transform the city that extends before the speaker so composedly:

> Now winter downs the dying of the year,
> And night is all a settlement of snow;
> From the soft street the rooms of houses show
> A gathered light, a shapen atmosphere,
> Like frozen-over lakes whose ice is thin
> And still allows some stirring down within.
>
> I've known the wind by water banks to shake
> The late leaves down, which frozen where they fell
> And held in ice as dancers in a spell
> Fluttered all winter long into a lake;
> Graved on the dark in gestures of descent,
> They seemed their own most perfect monument.
>   (*Poems*, p. 135)

Unlike art these are not represented leaves, merely frozen things; the poem deals with found rather than created artifacts. But their absence of movement makes them much like created images. They suggest a tactful coalescence of man-made fictions and the raw materials of nature's tableau. So close to perfection are objects in this season that a slight nudge turns them into statuary. The streets of the town, settled by snow, also assume certain qualities of art; the light is gathered as on a stage, and the atmosphere inside the houses is "shapen." The light that plays across the field of vision is diffused, reflected, and gathered into the focus of the inside vignettes. The placid lakes of the second stanza too are framed and sealed by the layer of ice, like rooms behind glass.

With respect to the flow of moments and sequence of perceptions that time imposes, Wilbur's attention fastens not so much on the things preserved as on the moment of transition and the quiet that still suggests movement—when the ice is thin and life almost stirs. As we see by the end of the poem, this quiet is roughly equivalent to memory's becalmed representations to the mind of some afterthought of clamorous reality: in pictorial still shots are inherent both the intense life of the present and a sense of remoteness. The poet's own presence—in language, technique, and artifice—is part of the icing. Indeed, the entire poem, not merely the first stanzas, pursues parallels between nature and art. Only after all changes are completed do monumentalized forms find their true perfection: art and the past isolate things and make them discrete. The preservation of fossilized gestures makes nature itself approach a vast museum of art and provides inhabitants for an icy Elysée.

It is not heaven that Wilbur considers as a tomb, however, but earth, which is a mausoleum and a memorial:

> There was perfection in the death of ferns
> Which laid their fragile cheeks against the stone
> A million years. Great mammoths overthrown
> Composedly have made their long sojourns,
> Like palaces of patience, in the gray
> And changeless lands of ice . . .

This quiescence, of course, comes at a certain expense. One who still hopes for a decade or two of personal future does not drop into that mummified peace without resistance. At Pompeii, the fourth stanza continues,

> The little dog lay curled and did not rise
> But slept the deeper as the ashes rose
> And found the people incomplete, and froze
> The random hands, the loose unready eyes
> Of men expecting yet another sun
> To do the shapely thing they had not done.

When we look back, the past may suggest repose, but to those who dropped into it, nothing was right about their transformation. Unlike the frozen leaves and the fragile ferns imprinted on the ancient stone, their hands were still random and their eyes restless.

Wilbur returns to this unexpected and inartistic way to enter fossilization in the final stanza:

> These sudden ends of time must give us pause.
> We fray into the future, rarely wrought
> Save in the tapestries of afterthought.
> More time, more time. Barrages of applause
> Come muffled from a buried radio.
> The New-year bells are wrangling with the snow.

Leaves, fern, mammoths, and dogs do not look into the future; they are dumb and go quietly. They are quickly part of what we call objectivity. But as the barrage of the new year testifies, people are strident in their resistance, and midnight releases a storm of greeting as the doorway of the new year opens. The poem is itself pried part way open by that intruding fire truck present that refuses settlement. But paradoxically, as the year winds up to that wrangle, the rhythm of the form and the conclusion of the meditation wind down to a placid couplet. The balance is precarious, as the demand for more time works counter to impulses in the poem that take as their ally the beguiling beauty of the snow and the implicit appeal of death.

The tension between the peace of art and the past on the one hand and an ever-uprising, gregarious reality on the other is finally dissolved—but not by any of the means that Wilbur's nineteenth-century predecessors might have chosen. The poem shows no need for the reverberations that romantics strain to hear from places farther off. Although in one sense "Year's End" refuses to end, its definition is complete, if not as pure thought, then as a rounding out of experience and statement. If the last day arrived like this, the apocalypse would be acceptable, reasonable: it would be a triumph of art, like a Keatsian equation of truth and beauty. Of course, the past is already a woven tapestry. The present comprises the frayed anxiety of an immediate future and the controls of formally arranged images, intelligible sequence, and statement rising calmly above its disturbed reference, in stanzas pursuing their own inevitable shape. From another angle, the journalism of that noisy medium the radio is modulated and filtered by the poet's means of reporting. In radio form, the message presses forward an unavoidable present and is very American; the old year is scarcely settled into history before it is crowded out and given no chance to collaborate with tradition. In the poem, the deeper rhythms of the organic world and the fixations of mind and memory keep us from rising completely to the surface. Past eons turn into view as the year progresses. They are ultimately the saving of the poet, because as objects press their singular, noisy claims, he sees in them laws and patterns thanks to which he is justified in his own formal means: if he gathers his selected images into a finely wrought tapestry, it is because they prompt him to do so. The marriage of verbal form to what the eye sees is precarious and fragile, but in chosen moments it manages. The result is neither an elevating nor an ironic view of nature's objects but a provisional joy and an indication of at least one modernist's wise acceptance of his limits.

IV

LITERARY

HISTORY?

CHAPTER 7

Ceres and the Librarians of Babel

A blasphemous sect suggested that all searches be given up and that men everywhere shuffle letters and symbols until they succeeded in composing, by means of an improbable stroke of luck, the canonical books. The authorities found themselves obliged to issue severe orders. The sect disappeared, but in my childhood I still saw old men who would hide out in the privies for long periods of time, and, with metal disks in a forbidden dicebox, feebly mimic the divine disorder.

JORGE LUIS BORGES, *"The Library of Babel," from* Ficciones

Ancient time contains vast durations without signals of any kind that we can now receive. Even the events of the past few hours are sparsely documented, when we consider the ratio of events to their documentation . . . [However] the total number of historical signals greatly exceeds the capacity of any individual group to interpret all the signals in all their meaning. A principal aim of the historian therefore is to condense the multiplicity and the redundancy of his signals by using various schemes of classification that will spare us the tedium of reliving the sequence in all its instantaneous confusion.

GEORGE KUBLER, The Shape of Time

Libraries and Poems

T O ANY KIND OF FORMAL STUDY, the past is a matter partly of archives, holdings, and surrounding knowledge for which the library is a collective source. In itself the library is a relatively neutral repository; it does not bring forth its items to preach them, sing them, lecture about them, or narrate them. It does not admonish, rejoice, or lament but merely stores information and potential performances for future reference. However, it is not totally transparent or devoid of implications. It has a method and maintains something akin to a living presence in the scholarly community. Nature, thought, and events are transcribed into various subcategories within its highly organized space as, piece by piece, it collects the exterior world in representations. Together with sister repositories (museums, galleries, monuments), it gives us a large part of our structured and labeled past.

The transportability of things into the smaller, lettered storage of the library makes them available in virtually any order, in defiance of their placement in the physical world or their chronology elsewhere: the library's system of storage is not respectful of the natural setting of the things it uproots and transplants. In effect, the library reduces all temporal settings to a single plane. Unlike the interpreters of ruins, the library researcher does not find strong evidence of age on the surfaces of most of the volumes he reads. The text is either there intact (assuming that vandals have not been at it) or is restorable by reprint. Very few other traces of the exterior world survive in rows of print and rows of books, which are always contemporary. As Borges' "Library of Babel" suggests, the library's holdings include numberless books that refer exclusively to other books, at several removes from primary experience. Of course for Borges, the Library is primarily a metaphor rather than a real institution; but for all our acquired, secondary experience—for the debt we owe to our educators—it is an appropriate representative precisely because it leads a "literal" existence. It is a suitable replacement for such older representatives of the world as the *theatrum mundi* and the book of nature, which were also figures for a totally ordered realm. No former model quite suggests the methodical and voluminous labyrinth that the modern world has become. Where other tropes remember at least vaguely some of the tangible sights and sounds of nature or society, almost no contamination from the physical world survives in the Library, which filters its subjects through codes, symbols, and categories. It renders learning as system as it transcribes reality into treatises.

This welter of codes and abundance of books add up to an immense interpretive problem. Of course, older tropes too were not totally free of that difficulty, and several of them anticipate Borges' Library. In the center of paradise itself—as Milton imagines it, with help from Genesis—the tree of knowledge stands near the tree of life, and the minds of the first man and woman, even with all newness before them, are very restless in its presence. Their wills are quickly infected by a desire for power over nature beyond what simple observation and horticultural arts provide. In effect, by initiating the movement toward civilization and all its celestial and terrestrial disciplines, they prepare for the prideful overreaching that brings first the Fall and then the Tower of Babel—which, with all its languages and indecipherable shouts and mutterings, takes a large step toward Borges' Library.

Closer to Borges' scholars are the projectors whom Swift satirizes in *A Tale of A Tub*—ingenious explorers of learning and the concealed will of God—or again, the scholars of the Academy of Lagado in *Gulliver's Travels*. There, Swift's version of academicians and scholars grants them a certain residual adamic charm. Primarily what the Academy's five hundred busy scholars do is pervert natural processes in subjecting them to method. Through their devotion to laboratory procedures, they manage such tricks as bottling sunbeams extracted from cucumbers, reversing the digestive metamorphoses so that waste again becomes consumable, and plowing fields with hogs. Simplicity and hopefulness run through these experiments, in the minds of whose inventors anything is possible under the right formula. Piece by piece, things from the natural world are pulled out of their original settings and subjected to the torture of professional science. The experiments of Lagado represent a triumph of the bookish over primary experience, and a triumph of the arbitrary and the seemingly logical. Especially clever is a section of learning that might now be thought roughly equivalent to computer linguistics. Those who hold that language is a purely arbitrary mechanism which intervenes between us and reality have nothing over Swift's professor of linguistics, whose machine can duplicate all the arts and sciences by the mere turning of handles. As his ranks of pupils flip over bits of wood fastened to wires, the words written thereon in all the moods, tenses, and declensions of the language turn up in new combinations. Transcribing the results as they appear, the professor has written innumerable original treatises for the ultimate Library, virtually without an obligation to nature. With his method, the chances of a stroke of luck that will deliver canonical books are at least no worse than those of Borges' old men with their metal disks in diceboxes.

One more example: almost as remote from the ordinary sensory experience of nature as Borges' desperate theologians are Flaubert's Bouvard and Pécuchet. Although as Eugenio Donato has pointed out, Flaubert's more privileged figure is the museum,[1] the library has a certain significance for his two quasiscientists, who are learned, well-read gentlemen. A museum arrangement of objects, without philosophic and scientific abstraction, would fall far short of the science they hope to attain. Flaubert also seems to agree with Borges that the methods of various disciplines are basically disconnected, although despite that the researcher cannot discontinue his always disappointed quest for definitive laws. Whatever nature's appeal to the senses and its responsiveness to the simpler sciences, our desire to know more and more, our love of networks, systems, and methods, forces us to take leave of ordinary objects and proceed into the labyrinths of learning—as Eve does when command of Eden's animal and vegetable life no longer seems sufficient. In the view of both Flaubert and Borges, men do not have the gift to be simple: the more they know, the more they require complex systems in which to affix their knowledge.

The study industry that their scholars pursue is farcical in its extreme; but it is not basically different from what they and Swift as well saw in the scholars and scientists around them. Of course, all three, and perhaps even Milton, are basically unfair to science by intention: they gain their satiric leverage by exaggerating the discrepancies between pretensions to control over nature and the actual futility of learning. Knowledge is always forbidden insofar as it drives men from nature's free gifts, from instinct—and in Milton's case, from God, Who happens to believe that creatures should keep to their assigned places. It would of course have been more just of them to acknowledge the usefulness of certain disciplines, especially those that settle for something less than completeness. But Milton's fatal Tree of Science and Tower of Babel, Flaubert's Museum, Swift's Academy, and Borges' Library idealize human error in the manner of utopian works; and scholars and scientists of the twentieth century *have* realized some of their wildest dreams.

But before we go farther in that direction, I want to begin from another angle and consider the literary text within the world of learning that the library holds ready for us, to see whether or not we can locate some suitable compromise between its immediate presence and the distancing, neutralized research that the absolute equality of call numbers and catalogues encourages. Let us suppose initially, for the sake of argument, that all aesthetic performances celebrate something, that even novels and tragedies convert facts into the sort of perceptions that we may glory in. A number of things impede the audience's complete presence at such celebrations, which come in their briefest and most intense form in the lyric: anxieties of one kind or another may intervene, or dulness, or the sloth of inattentive reading. The one I want to touch on here is the one most native to libraries: specifically, the profession of letters itself, by which I mean not the society that gathers in colloquia and MLA conventions but the collection of methods and ways of processing information that, because libraries are there, we seek to use. One of the paradoxes of graduate study in literature is the great discrepancy between the talent that a reaction to *Hamlet* calls for and the labor exacted by bibliographical aids to research. One talent deals with a living text, the other with allied and scattered resources, in extensive accessory reading. Where one takes us to the theater, the other leaves us alone at desks among books and periodicals. The difference reminds one of Donne's contrast between the ordinary, more or less dispersed, selves with which we greet daily events and the collected selves that he imagines gathering at the ultimate Resurrection—that climactic moment when movement toward becomes presence at:

> I shall be all there, my body, and my soul, and all my body, and all my soul. I am not all here, I am here now preaching upon this text, and I am at home in my Library considering whether Saint Gregory, or Saint Hierome, have said best of this text, before. I am here speaking to you, and yet I consider by the way, in the same instant, what it is likely you will say to one another, when I have done. You are not all here neither;

you are here now, hearing me, and yet you are thinking that you have heard a better Sermon somewhere else, of this text before . . . I cannot say, you cannot say so perfectly, so entirely now, as at the Resurrection, Ego, I am here; I, body and soul; I, soul and faculties; as Christ said to Peter . . . *Fear Nothing, it is I.*[2]

For Donne, the single cause for total celebration is the opening up of heaven to immediate perception. But that great Type of Clarification might be taken as a figure here for the disclosure of perceptions that aesthetic moments bring, when details fall into place. Certainly, insofar as a poem speaks not merely to the intellect but to the senses and feelings, it may be the occasion of a completer gathering of soul and body than most occasions are. As Wilbur Sanders has suggested, critical scrutiny and appreciation become one and the same under the influence of classics: "We hail a writer as a classic precisely because of his capacity to incite to the finest kind of consciousness: his very excellence is what animates and empowers the critical scrutiny of it. And as the mind finds increasing satisfaction in that task, as the conviction of excellence grows, so the author's capacity to sustain the scrutiny becomes a source of multiplying pleasure—criticism and appreciation become a single complex act."[3] As a discrete and relatively closed performance, a classic brings into the act of its perception something like a total reader, if only momentarily, whereas informational writing and nonperformable texts instruct us implicitly to put a good deal aside in order to think analytically. Normally we are not all here in our own present or in someone's discourse; we are more or less here, more or less elsewhere; and the activities of the minuter forms of scholarship carry many places, unarranged in any order of climax that might deliver us intact to a finished view of a subject.

The great divergence between what literary texts call for and what the scholar (as opposed to the entranced reader) brings to them is evident the moment we imagine a given reader pulling down from the library shelf a volume and turning to a particular poem. Let us suppose that we select Herrick and become thereby readers of "The Argument of his Book":

> I sing of brooks, of blossoms, birds, and bowers:
> Of April, May, of June, and July-flowers.
> I sing of Maypoles, hockcarts, wassails, wakes,
> Of bridegrooms, brides, and of their bridal cakes.
> I write of youth, of love, and have access
> By these, to sing of cleanly-wantonness.
> I sing of dews, of rains, and piece by piece
> Of balm, of oil, of spice, and ambergris.
> I sing of times transshifting; and I write
> How roses first came red, and lillies white.

> I write of groves, of twilights, and I sing
> The Court of Mab, and of the Fairie-King.
> I write of hell; I sing (and ever shall)
> Of heaven, and hope to have it after all.

To bridge the distance between a twentieth-century reading and Herrick's 1648 book—to bring the book into the present or to go to meet it—the reader needs to do a number of things, some of them more scholarly and more likely to postpone the full presence of the text than others. Actually, not a good deal has aged in the imagery and diction, and an astute reader will fare pretty well even in an initial attempt to plunge in. Obviously he will still know the meaning of the seasons and of bridal celebrations, Mayday games, heaven and hell in approximately the way Herrick knew them, though perhaps with less resonance and fewer personal associations. Even if he is unfamiliar with Ovidian metamorphoses, he can make an intelligent guess about the origins of the rose's red and the lilies' white, and he needs only a bit of Elizabethan folklore to locate Mab and the fairy king, especially since Herrick's volume describes them at length, and he has the entire volume in hand. Most of his research, in fact, can be conducted within the book itself, to which this first poem offers a compressed table of contents, and so the reader and scholar in one sense are joined as Herrick's guests. Herrick's introduction beckons both of them in at the same time that it gestures toward Catullus, Ovid, Jonson, seventeenth-century ideas and taste, and certain biographical matters. As an encapsulating index, "The Argument" suggests that the poem itself is an act of scholarship, like a catalogue listing. In some sense, certainly, it offers a brief manual for reading: It alerts us both to topics and themes to be found in the book and to the poet's attitudes toward them. The poet will not treat these things in any discursive manner but will sing of them, for reasons that the poem proleptically enumerates and illustrates. His various subjects are both orderly and plentiful; they yield verbal music, alliteration, rhyme, meter, and various vowel and consonant patterns; they can be arranged in a progressive order that goes from more tangible things to more elusive and abstract matters of transshifting times, metamorphoses, and fairies, and finally to transcendent matters of hell and heaven, with their demonic and angelic extremities.

The positive conclusion of "The Argument" suggests that in at least one respect, Herrick is with Donne: the hope of heaven collects the world's scattered blessing; it draws the activity of Herrick's verbs "sing" and "write" into the culminating possession of "have." The blessings of this world are not so much possessed by the poet as transcribed, but the blessings of heaven he expects to own—though that lies in the future and for the moment must be screened through hope. The poem is therefore predictive on at least two levels: it sums up the store of the volume—a store worthy of celebration in the nonprophetic mode of the brief lyric—and it looks forward "after all" to another order of things beyond ordinary words.

"The Argument of his Book" conducts us through an apparently loosely arranged miscellany to a structure completed in the closure of hell and heaven, the very names of which raise curse and benediction to a realm of ideas beyond renewed search, or research, since the world offers only a dispersed guess at the content of "heaven." "Hell" and "heaven" clang down like iron doors, framing the universe of the book, stationing earth in its middle place in the cosmos, and putting its delights in perspective. By that expansion to a total, bounded cosmos, Herrick seeks to gather his reader entirely into the book and leave no other worlds and seas to detour him. The book will be spacious and complete; it will contain the main types of joy and the representative occasions, and it will point toward that which gives them foundation and prevents time from becoming merely a succession of cycles.

However, as fine a poem as "The Argument" is, and as effectively as it leads the reader into a reasonably self-contained volume, it is not itself particularly stirring, as "Corinna's Going A'Maying" might be said to be, nor is it as surprising in perceptions as a poem like "Delight in Disorder." Instead it performs its indexing of the volume and makes its gestures toward the outside world without great urgency. Nothing like the excitement that attends Herbert's overcoming of obstacles in the locating of heaven stirs in Herrick's somewhat perfunctory last couplet. The voice is a little complacent, the enthusiasm of discovery a little blunted by the indexing or library function of the poem as a learned preface. For more active dramas, the reader must await the other demonstrations that the volume promises. In this respect, the poem forces him to remain partly a scholar and to bring to the initial poem the information and culled experience that related texts provide, some from inside *Hesperides*, some from predecessors. The present poem's anticipatory nature makes him not all "here," in Donne's phrase; it spots his attention forward and outward as, for instance, among those things in the real world that "piece by piece" make up a "cleanly-wantonness."

Of all forms of verbal representation, one might expect small lyrics to be the most removed from the labors of encyclopedia or treatise, the most immune to learned dismemberment; certainly no lyric makes the demands for research that the cosmology, doctrine, and history of *Paradise Lost* do, for instance. But here Herrick incorporates into the poem precisely those tasks of analysis, of sorting and classifying, remembering, and anticipating that enable us to make subsystems of related information and experience out of library holdings. Just this sort of labor the Library and the Academy exact from the reading of most poems, as scholars and critics subject the text to the labors of taxonomy, of detailed indexing, and interpretation that extrapolate and translate the "argument of the book."

The difference between the initial vision of the poet and the fully processed poem—once the poem has been committed to paper, submitted to an audience, and attracted the interest of Ph.D.s—is as drastic as the difference, say, between Colin Clout as the piper of dances on Mount Acidale and Colin Clout as the explicator of his own vision. For once the dancers have vanished from sight—to dwell a bit on Spenser's instructive example—Colin immediately becomes a critic, studious allegorist that he is. He knows his duties to the queen and to the knight of courtesy and partly fulfills them in that role. The difficulty is that he cannot be both critic and visionary at once. And if Borges' figure has any applicability, the problem with our submitting especially the poetic past to systematic study and to stored-away learning is that intellectual scheme making threatens the efficacy of words and the harvest of ideas with the complexity of relationships and with translation into foreign forms of discourse. The compromise between immediate reading and research that we seek is not easy to locate. Colin Clout's explanation of his dancers and their history is followed by other explanations from Spenserian scholars, each of whom absorbs, critiques, and modifies his predecessors; and this series of interpretations of interpretations moves us ever farther away from the first-hand engagement of poetry. It becomes a progressive retreat, a new historical factor, a substitution—for the dance of the hundred bonny graces—of the labors of a hundred scholars armed with the Latin Patrology and Elizabethan lore.

The language of any late text is so strategically dependent on predecessors, in our rearward view, that it cannot exist alone, any more than a single word in the language escapes receding definition through chains of words: all are implicated in a ramshackle entourage whose components jostle each other side by side on the shelves. Mount Acidale exists nowhere but on those shelves, unless here and there a few imaginations reduplicate Spenser's vision in defiance of Colin Clout and his many good students. However strongly the modernist wishes to deny this backward trail of entanglements, then, however much he might want to return to the poem itself, he finds it difficult to do so. As Frank Kermode has remarked, the main temporal agency of the survival of classics "is a more or less continuous chorus of voices asserting [their] . . . value."[4] We cannot listen to classics, in academic circumstances, without listening to that chorus.

Literary History

Yet one brand of formal study that forms its own discipline and sub-system of learning—literary history—has always led a precarious exis-tence and does so still, as more and more disciplines and influential critics take sides against it. That resistance comes in part from the im-mediate appeal of great texts. After all, why should a reader take an extensive detour through scholarship of a peripheral sort when the poem speaks directly to him? Must he, in Herrick's case for instance, become a seventeenth-century and classical scholar? How important are the ancillary matters of linguistic system, recurrent social structure, anthropological rites, communal values, courtship, and group psychol-ogy? No doubt all of these figure to some extent in Herrick's highly cer-emonial version of social relations, but the poems tend to explain themselves as they go along. Also resistant to historical study are many of literature's interdisciplinary entanglements, which have synchronic rather than diachronic leanings. In the interests of descriptive, system-atic analysis, they divest linguistics of its philology and literature of its precedents. Jan Corstius finds it reason to think that "beyond doubt . . . the historical sense is weakening":

> The shared opinion that literary history is of no value to the study of lit-erature is a common ground whereupon an alliance between structural-ists and neomarxists has come about. Literary history is relegated to soci-ology and literary study comes to be the study of language, i.e. poetic language, ideologically considered a means by which capitalist society manipulates the reader in order to keep him a true member of the bour-geoisie.[5]

Neither the groups that Corstius cites nor the new critics before them were there first, however, in their complaints against literary history, which has always encountered at least passive resistance if not outright opposition. F. W. Bateson finds the very phrase *"literary* history" to be a contradiction in terms.[6] Opposition to literary history crops up even in sociology, where one might expect to find some sympathy for the re-construction of milieux. Jeffrey Sammons echoes Robert Escarpit and Karl Rosengren in pointing out that "all literature, even that we canon-ize as great, is ultimately ephemeral." Classics exist only for a limited group with vested interests. Otherwise a text "vanishes from the cul-tural memory once the social context to which it is related has passed away." It might be argued that Homer has lasted long enough not to be considered ephemeral, but Sammons is supported by the reading habits of the mass public and by analysts of popular taste. The latter, for in-stance, find that only the smallest percentage of what is written survives beyond a few years, outside of systematic study. According to Sam-

mons, one must therefore conclude that even Shakespeare is the orna-
mental possession of a minority: "It would seem that the preservation
and transmission of past literature in the educational process is unnatural from a sociological viewpoint."[7] Forced preservation is even more
unnatural from the structuralist viewpoint, because it is methodologi-
cally faulty: it presupposes continuities and coherent fields that prove
upon closer inspection to be illusory. Neither Lévi-Strauss's anthropology nor Foucault's archaeology permits the conclusion that civilized
societies convey ever-refined orders from generation to generation or
that progress is anything but an illusion in humanistic affairs.[8]

At the same time, classic texts in their own right defy historical placement; they have ways of breaking loose from the connections that historical study would weave around them. On one end of its transaction
with the public, the symbol-using imagination breaks with the milieu;
on the other end, the impact of the reperformed work is usually unrecorded and unmeasured, and therefore beyond either historical or systematic investigation. The same free play with the real world that generates an imaginative text is repeatable in its reception. Thus one may
learn a good deal about Elizabethan England, Donne's philosophy of
love, and literary traditions, discover what dictionaries have to say
about tapers, the phoenix, and canonizations, and yet, upon hearing the
voice of the poet say in "The Canonization," "For Godsake hold your
tongue, and let me love," set aside almost everything but the immediate
sound and sense of the poem. To turn from the introductory explanations of an anthology or from the headnotes to the poem itself—to put
aside the commentary of critics and historians and listen strictly to a
declaration such as "That is no country for old men"—is to undergo a
great forgetfulness, if only a momentary one. The reader, as opposed to
the scholar in his network of categories and codes, declassifies the text.
Its call number and the adjacent work on the shelf no longer matter.
Only what *it* remembers of history, science, and other arts exists, at
least in the dominant perceptions of reading. In that forgetfulness, the
poem—perhaps with some residual, implicit field of like poems in the
background—generates an always current activity of consciousness.
Certainly, the reader as such is not the same as the explicator, the
theorist, or the influenced poet. Like Colin Clout before he becomes a
critic, he remains entranced in the vision and will be recalled from it
only with unease into an act of explanation.

Any rapt, exclusive attention that the text commands simultaneously
resurrects a piece of the past, however, and thereby opens an avenue
backward that is potentially historical. As Poulet remarks in "The
Phenomenology of Reading," "The extraordinary fact in the case of a
book is the falling away of the barriers between you and it. You are in-

side it; it is inside you; there is no longer either outside or inside." The interior universe "constituted by language does not seem radically opposed to the *me* who thinks it. Doubtless what I glimpse through the words are mental forms not divested of an appearance of objectivity. But they do not seem to be of a nature other than my mind which thinks them."[9] That much we owe to the true revival of a text: it returns to us not as a salvaged network of ideas and facts from other places but as an experience that rivals other current things. As Hayden White points out, with some cultural phenomena we have the right to choose our associations with almost complete disregard for chronology or national proximity.[10] Though we must accept the governments, economics, and weather that fate deals us (or go to great lengths to change them), we can easily elect or not elect to read Homer or listen to Gershwin. But the moment we have made our selection, it opens the door to historical placement; we are ushered into the times of the text *through* the text.

As I remarked earlier, the discrediting of literary history is by no means of recent origin; the problematic relations of art to its temporal settings are age old. The main critics in Western traditions have seldom established close links between texts and their historical settings, particularly before the upsurge of antiquarian research in the eighteenth century and its development of a chronology-oriented social criticism. Even the concept of highly articulated periods and movements within literature itself—to take a phase of the problem less dependent on the social environment—is relatively new, as is the creation of the closely defined specialties and areas of scholarship that accompany them. Until the nineteenth century, antiquity was entrusted to overall cultural historians rather than to guardians of local research areas. Before the rise of comparative cultural analysis and the growth of national histories (in the detail in which we now know them), historians were more or less content with several broad "ages of man." Plato and Aristotle were interested not in the Greekness of their models (by comparison to Egyptian or Asian examples, for instance) but in their universality. Though Hebraic-Christian thought took note of contrasting Mediterranean cultures and had a concept of period and development, it did not possess an accompanying theory of literature or poetics. Augustine discredited polytheistic cultures as errors along with their endless, meaningless cycles—again in the interests of a totalized history under Providence. The foundations of a comparative treatment of times, places, and movements were missing not only in Augustine himself but in Christian and Platonist poetics generally.

The same outlook dominated Renaissance historiography and its scanty vision of literary history.[11] Although Italian critics developed a theory of genres, they did not sufficiently nationalize the examples or periodize the phases of growth in each genre to predict modern practice. They did not require elaborate systems of classification and scholarly specialty. As René Wellek points out, Samuel Daniel's *Defence of Rime* has a sense of national differences and literary development but in a primitive form.[12] To Sidney in *Apology*, all types and kinds coexist on virtually the same temporal plane. Bacon's *Advancement of Learning*, as the title suggests, stresses scientific advancement and makes a basic connection between literary expression and the spirit of a given age; but it is not itself a detailed history or a theory of literature. Dryden's *Discourse Concerning the Origin and Progress of Satire* (1693) is more explicit about growth and change but limits itself to a single genre. When classics such as Virgil's *Georgics* were translated, the prevailing practice in neoclassical poetics was to modernize and transpose them into the receiving climate without preserving everything Roman or Greek about them.[13] And so on.

Given this slighting of the his rical dimensions of classics, it is no great exaggeration to say that literary history reached a sophistication sufficient to generate separate, specialized research areas and close relations between societies and works only in the late eighteenth century. For the first real step in the breakdown of the subject into high-definition topics, literary history required the idea of general cultural advancement and relations between national cultures and literary forms (as Adam Ferguson begins to suggest them).[14] It was not really until cultural evolution, national differences, and social dynamics combined in Johann Herder, Madame de Staël, and Taine that literary history was established as the discipline that universities now assume it to be.

One added remark along that line: the romantics did not very much influence the modern developments in literary historiography. It is true that Wordsworth thought of the literary past in terms of the ages of Catullus, Shakespeare, and Dryden; that Peacock listed four ages of poetry, each revisited; that Hazlitt delivered extensive and influential lectures on literary history. But chronological categories run counter to the main drift of romantic theory, which is more sympathetic to the antihistorical tendencies of modern criticism. Wordsworth does not so much periodize literature as catalogue its audiences, on the grounds that the "exponent," or symbol, that the poet holds forth in metrical language excites different expectations in different eras. His main concern is that he may "not have fulfilled the terms of an engagement thus voluntarily contracted" with his own readers. Also, when one gets beyond capricious habits and fickle tastes, the same purified and simple nature speaks to all times alike. Over and above the types and periods that national cultures create stands a uniformity of poetic language that makes it universal:

In spite of difference of soil and climate, of language and manners, of laws and customs: in spite of things silently gone out of mind, and things violently destroyed; the poet binds together by passion and knowledge the vast empire of human society, as it is spread over the whole earth, and over all time. The objects of the poet's thought are everywhere . . . Poetry is the first and last of all knowledge—it is as immortal as the heart of man.[15]

Coleridge and Hazlitt provide similarly generalized views of poetry's mission. Though Hazlitt's *Lectures on the English Poets* proceeds chronologically, its separate chapters are not profoundly historical, nor is his view of the progress of letters.[16] Shelley is more positive still in denying that one can connect poets meaningfully to time or circumstance: "A poet participates in the eternal, the infinite, and the one; as far as relates to his conceptions, time and place and number are not."[17] The appreciation of masterpieces for their own sake and of art for art's sake later in the century was also basically antihistorical.

Thus the romantics and their successors generally refuse to classify or anatomize literature along historical lines. In this respect, they too prepare for new criticism, in the explications and taxonomy of which texts reenter the present as pinpointed stars in a timeless field, either standing aloof from other texts or constellated with them by kind, proximity, and magnitude rather than by dates of origin and social and historical contexts.

Although it is an incidental point, we might also note that this separation of poems from their surroundings receives support from the writer's concept of himself either as a modernist divesting himself of the past or as a man for all seasons. In either case, the writer himself seeks to drop all compromising affiliations with social history. As Hemingway puts it representatively: "A writer is an outlyer like a Gypsey . . . If he is a good writer he will never like the government he lives under . . . He can be class conscious only if his talent is limited. If he has enough talent, all classes are his province. He takes from them all and what he gives is everybody's property . . . A true work of art endures forever; no matter what its politics."[18] Such a writer, in his creative independence, is supposedly not beholden even to other good writers: he is his own classification. Classics are not to be strung like beads along a line of inescapable influences. "A new classic," Hemingway argues, "does not bear any resemblance to the classics that have preceded it. It can steal from anything that it is better than, anything that is not a classic . . . But it cannot derive from or resemble a previous classic."[19] Thus the robustly independent modernist shaves his debts and enlarges his own domain.

Despite all of these resistances to the chronological placement of texts, the antihistoricist bias is deficient in many ways and has obviously not succeeded in eliminating the scholar's impulse to classify and retrieve information or to align texts in serial ways. Everyone now realizes, for instance, how important influence is. The historian who reads one writer in the light of others may no longer simply trace open lineages, transitions, and parallel styles without thinking occasionally about less witnessed mechanisms of imitation and repression. He may also counter the independence of creation with the observation that although good writing need not be political in Hemingway's narrow sense, it is always social: beyond the Library is a codified social system that has taught us virtually all we know. Not only the need to invent poems but the direction they take may be thrust upon them by historical provocations and their expected receptions. Because each successive moment of a presumed period changes the circumstances of utterance, and language passes from party to party with steady alterations, the historical disciplines are justified in finding kinds to be gradual outgrowths from predecessors or reactions and counterreactions. Even dramatic overturnings and reversals often bring forward what has been latent in a previous orthodoxy. Certainly literature is a sensitive register of past idioms under gradual modification. If we wish to know the details of bourgeois marital institutions in the eighteenth century, the sociological historian of literature might well say, we can find few better places to look than Richardson's novels; if we wish to know the rhetoric of warriors or the place of women in Greek feudalism, we obviously profit from Homer. The details of courtship, negotiation, concerted public acts and private, the relations of courage to fidelity, and the structure of discourse and of thought itself we find modeled to some extent in literary texts. Granted, this is not all we find there, and granted that we violate the parenthetical, nondocumentary nature of the texts to look only for those things in them; yet even in imaginative literature, certain elements of pointed language come forward in detailed, fully textured imprints, both immediate and historical, both digressive and pertinent.

The fact remains that unlike stars in a constellation, which appear to the eye to be ever present and almost uniform, literary texts differ from one another in ways that can be explained only on historical grounds. A text engages in a constant tug of war with materials fastened in chronological place, which it tries to enshrine in such a way as to convert them into general truths. On one hand, it brings these materials into the single current field of a performance, a field in which Shakespeare's Caesar exists on the same footing as Lear. On the other hand, the historicity of a Caesar or a Lear and the datability of Shakespeare himself tug back; the world of reference and authorial experience will not totally relinquish the work to some galaxy of timeless masterpieces. A given text follows or precedes others; it is shaped by some and has formative influences on others, however reactive or twisted by misreading it may be. Hemingway's desire to reach a dateless immortality notwithstanding, Hemingway's own subject and prose style bear a certain stamp. They came from a series of training exercises in which Ezra Pound and Gertrude Stein, among others, issued commands and encouragement. Moreover, every particular text has a genesis and a case history, including a reception and a record of reactions, however sketchy our reports of these may be. It is not fixed in mosaic but stands against a backdrop of processional events.

The study industry thrives on this range of historical implications in literature and, notwithstanding reports of its demise, grows more remarkable every year—in the company of such fields as anthropology, geology, archaeology, history, and philosophy. These and other areas together employ thousands in the teaching of millions. The number of secondary bibliographic entries for literature and language alone in 1963 in the Modern Language Association *Bibliography* was 15,679 from some 1150 periodicals and books—already a discouraging quantity. In 1969, when the *Bibliography* fractured into four volumes in different fields, the number climbed to 24,126 from 1300 periodicals. Every year since then has realized a similar proliferation. The combined library holdings and the labor devoted to cataloguing, filing, and retrieving information in the ultimate Library of Babel will not have to gain much to be inestimable. Borrowing from a UNESCO study, J. W. Saunders in *The Profession of English Letters* cites an annual global output of five billion copies of books over fifty pages in length in over three thousand languages.

Since the proliferation of disciplines began some two hundred years ago (at the height of what scholars once cheerfully took to be an Enlightenment), the pursuits that lead scholars into the periodical room of Babel's library have become legion and their refinements and combinations endless. Some primary works have virtually disappeared beneath commentary, the perusal of which is one of the preliminary tasks of further research. Anyone who was required to read all that has been written on Shakespeare in English (disregarding Germanic, Romance, Slavic, and Asian languages) would be in for several melancholy decades, during which he would find an accelerating mass of new materials piling up faster than he could dispose of the old—like Tristram Shandy gaining experience faster than he can narrate it. The modern scholar has ample new tools for sorting, measuring, transporting, and representing a good many things; and with the invention of each new one, tools themselves become a greater part of his concern. In all the systems of law, transportation, social institutions, language, business, and government put together—in mounting a massive systematic expertise to transmit the training and knowledge of one generation to another—we have created procedures and vocabularies as difficult to master as the subjects they were meant to serve. An extraordinary quality is required of anything that would resist that bureaucratic assault. Research and scholarly prose are not in themselves ideal resuscitators, nor are they sufficient to prevent literary texts from fading into vaguer and vaguer distances or more and more complicated jargons. They seldom manage to reparaphrase or translate the brilliance of what is brilliant.

But the main burden of that sort of historical study weighs mostly on scholars. The influenced poet and the reader can afford to be more selective. Even for serious students of literature, we can find some relief in remembering that while it might be said that no one understands the stars or the properties of matter without a detailed study of modern astronomy or physics, it cannot be said that no one understands *Hamlet* without training in psychoanalysis, linguistics, existentialism, structuralism, new criticism, or old historicism.

What does a serious reader possess if not some portion of the field of learning within which scholars situate the text? That question serves as a pretext to leave the library a moment and go into the field again, since one of the keys to the retrievability of classics is the common experience they find in the answerable reader's imagination across language barriers. By "common experience" I do not mean primarily facts, though concrete detail is often part of it, but the response that symbolic epitomes raise in readers, as augmented by the store already in the reader's mind. The bounty of a text like Herrick's "Argument of his Book" is partly natural in that it capitalizes on the reader's firsthand reservoir of creaturely images, feelings, and common ideas. Analogies between common experience in the poet's then and the reader's now open a broader passageway through the historical corridor than formal study normally can—though I again remind the reader that I am seeking to work both sides of the fence in seeing what literary scholars and readers normally do or might do about salvaging both the spontaneous bounty of texts and the added resonance that a learned reading provides.

Poets in Pomona's Fields

These ready, translatable analogies between the authorial pool of experience and the reader's suggest another figure to set beside the Library and its industrious research: the poet as husbandman or the sower of the "seeds of things." More than a few poets have fallen back on that georgic notion to express the unsystematic bounty of poems before (and sometimes even after) we have subjected them to methodical interpretation.

The analogy between poets and cultivators is again illustrated by Milton's paradise, in this case the one that exists before the Tree of Science has worked its magic on Eve. Adam learns to name Eden's objects and creatures in utmost simplicity and with a certain ceremonial reverence; he finds nothing arbitrary in passing from what the eye sees to what the brain classifies: science and poetry are not yet at odds, nor do signs themselves intrude between the intelligence and exterior forms. Naturally he knows no form of writing or prepared speech. In this regard, Adam's reaction to the Tower of Babel is the opposite of his reaction to nature's plenty. Though the tower is not yet a library, he finds it extraordinarily presumptuous in its assault on knowledge; its builders are appropriately punished with unintelligibility and a proliferation of tongues. If God rewards adamic naming with a sense of satisfaction in the meeting of names and objects, he rewards the builders of the tower with an excess of names, "and in derision sets / Upon thir Tongues a various Spirit":

> Forwith a hideous gabble rises loud
> Among the Builders; each to other calls
> Not understood, till hoarse, and all in rage,
> As mockt they storm; great laughter was in Heav'n
> And looking down, to see the hubbub strange
> And hear the din; thus was the building left
> Ridiculous, and the work Confusion nam'd.
>   (XII.56-62)

Milton accounts for the obvious fact that the nations we see about us are confused and cannot understand one another, as he and the writers of scripture reason backward to a primal rupture that shattered the one native language. The apple of science is divisive precisely because it entices the intellect into a search for perspectives closer to God's own omni-science.

Strangely, it is the image of feasting that governs Adam's view of Babel, just as it has governed the discourse on knowledge between him and Raphael. Food and talk are the link between Babel and paradise. Talk is food for "pure / Intelligential substances," as though the ripened blessings of paradise must be not only nameable but digestible if they are to satisfy both corporeal and incorporeal nourishment. The prelapsarian feast is a banquet of words, ideas, and things harmoniously and mutually sustaining. Coming to the lodge "that like Pomona's Arbor smil'd," the feasters find their table fully laden: "Here on Earth / God hath dispenst his bounties as in Heav'n." Eve's preparations for lunch are careful and artful:

> She turns, on hospitable thoughts intent
> What choice to choose for delicacy best,

> What order, so contriv'd as not to mix
> Tastes, not well join'd, inelegant, but bring
> Taste after taste upheld with kindliest change.
> (V.332-336)

The accommodation of fruits to taste is parallel to the accommodation of words to things and of reason to objects; each seeks out the hidden harmony of compatible and complementary elements. Thus Milton develops in several places parallels between the harvest of Pomona-Eve and the feast of words that angel and man consume as part of the digesting intellect. Raphael draws similar parallels in his lecture on "alimental recompense" and its place in the hierarchy, in which one intelligence visits another, accommodates its language, and exchanges perspectives. The "Empiric Alchemist" of the mind is like the sun, ingesting what lies before it. Hence, not surprisingly, when Adam and his guest have eaten, sudden mind arises within Adam, and Raphael fills him in on ranges of the divine reciprocity or grateful vicissitude that lie beyond his immediate experience. The passage from fruits to reason to discourse proceeds without a hitch. Thinking and talking learnedly are as natural as eating; all these are analogous in their possession on one level of comparable things on other levels.

Milton's treatment of Adam is revealing in its association of the primal poet with simple naming, tasting, and harvesting and in its association of forbidden learning with confusion. But Adam's language is after all special. Closer to the poet's own task than the celebration and consumption of the harvest that piles up on Eve's "ample Square from side to side" is Adam's post-Fall historical labor. Adam must generate or bring forth from the mysterious "seed" several things. One of them is quite literally food for the table, as the primal curse of Genesis draws him into the *ponos* or hard labor of the fields. Paralleling that labor and exceeding it in difficulty is the intelligence's labor with signs and symbols: he must now strive for epiphanies that once came handily. Deciphering the seed of the curse becomes an extended exegetical task that requires the instructor Michael and a theory of Old Testament types. Nature, too, becomes protean; it is veiled and changes shapes. It is a wilderness that requires guidance, a set of multilayered symbols demanding laborious explication.

I do not want to imply that Milton's is a privileged version of the tension between spontaneous harvests and the labors of intellect; it is merely an instructive one. Spenser, Marvell, Keats, Shelley, Shakespeare, and Pope also have something to say on the subject and together make up a reasonably diverse English panel of those who associate natural gifts with the bounty of poetry. Equally important, some of them are aware of the ghostliness of the poet's illusions in the midst of abundance, as language and reality draw apart.

As Spenser and Keats illustrate, the preference in some forms of poetry for a bountiful paradise runs very deep. In certain forms of romance, for instance, the questing hero drops out of the race for honors
in order to gain the peace of shepherds. Some of the bowers, caves, and
isolated small societies into which he passes are analogous to the harmony of poetry, as when Spenser's Calidore subscribes to Meliboe's
description of the retired life and thereby approaches a step nearer the
aesthetic perfection of the dancing graces. Meliboe's case for retreat,
which Calidore finds convincing partly because of its intrinsic merit
and partly because Meliboe puts it with such simple eloquence
(VI.9.26), is based on his conviction that the world where history is
made is but vanity and "gay showe": it is "but vaine shadowes to this
safe retyre / Of life." The pastoral interim in contrast is a step toward
Calidore's riddance of the barriers to higher vision, the "pleasaunce" of
which surpasses all others in the poem:

> One day as he did raunge the fields abroad,
> Whilest his faire Pastorella was elsewhere,
> He chaunst to come, far from all peoples troad,
> Unto a place, whose pleasaunce did appere
> To passe all others on the earth which were:
> For all that ever was by Natures skill
> Devized to worke delight was gathered there,
> And there by her were poured forth at fill,
> As if, this to adorne, she all the rest did pill.
>   (VI.10.5)

Mount Acidale lies across a stream that prevents the access of beasts
and rude wildness. Calidore finds there not the sacred or the holy but
the natural and the artful. Where earlier Adonis has imported into his
bower a concern with fertility and hence with cycles of generation, here
even that dimension of time is set aside. Only when Venus divests herself of projects of serious love and war may she enter here—when she
does "dispose / Her selfe to pleasaunce" (VI.10.9). She must become in
effect an unhistorical goddess. Mount Acidale is therefore a place of
pure play and sport, on a level assisted by lower spirits and goddesses.
That it substitutes for the queen a lady of no particular standing suggests a further divesting of accumulated, contracted social attributes.
The vision is reductive; it discards both the duties and the niceties of
manner that courtesy normally insists upon.

Before Colin explains it, that vision is of pure harmony and movement for their own sakes, and Calidore's approach is a progressive retraction from heroic labor, a return to paradise, not as the first parents
knew it in their simplicity and solitude but as one of a goodly throng
enacting a sophisticated art. As a preliminary to that art, Calidore has
watched Pastorella earlier upon a "litle hillocke" surrounded by lovely

lasses and "lustie shepheard swaynes" who pipe and sing her praises "As if some miracle of heavenly hew / Were downe to them descended in that earthly vew" (VI.9.8). The central vision Spenser prepares for more elaborately, with a description of landscape that sets Colin Clout apart from the society of normal shepherds

> Unto this place when as the Elfin knight
> Approcht, him seemed that the merry sound
> Of a shrill pipe he playing heard on hight,
> And many feete fast thumping th' hollow ground,
> That through the woods their eccho did rebound.
> He nigher drew, to weete what mote it be;
> There he a troupe of ladies dauncing found
> Full merrily, and making gladfull glee,
> And in the midst a shepheard piping he did see.
> (VI.10.10)

The journey to Mount Acidale that climaxes here models in a striking way one extreme of poetry's riddance of all motives beyond joyful play and its digressive sidestepping of history. The fair one at the center of the concentric rings inspires Colin Clout to pipe "so merrily, as never none" (VI.10.15). The only measure is the thump of dancing rhythms: the music that Calidore hears is without words and hence without the tug of signification that pulls in an outside world.

Spenser's point in Calidor's interruption of Colin's vision and the brigands' interruption of Calidore's pastoral sojourn is that two distinct dimensions of fairyland cannot be easily joined: no suturing makes a smooth connection between pure aesthetic play and responsible, educative poetry of a kind that learned interpretation may apply to the historical setting. The call to duty and the pursuit of the Blatant Beast come as abrupt interjections. Whatever aloofness paradise has, it is always as a contrast to normality that we perceive it. The raid of the brigands, like the Fall of Milton's first parents, is inevitable. Poetry's impulse to commemorate is thus brought up sharply before the necessities of the hard life; insofar as it dwells with those necessities, it must engage the record of societies in their actual histories.

In both Milton's and Spenser's versions, then, the poet's close contact with the blessings of paradise is interrupted and spoiled by an inevitable fall. The adamic poet and the shepherd possess an instinctive harmony between mind, word or music, and thing that issues in the spontaneous delights of art. For Spenser, the momentary escape of the shepherd piper from the obligations of the educative vision that didactic allegory undertakes implicitly reproaches lesser ideals, yet is itself reproached. Turning this around one more time, Milton finds history itself a kind of postponement of what the poet knows to be a new paradise awaiting the blessed.

Michael's intepretive discourse in the education of Adam and Colin Clout's explanation of the dancing graces move poetic vision some distance away from the easy plenty of nature and art and toward the earned gleanings of the trained intellect. Exegesis in those instances may not yet be a library-oriented discipline, but the expounder of the text does add a certain amount of learning to spontaneous vision. Even so, neither teacher expresses any reservations over the accountability of the explanation to the vision itself, which does not evaporate under scrutiny (though Colin's graces have already disappeared before he starts to expound them).

The relations between nature's own bounty and what words can deliver become more problematic when the poet stops to consider the medium through which he screens his subject. Whereas neither Spenser nor Milton considers poetry's distillation and reduction of natural blessings, for instance, it is precisely this aspect of the "harvest" that Shakespeare dwells upon in the sonnets and that reenters in another form in Keats and Shelley. Distillation points up the problem of language and its transfiguration of everything it touches, though Shakespeare does not look at it quite that way himself. His conventional assertion of poetry's timelessness against the ravages of change depends on the transformation that objects undergo in the act of verbalizing. When the poet remarks that "All in war with Time for love of you / As he takes from you, I ingraft you new," we are willing to concede that limited point, granted the slight exaggeration of the grafting he promises; but the loss of the addressee's identity and the lack of specific characteristics in his portrait discredit to some extent the assertion that poetry salvages something equivalent to him. Certainly the graft has not produced quite the fruit the husbandman intended. However, Shakespeare can take advantage of the fact that though we lose many things, good poems return without the tarnish of memory or the scars that unique things carry in time. They are effortlessly renewable and timeless:

> Time doth transfix the flourish set on youth
> And delves the parallels in beauty's brow,
> Feeds on the rarities of nature's truth,
> And nothing stands but for his scythe to mow;
> And yet to times in hope my verse shall stand,
> Praising thy worth, despite his cruel hand.
>   (Sonnet 60)

A last step in the harvest: verse distills young beauty from the original flower to keep it from vanishing. The metaphor is especially useful because, though the poet as harvester puts the plant itself to death in the reaping, he does so as a transformer of good intent and keeper of essences: the rarities that time destroys he makes into equivalent verbal rarities (like those anthologies of rhetorical and poetic flowers in the Renaissance in which "posies" distill thought into mottos). The poem is a chemical transfer of spirits from one form to another.

Even so, several things intervene between an original subject and the delivery of such a memorial. The poetic text does not guarantee the renewal of its distilled essence unless readers are capable of receiving it, and they may have to approach from outside, as Keats's observer does the Grecian urn. Indeed, the differences between the distilled—and stilled—world of art and the living world of the reader are precisely what troubles Keats in "Ode on a Grecian Urn," which makes its own comment on those ultimately extracted essences of things: truth and beauty. Like Shakespeare's verbalized essences that capture the beloved's beauty, Keats's abstractions drop all identifying characteristics on the way to permanence. The observer's reaction to the art work grows out of negotiations between what lasts in its fixity and what he brings to it from his own realm of change and suffering. The urn is both tantalizing and distressing to such an observer, who is aware that art intrudes its relative timelessness between him and a far-off sylvan ideal that once consisted of warmth, music, and growing things and is now iconographical silence. The distilled message the urn delivers leaves no conceptual bridge from art to the desolation that wastes human generations; the time of the urn's original making draws apart from the time of its reception.

While the speaker observes his own era and thinks of new woes still to come, the urn will continue to repeat its aphorism—extending itself to all listeners alike, drawing them into its mysteries, idealizing its truth and beauty, but applying no direct force to the observer's world and giving him no concrete bounty. If the viewer is somehow to get past the marble surface, he must imagine the rest of the urn's flowery tale. Yet when he proceeds to fill in the before and after of the lovers or the procession of villagers, he finds the contrast between linear time and monumental art more troubling than ever. The urn's stopped momentum so removes it from the animal and vegetable world that he is unable to harvest it; the invisible village remains beyond retrieval, despite the procession that leads the heifer forth. Thus while Keats emphasizes the naturalness of everything the urn depicts and the linear time in which its depiction seems to exist, its surface remains insistently cold and detached. The problems of the observer's approach to the urn's history linger on as those of the reader approaching the poem and what it represents. *Its* forbidding surface is composed of impenetrable abstractions on a high plane, and of muteness.

Equally telling in its distrust of poetry's capacity to deliver a reinstated, concrete nature is *The Fall of Hyperion.* In a garden of plenty like

Milton's, Keats's dreamer finds the fruits of Ceres palpable evidence of a ruined paradisal vision. The poet has no way to reclaim the past of the aged gods. Instead, his creative swoon brings him to an abundance turned to mere spoilage. Keats's reference to "our Mother Eve" suggests that part of what lies in wreckage is in fact the Miltonic edifice itself, due to be replaced by a new heroic style if one could be managed:

> Turning round
> I saw an arbour with a drooping roof
> Or trellis vines, and bells, and larger blooms,
> Like floral censers, swinging light in air;
> Before its wreathed doorway, on a mound
> Of moss, was spread a feast of summer fruits,
> Which, nearer seen, seem'd refuse of a meal
> By angel tasted or our Mother Eve;
> For empty shells were scattered on the grass,
> And grape-stalks but half bare, and remnants more,
> Sweet-smelling, whose pure kinds I could not know.
> Still was more plenty than the fabled horn
> Thrice emptied could pour forth, at banqueting
> For Proserpine return'd to her own fields,
> Where the white heifers low.
>   (24-38)

Whereas in the Autumn ode poetry works under the aegis of autumn to load every image, in *The Fall* the poet-dreamer discovers not a seasonal abundance but one among many cycles. If Shakespeare's concept of poetic distillation carries poetry one remove from its object, Keats's ruined paradise withdraws to the farther distance of the gods; and the horn of plenty is half consumed.

Still stronger doubts about poetry's capacity to materialize an inventory of natural gifts are evident in "Adonais," where the dying of the hero and his eventual apotheosis indicate the perishability of earthly paradises. Also, as in "Ode on a Grecian Urn," the ideal place lies beyond any medium we might employ to approach it. In the urn, a portion of what has passed away is transposed into the near eternity of marble; in Shelley, Keats (as Adonais) is installed in an imageless paradise that leaves art and the poet entirely behind. As Earl Wasserman points out,[20] the poem's imagery is therefore set up as an erroneous surmise about reality; pastoral conventions are intrusions between us and eternity's immutable ideas, not seeds to be harvested in the reader's fertile store but gestures that direct him to set aside sensory forms. The pastoral tradition is not a series of images and texts to be revered and continued for its transparent revelations but a falsifying set of masks and disguises. Insofar as the poet himself must speak from within a tangible world, he is torn between it and the ascendant Adonais; he must ultimately leave the world behind as a general ruin even more pervasive than Keats's spoilage of Milton's Eden:

> Die,
> If thou wouldst be with that which thou dost seek!
> Follow where all is fled!—Rome's azure sky,
> Flowers, ruins, statues, music, words, are weak
> The glory they transfuse with fitting truth to speak.
> (Stanza 52)

Whereas Milton's *Lycidas* finds classical pastoral and the husk of its conventions at least a rough estimation of the Christian archetype of restoration, Shelley, in searching out the "abode where the eternal are," discards time, place, and all concretions of presentation, both from poetry and personal experience.

Shelley's neo-Platonism gives poetry's involvement in concretion and in universals a special twist that stresses the interference of surfaces and the evasiveness of the poet's true subject. Less dubious about the deliverability of nature's plenty is Marvell. Although he too is at times strongly neo-Platonist, he also discovers traces of Providence in gardens, forests, and tropical isles. In "The Garden," perhaps the best example of his association of poetry with natural bounty, the mind's creative play and the soul's song have significant footing in the garden's forms, colors, and kinds, while they also range beyond them. As a fully tangible place, the garden presents a selected but generous sampling of nature's gifts to the happy wanderer. The imagistic soul's harvest is both a refinement of the body's world and a particularization of the mind's transcendence. Its intermediate state converts natural objects into song as though pursuing an adamic absorption of forms:

> My soul into the boughs does glide:
> There like a Bird it sits, and sings,
> Then whets, and combs its silver Wings;
> And, till prepar'd for longer flight,
> Waves in its Plumes the various Light.

The physical garden lives a distinct second existence in the soul-bird's plumage and in the song. The soul's purifications of light may free it from the heavier burden of melons and apples, but it nonetheless takes from nature, as though patterns of color, for instance, were directly translatable into imagery and music. In mind too the poet discovers a repetition of nature's kinds before projecting a paradise beyond them:

> The Mind, that Ocean where each kind
> Does streight its own resemblance find;
> Yet it creates, transcending these,
> Far other Worlds, and other Seas,

> Annihilating all that's made
> To a green Thought in green Shade.

The ruthless devouring of nature's plenty that the word "annihilating" suggests is countered in context by the creative fury of mind, the body's contact with nature's abundance, and the soul's contented song. The bond between nature and art is refreshing and innocent. The distance between Eden and the present is quickly abridged. Indeed, no other poem in the language is so confident of the easy identity between the poet's anthology of images and the world's delights, as Providence provides them.

Had Marvell's supreme moment had more impact, had it filtered into romantic and modern poetic theory—and had it not sent so many scholars to far-flung libraries—one would be tempted to accept its harvest of the garden's plenty as perhaps the most that poetry can offer by way of support in the outdoor trope for common, transferable abundance. Not only would Eden return to Marvell's adamic wanderer, but Marvell would deliver himself easily to us across the historical distance. But unfortunately, Marvell went largely unnoticed through most of the eighteenth and nineteenth centuries, which argues against his automatically finding common ground with every audience; and the simplicity of "The Garden" still escapes and baffles a practiced, learned, and ingenious body of interpreters. We insist on taking detours through Platonists, the Church Fathers, Stoics, Epicureans, and other poets in search of analogues; we convert Marvell's well-endowed place into a garden of learned figures, disbelieving in gardens that do not require incessant care and trips to the library. Paradoxically, the more beguiling the poem, the more it guarantees scholarly productivity. Except in special moments of suspended disbelief, we probably cannot share Marvell's confidence in the mind's duplication of the world's kinds and its creation not of fictive but real worlds and seas beyond this one. We may well concede the body's delight in nectarines, but even that no doubt seems a truancy from some more rigorous training we ought to be undergoing.

And so, jogging down the isles of the library, we look for less complacent versions of the poet as husbandman and revisitor of edenic gardens. For several reasons, one is tempted to seek a more conclusive word in *The Tempest,* especially since Shakespeare is aware not merely of the poet-magician's harvest of images but also of the fragility of his illusions. While Marvell does not question the powers of mind and soul to regain their edenic heritage through the setting that Providence gives, Shakespeare is much more cautious. Although he has faith in the conjurer who governs the island, one difficulty in *The Tempest* is that Prospero governs only there, at least in his full range of powers, in a geographical equivalent to a theater of illusions. The island is an imaginative place for the restoration of sanity to certain people who have lost it, as Prospero counters their lust for power with songs, pinches, and visions. But just as surely as the play ends, he must leave his charmed place and break the spell. As Shakespeare imagines the sequence in the play's most impressive pageant, first comes the specter of Ceres, then a share of the world's bounty as poets are wont to recite it:

> Ceres, most bounteous lady, thy rich leas
> Of wheat, rye, barley, vetches, oats, and pease;
> Thy turfy mountains, where live nibbling sheep,
> And flat meads thatch'd with stover, them to keep;
> Thy banks with pioned and twilled brims,
> Which spongy April at thy hest betrims,
> To make cold nymphs chaste crowns . . .
> > the Queen o' th' sky . . .
> Bids thee leave these.
> (IV.1.60-71)

Along with these gifts come "honour, riches, marriage blessing, / Long continuance, and increasing":

> Earth's increase, foison plenty,
> Barns and garners never empty;
> Vines with clust'ring bunches growing,
> Plants with goodly burden bowing;
> Spring come to you at the farthest
> In the very end of harvest!
> Scarcity and want shall shun you,
> Ceres' blessings so is on you.
> (IV.1.110-117)

We need not be told that a full larder and the satisfactions of such a poetic inventory go well together. But this abundance has scarcely been realized when, after a "strange, hollow and confused noise," the spirits who have presented it "heavily vanish." The magician confesses to the onlookers, as Shakespeare does to the audience at the end of the play (and therefore to us reading in the library), that he has no power over actual things, only over spirits and appearances.

That does not entirely discredit his own conjuring. Under the sway of time's dissolving, life is no more durable than conjured visions are. In that observation, Shakespeare doubles the paradoxes: art as an illusion has the power to renew the world's plenty in our minds; but the world's plenty is itself phantomized in greater vistas. Unlike Milton, Marvell, Keats, and Shelley, Shakespeare does not draw attention to separate realms of fiction or lasting essences at that point. No permanent ideas sustain nature's forms or rise to consciousness in their dissolution:

> Our revels now are ended. These our actors,
> As I foretold you, were all spirits, and

> Are melted into air, into thin air:
> And, like the baseless fabric of this vision,
> The cloud-capp'd towers, the gorgeous palaces,
> The solemn temples, the great globe itself—
> Yea, all which it inherit—shall dissolve,
> And, like this insubstantial pageant faded,
> Leave not a rack behind. We are such stuff
> As dreams are made on; and our little life
> Is rounded with a sleep.
> (IV.1.148-158)

The combination of vaporous reality and the hurt of metamorphosis is suggested by the ambiguity of the word "rack," which means light or smoky clouds, the torture rack, and the wrack that goes with ruin. The play returns frequently to an elegiac view of those painful disappearances. As Shakespeare's most autumnal play, filled with retrospective narration and a greater than usual focus on the older generation, *The Tempest* thus suggests both the plenty and the limits of the poet's fictions. Though Prospero clings to no illusions himself, he would obviously prefer a sturdier world. When Caliban too is stirred to heights beyond himself by dreams that Prospero and Ariel have planted in him, he awakens from visions that have melted into harsher realities:

> Be not afeard; the isle is full of noises,
> Sounds and sweet airs, that give delight and hurt not.
> Sometimes a thousand twangling instruments
> Will hum about mine ears; and sometimes voices,
> That, if I then had wak'd after long sleep,
> Will make me sleep again: and then, in dreaming,
> The clouds methought would open and show riches
> Ready to drop upon me; that, when I wak'd,
> I cried to dream again.
> (III.2.133-141)

It is Ferdinand, however, who predicts the ambiguity of Prospero's "rack" in an earlier notion about recollection, in which his departed friends are supplanted by the brave new vision of Miranda:

> My spirits, as in a dream, are all bound up.
> My father's loss, the weakness which I feel,
> The wrack of all my friends, nor this man's threats,
> To whom I am subdued, are but light to me,
> Might I but through my prison once a day
> Behold this maid.
> (I.2.489-494)

The wrack of his father's memory is one phase of the insubstantial pageant and of "the dark backward and abysm of time," which he too sees as in a dream.

From Garden to Library Again

Other tropes besides the poem as a harvest suggest a similar evaporation of the world's body from any container in which the poet would
put it. Reversing the passage of things into the poem as an index of distilled plenty, for instance, is the figure of nature itself as a book. As the
fields and bowers that poets cultivate and harvest naturalize words, so
nature's bookishness undermines the world's substance and reduces it
to signs, images, emblems, and symbols. The poet who reads in such a
book becomes akin not to husbandmen but to scholars nurturing icons.
His granary becomes the library once again. In the light of that trope,
the paradise of Lycidas, the pastoral realm of Calidore, the pageant of
Ceres, and the star of Adonais would all have to be said to derive not
from observations of nature or some realm of ideas but from a reading
of previous books—which, after all, is where nature's book gets its
code. In a sense, the library and the georgic harvest, though slightly incompatible figures, enter a forced marriage in every poetic text: nature's
essences are distilled only in words submitted in due course to the systematic interference of discourse, exegesis, and redigestion in other
poets. Shakespeare's Ceres, Milton's and Shelley's pastoral conventions, even Marvell's enclosed garden have precedents that the literary
historian must acknowledge. Their "flowers" are rhetorical and poetic
devices that have developed over a period of time.

Whatever the value of other figures here, we obviously require another sort of poet on our panel if we are to balance the case for the
poet's natural harvest with his re-presentation of predecessors—a poet
who confesses his precedents more openly and thereby bridges the gap
between the innocent reader and the history-minded critic, and who
keeps that auxiliary scholarship by which we particularize and refine
the historical flow between author and reader.

I mentioned earlier the desirability of salvaging the resonance of
learned reading. No one outside of Eliot makes the reasons for doing so
more persuasive than Pope. Luckily, however, though he points us toward the library again, his is a more humane institution than Borges'
Library. No one knows better than Pope, in fact, both the vitality of re-
vived classics and the destructive power of traditions under certain
types of dulness. That the language of later writers is always indebted
to the language of earlier ones would of course come as no surprise to
him. In his view, classics have told us nearly all we know about nature
itself: they *are* our garden. Although the integrity of an individual text is
not totally destroyed by language, it is challenged by its network of allusions and reduplicative forms. Nature is as thoroughly processed and
refined in its journey through predecessors as the elephant and the tortoise are in Belinda's cosmetic collection:

The tortoise here and elephant unite,
Transform'd to combs, the speckled, and the white.
Here files of pins extend their shining rows,
Puffs, powders, patches, bibles, billet-doux.
Now awful beauty puts on all its arms;
The Fair each moment rises in her charms,
Repairs her smiles, awakens ev'ry grace,
And calls forth all the wonders of her face;
Sees by degrees a purer blush arise,
And keener lightnings quicken in her eyes.
       (*The Rape of the Lock* 1.135-144)

We impose art on nature by received custom and common standards.

These typical forms and standards, in fact, are what unite the poet with both his predecessors and his readers across time's gaps. Nature does not evolve or change for Pope, nor do human feelings and inclinations. They are everywhere the same except for cosmetic changes. Hence what one great text says another will affirm, necessarily. We do not leave cultures and their products behind to an ever-increasing unintelligibility. Pope's solution to the contest between nature's bounty and learning, which is a related matter, revolves around the translation and reuse not of everything in the library but of specific masterworks as the source of normative standards. The modern poet may play with these in a mock-heroic way, as *The Rape of the Lock* does with *Paradise Lost*. But he and the man of letters too must make the same choices and establish the same priorities as their leading predecessors. In *An Essay on Criticism*, Pope offers certain rules for the poet's doing so, in reworking particularly the fields that Homer and Virgil worked: "Learn hence for Ancient rules a just esteem; / To copy Nature is to copy them" (139-140). Thus when Virgil came to consider *The Aeneid* and scorned to take any part except from "nature's fountains," he was amazed to discover on examining Homer that "Nature and Homer were . . . the same." Pope himself is happy to substitute a hymn of praise to the ancient bards for a direct celebration of nature:

See, from each clime the Learn'd their incense bring;
Hear, in all tongues consenting Paeans ring!
In praise so just, let ev'ry voice be join'd,
And fill the gen'ral chorus of mankind!
Hail bards triumphant! born in happier days;
Immortal heirs of universal praise!
Whose honours with increase of ages grow,
As streams roll down, enlarging as they flow!
Nations unborn your mighty names shall sound,
And worlds applaud that must not yet be found!
Oh may some spark of your celestial fire
The last, the meanest of your sons inspire,

(That on weak wings, from far, pursues your flights;
Glows while he reads, but trembles as he writes).
   (185-198)

The language of the bards is a second nature, then, without the dire effects of a Bouvard or Pécuchet copying everything indiscriminately. One finds in the fields that true wit has tilled a small collection of central texts, well conceived and well phrased. We may declare these central on the basis of the human values and literary qualities we find in them. This central library, as opposed to the confusing totality of all books, is established by a consensus of educated readers, scholars, and poets over a long period. Neither in unsifted nature nor in the miscellaneous run of scribblers and scientist-projectors do we find any sense of the hierarchy of the Creation or of human products that arrange learning in a particularly human order. The kingdom of dulness swarms with those who disregard or mutilate the best of the ancients in setting up shop on their own (as modern museums and libraries necessarily abandon the order of value for the relatively unsifted order of parallel listing). As types of the antilogos hatching a new saturnalian age of lead, Pope's new breed of writers and scholars undo with egalitarian fervor the spirit that brooded over the deep and brought forth Eden's hierarchical order.

Actually, just as there are two sorts of heritage, Pope finds two kinds of dulness—one learned and one ignorant. In *An Essay on Criticism* he takes note of "the bookful Blockhead, ignorantly read, / With loads of learned lumber in his head" (612-613). In *The Dunciad*, on the other hand, the legions of the dull, beginning with the Chinese and proceeding to Egypt and on to Rome, have been great burners of libraries ("Heav'ns! what a pile! whole ages perish there: / And one bright blaze turns Learning into air," III.77-78). As the three-book version of *The Dunciad* begins, its central subject is precisely the fate of books. Dulness, as the first type or antitype of learning, is all we possess if we lack the imprint of method, art, or judgment on nature—in short, if we lack great books. Thus Pope brings the library to the defense of nature: we would have precious little use for either without the other.

Luckily for the study of literature, Pope, like Eliot, includes critical reading as an added factor in the new life of old books. Along with nature, criticism can, at a minimum, exercise correctives. The son of bards not only trembles as he writes but glows as he reads; and paralleling the line of bards is a line of "long succeeding critics" who reign justly and ordain useful laws. Though Pope's praise of them is not as warm as his praise of bards, it is enthusiastic, beginning with the "mighty Stagyrite" and proceeding to Horace, Dionysius, Quintilian, and Longinus. *An Essay on Criticism* testifies to his own fusion of poet and critic and his maintaining of a line of praise for the light of reason and judgment that reigns alike in reading and good writing. Both of these follow the establishment of empire, as "learning and Rome alike in empire grew / And arts still follow'd where her eagles flew." Where empires fall, learning falls, and tyranny and superstition join in a deluge of false beliefs.

All of this is easier for Pope to say than for later poets and critics. When he sorted out his classics, the main line of critics and poets had not been displaced by new poetries, new criticisms, new waves of science and learning, and the questioning of canonical literature. A similar doctrine of classical revival and empire looks anachronistic in Eliot, despite the eloquence of his defense of it, and again in Frank Kermode's recent modifications of it. Certainly for Borges, the succession of bards is less clear; if one wishes to decode nature and discover a single logic behind the library's holdings, one may have to shuffle letters and symbols endlessly. What to Pope is an antitype of the Logos—a creative spirit that hatches nonsense in the deep—becomes for Borges "the divine disorder" itself. Pope's traditions are learnable, and nature itself is summed up in a limited number of genres—codified, systematized, reimagined by a family of poets more or less in accord. As two more centuries of writers have filled the library to overflowing, the tradition's sifted and methodized nature has become less definitive.

I nonetheless find Pope a useful model with which to conclude because he manages a sensible compromise between learning's vast enterprise and the simple view of the enthusiastic reader. It is doubtful that he would have sanctioned all branches of the modern study industry, but he treasured the deep past that poets extend to us and the judgment of critics in screening it. Something like a pluralism of institutions following their own momentum surfaces in his discriminating sense of genres; and at the same time, he controls that pluralism with the dominance of certain universals. In aiming for a more complete storage and recall, modern scholarship has come closer than Pope would advise to dissolving the integrity of texts into what can be said about them and into what surrounds them. What we instinctively fall back on is a finite number of good fictions that reward reading.

Certainly our better fictions, thus submitted to systematic study and repossessed intelligently, represent a different past from any other that we possess. In doing so, they construct a different present from the one we would otherwise have and urge us to develop powers of listening that we would not otherwise cultivate. Pope acknowledges the indebtedness that makes all literature and its commentary a related network. Because texts come forth in a historical context and a serial order, they require that we understand both the author's intent and his reconstruction of predecessors. Reading must also acknowledge the intervening time and the changes it has wrought as barriers we must overcome and as sources of the detachment in even the most intimate collaboration between text and reader. We cannot wish that historical distance away, and we must not forcefully uproot the text and bring it to us on our terms. But in between our destroying of its context and the loss of our own is a practiced mean in which we may keep the historical corridor open and active. The experience at each end of it is the more resonant for the connection and for the finesse that scholarship at its best contributes to it. Nature's represented, reordered, reconstituted bounty is redoubled in that momentary contact. The final irony of Prospero's Ceres and her quick exit is that, next evening on the same stage, or a century later on another stage, other actors who follow the script may coax her back again and reopen the corridor.

NOTES

INDEX

Notes

Introduction

1. T. S. Eliot, *The Classics and the Man of Letters* (London: Oxford University Press, 1942), p. 8. The citation from Marcel Proust is from *The Past Recaptured*, trans. Frederick A. Blossom (New York: Random House, 1932), p. 401.
2. T. S. Eliot, *What Is a Classic?* (London: Faber and Faber, 1945), p. 11.
3. Marcel Proust, *The Past Recaptured*, p. 197.
4. Sir Philip Sidney, *An Apology for Poetry*, ed. Geoffrey Shepherd (London: Thomas Nelson, 1965), p. 100.

1. The Wayward Temporality of Literature

1. The thrust of recent criticism is primarily in another direction. See, for instance, Michel Foucault, *The Archaeology of Knowledge*, trans. A. M. Sheridan Smith (New York: Random House, 1972), and *The Order of Things: An Archaeology of the Human Sciences* (New York: Random House, 1970). See also Warner Berthoff's review of literary making and unmaking in recent critics and reestablishment of the privileged literary text in "The Way We Think Now: Protocols for Deprivation," *New Literary History*, 7 (1976): 599–617. For other views of literary pastness, see Robert Escarpit, " 'Creative Treason' as a Key to Literature," *Yearbook of Comparative and General Literature* 10 (1961): 19; see also W. Jackson Bate, *The Burden of the Past and the English Poet* (Cambridge, Mass.: Harvard University Press, 1970); Harold Bloom, *The Anxiety of Influence* (London: Oxford University Press, 1973), *A Map of Misreading* (New York: Oxford University Press, 1975), *Kabbalah and Criticism* (New York: Seabury Press, 1975), and *Figures of Capable Imagination* (New York: Seabury Press, 1976); Geoffrey H. Hartman, "War in Heaven," *Diacritics* 3 (1973): 26–32; Harold Bloom, "Poetry, Revisionism, Repression," *Critical Inquiry* 2 (1975): 233–252; Claudio Guillén, *Literature as System: Essays toward the Theory of Literary History* (Princeton: Princeton University Press, 1971); Ihab H. Hassan, "The Problem of Influence in Literary History," *Journal of Aesthetics and Art Criticism* 14 (1955): 66–76; Alice S. Miskimin, *The Renaissance Chaucer* (New Haven: Yale University

Press, 1975), pp. 1–29; Joseph Anthony Wittreich, Jr., "A Theory of Influence," in *Angel-of-Apocalypse: Blake's Idea of Milton* (Madison: University of Wisconsin Press, 1975), pp. 223–229. Here and in " 'A Poet amongst Poets'; Milton and the Tradition of Prophecy," in *Milton and the Line of Vision* (Madison: University of Wisconsin Press, 1975), pp. 97–142, Wittreich argues convincingly against the anxiety of influence in the line of Western prophetic poets: "The prophet makes two assumptions about his art: one is that he must offer a sharper articulation of his precursor's visions; the other, that he is the recipient of a new revelation which he is charged with purveying (*Angel-of-Apocalypse*, p. 225).

2. Northrop Frye, *The Critical Path* (Bloomington: Indiana University Press, 1971), p. 98. As Henry Focillon writes even more emphatically than Frye: "The life of forms [in art] is not the result of change. Nor is it a great cyclorama neatly fitted into the theatre of history and called into being by historical necessities." Instead, literary forms "obey their own rules—rules that are inherent in the . . . regions of the mind where they are located and centered." If it is to exist at all, the historical study of art and of literature must proceed as "an investigation of how these great ensembles . . . behave throughout the phases which we call their life" (*The Life of Forms in Art* [New York: George Wittenborn, 1948], p. 10). Or as W. Wolfgang Holdheim has observed, along with other arts, literature is "antihistorical and antitemporal"; it "dehistoricizes" history, remaining aloof from whatever causal and behavioral theories we might propose for classes, economic institutions, or technologies ("The Aesthetic-Historical Paradox," *Comparative Literature Studies* 10 [1973]: 1–8).

3. Maurice Merleau-Ponty, *The Primacy of Perception*, ed. James M. Edie (Evanston: Northwestern University Press, 1964), p. 25. See also Alex Gelley, "Toward a Theory of History in Literature: Merleau-Ponty and Gadamer," *PTL, a Journal of Descriptive Poetics and Theory of Literature* 1 (1976): 357–377.

4. See Geoffrey Hartman, "History-Writing as Answerable Style," *NLH* 2 (1970): 73–84; Fred Chappell, "Six Propositions about Literary History," *NLH* 1 (1969): 513–522; Douglas Bush, "Literary History and Literary Criticism" in *Engaged and Disengaged* (Cambridge, Mass.: Harvard University Press, 1966), pp. 234–251; Helen Gardner, "The Historical Approach," in *The Business of Criticism* (London: Oxford University Press, 1959), pp. 25–51; Robert Heilman, "History and Criticism: Psychological and Pedagogical Notes," *College English* 27 (1965): 32–38; Edwin Greenlaw, *The Province of Literary History* (Port Washington, N.Y.: Kennikat Press, 1931); Roy Harvey Pearce, *Historicism Once More* (Princeton: Princeton University Press, 1969); Leo Spitzer, *Linguistics and Literary History* (New York: Russell and Russell, 1962), pp. 1–40; Robert Weimann, "Past Significance and Present Meaning in Literary History," *NLH* 1 (1969): 91–109; René Wellek, "Literary History," in *Literary Scholarship*, ed. Norman Foerster et al. (Chapel Hill: North Carolina University Press, 1941), pp. 91–130, and "Literary Theory, Criticism, and History," in *Concepts of Criticism*, ed. Stephen G. Nichols, Jr. (New Haven: Yale University Press, 1963), pp. 37–53; Warner Berthoff, *Fictions and Events* (New York: E. P. Dutton, 1971), especially "The Study of Literature and the Recovery of the Historical," pp. 15–29; Wesley Morris, *Toward a New Historicism* (Princeton: Princeton University Press, 1972); F. W. Bateson, "Literary History: Non-Subject *Par Excellence*," *NLH* 2 (1970): 115–122; Elemér Hankiss, "The Structure of Literary Evolution: An Essay in

Diachronic Poetics," *Poetics* 5 (1972): 40–66; Ralph Cohen, "Innovation and Variation: Literary Change and Georgic Poetry," *Neohelicon* 3 (1975): 149–182.

5. Friedrich Kümmel, "Time as Succession and the Problem of Duration," in J. T. Fraser, ed., *The Voices of Time* (New York: George Braziller), p. 38.

6. Harry Levin, "Literature as an Institution," *Accent* 6 (1946): 167.

7. See Eugene McNamara, ed., *The Interior Landscape: The Literary Criticism of Marshall McLuhan, 1943–1962* (New York: McGraw-Hill, 1969). pp. 23–24.

8. Hippolyte Taine, *History of English Literature*, vol. I, pt. 1 trans. H. Van Laun (London: Chatto and Windus, 1897). See Harry Levin, "Literature as an Institution," p. 159; Guillén, *Literature as System*, pp. 24–25; Madame de Staël, *De la littérature* . . . , ed. Paul Van Tieghem (Geneva and Paris: Droz, 1959); Thomas Monro, "Taine's Theory of Determining Factors in Art History," in *Evolution in the Arts* (Cleveland: Cleveland Museum of Art, n.d.), pp. 105–117.

9. Vilfredo Pareto, *Sociological Writings*, ed. S. E. Finer, trans. Derick Mirfin (New York: Frederick A. Praeger, 1966), and *The Mind and Society*, trans. James Harvey Rogers, ed. Arthur Livingston (New York: Dover, 1963). Pareto makes nonlogical human impulses, or "residues," a central subject of his sociological inquiry and allows for their conversion (or masking) in habits and ideologies, or what he calls "derivations." Both residues and derivations particularize more general concepts of tradition. As Renato Poggioli remarks, great literature, in Pareto's view, expresses "residues of which we still partake; culture itself is a sublimation of residues" (see "For a Literary Historiography Based on Pareto's Sociology," in *The Spirit of the Letter* [Cambridge, Mass.: Harvard University Press, 1965], pp. 291–322).

10. Georgi Plekhanov, "The Role of the Individual in History," in Patrick Gardiner, ed., *Theories of History* (New York: The Free Press, 1959), pp. 139–165; *The Materialist Conception of History* (New York: International Publishers, 1940); *Fundamental Problems of Marxism* (London: Martin Lawrence, 1928); and *The Development of the Monist View of History*, trans. Andrew Rothstein (Moscow: Foreign Language Publishing House, 1956). See also Mikhail Lifshitz, *The Philosophy of Art of Karl Marx*, trans. Ralph B. Winn, ed. Angel Flores (New York: Critics Group, 1938); Gaylord C. LeRoy and Ursula Beitz, eds., *Preserve and Create: Essays in Marxist Literary Criticism* (New York: Humanities Press, 1973); Neil J. Smelser, ed., *Karl Marx on Society and Social Change* (Chicago: University of Chicago Press, 1973); John McLeish, *The Theory of Social Change* (New York: Schocken Books, 1969); Karl Mannheim, *Essays on the Sociology of Culture*, ed. Ernest Manheim (London: Routledge and Kegan Paul, 1956), "Historicism," in *Essays on the Sociology of Knowledge* (London: Routledge and Kegan Paul, 1952), and *Ideology and Utopia* (New York: Harcourt, Brace and World, 1936). See also Jost Hermand and Evelyn Torton Beck, *Interpretive Synthesis* (New York: Frederick Ungar, 1975), pp. 74–94; Hugh Dalziel Duncan, "Rhetoric and Dialectic in Marxism," in *Communication and Social Order* (New York: Bedminster Press, 1962), pp. 181–188; see also Duncan's bibliography in *Language and Literature in Society* (New York: Bedminster Press, 1961); C. M. Bowra, *Poetry and Politics, 1900–1960* (Cambridge: Cambridge University Press, 1966); Leonard Meyer, *Music, the Arts and Ideas* (Chicago: University of Chicago Press, 1967), p. 108.

11. Lucien Goldmann, "Genetic Structuralism and the History of Literature," in *Velocities of Change*, ed. Richard Macksey (Baltimore: Johns Hopkins

University Press), p. 91; see also *Pour une sociologie du roman* (Paris: Gallimard, 1964); *The Human Sciences and Philosophy*, trans. Hayden V. White and Robert Anchor (London: Jonathan cape, 1969); and "The Sociology of Literature: Status and Problems of Method," *International Social Science Journal* 19 (1967), also published in *The Sociology of Art and Literature: A Reader*, ed. Milton C. Albrecht, James H. Barnett, and Mason Griff (New York: Praeger Publishers, 1970), pp. 582–609. See also David Morss and Sandy Petrey, "Literature and History in Contemporary French Scholarship," *Clio* 5 (1975): 45; Robert Weimann, *Structure and Society in Literary History* (Charlottesville: University of Virginia Press, 1976), pp. 163–164; P. V. Zima, *Le désire du mythe: Une lecture sociologique de Marcel Proust* (Paris: A. G. Nizet, 1973); Radhakamal Mukerjee, *The Social Function of Art* (Westport, Conn.: Greenwood Press, 1971); Hermand and Beck, "Sociological and Marxist Literary Scholarship," pp. 74–95; Patrick Brady, "Socio-Criticism as Genetic Structuralism: Value and Limitation of the Goldmann Method," *L'esprit créateur* 14 (1974): 207–218; Raymond Williams, "Literature and Sociology: In Memory of Lucien Goldmann," *New Left Review* 67 (1971): 3–18; Miriam Glucksmann, "Lucien Goldmann: Humanist or Marxist?" *New Left Review* 56 (1969): 49–62; Priscilla Clark, "The Comparative Method: Sociology and the Study of Literature," *Yearbook of Comparative Literature* 23 (1974): 5–13. See also Louis Althusser and Etienne Balibar, *Reading Capital*, trans. Ben Brewster (London: NLB, 1970), pp. 274–275; cf. Bertrand Russell, *Freedom and Organization, 1814–1914* (London: Allen and Unwin, 1952), pp. 173–258; John McLeish, *The Theory of Social Change* (New York: Schocken Books, 1969); Robert Weimann, " 'Reception Aesthetics' and the Crisis in Literary History," *Clio* 5 (1975): 17; Hans Robert Jauss, "The Idealist Embarrassment: Observations on Marxist Aesthetics," *NLH* 7 (1975): 191–208; Thomas Monro, "The Marxist Theory of Art History," in *Evolution in the Arts*, pp. 92–104; George Bisztray, *Marxist Models of Literary Realism* (New York: Columbia University Press, 1978); Nicolai Bukhurin, "Poetry, Poetics and the Problem of Poetry in the U.S.S.R.," in *Problems of Soviet Literature*, ed. H. G. Scott (Moscow: Co-operative Publishing Society, 1935).

12. Cf. George Plekhanov, *Fundamental Problems of Marxism* (London: Martin Lawrence, 1928), pp. 97–111; "The Role of the Individual in History," in *Theories of History*, ed. Patrick Gardiner (New York: The Free Press, 1959), pp. 139–165. Cf. Leon Trotsky, in *Critical Theory Since Plato*, ed. Hazard Adams (New York: Harcourt, Brace, Jovanovich, 1971), p. 822.

13. Louis Althusser, *For Marx*, trans. Ben Brewster (New York: Random House, 1969), p. 121.

14. Karl Marx, *Capital*, vol. I, trans. Eden and Cedar Paul (London: J. M. Dent, 1930), p. 59; cf. *Karl Marx on Society and Social Change, with Selections by Friedrich Engels*, ed. Neil J. Smelser (Chicago: University of Chicago Press, 1973); Karl Marx and Frederich Engels, *Literature and Art* (New York: International Publishers, 1947); Lifshitz, *The Philosophy of Art of Karl Marx*; essays by Lukacs, Petrov, Weimann, N. K. Gay, and others in *Preserve and Create: Essays in Marxist Literary Criticism*. See also Fredric Jameson, *Marxism and Form: Twentieth-Century Dialectical Theories of Literature* (Princeton: Princeton University Press, 1971); Mark Poster, *Existential Marxism in Postwar France: From Sartre to Althusser* (Princeton: Princeton University Press, 1975), especially "The Dialectic and Its

Limits," pp. 270–276; Louis Althusser, *Lenin and Philosophy and Other Essays*, trans. Ben Brewster (London: NLB, 1971); Terry Eagleton, *Marxism and Literary Criticism* (London: Methuen, 1976); Maurice Godelier, "Myth and History," *New Left Review* 69 (1971): 93–112; Lewis A. Coser, *Continuities in the Study of Social Conflict* (New York: The Free Press, 1967), pp. 137–152; *The Open Marxism of Antonio Gramsci*, trans. Carl Marzani (New York: Cameron Associates, 1959); Raymond Williams, *Marxism and Literature* (London: Oxford University Press, 1977), pp. 75–144.

15. Cf. Paul J. Korshin, *Studies in Change and Revolution* (Menston, Yorkshire: Scholar Press, 1972), p. 100.

16. On the reader's aesthetics, see Weimann " 'Reception Aesthetics,' " and Jauss, "The Idealist Embarrassment"; Wolfgang Iser, *The Implied Reader*, and "The Reading Process: A Phenomenological Approach," *NLH* 3 (1972): 279–300; Stanley E. Fish, "Literature in the Reader: Affective Stylistics," *NLH* 2 (1970): 123–162.

17. As Fredric Jameson marvels in *The Prison-House of Language* (Princeton: Princeton University Press, 1972), p. vii, we have had several models, including the universe as machine and organic system, and now language—now "to rethink everything through once again in terms of linguistics!" See also Wesley Morris, "Aesthetics and Structuralism," *Clio* 4 (1975): 266–275; Jonathan Culler, *Structuralistic Poetics: Structuralism, Linguistics and the Study of Literature* (Ithaca: Cornell University Press, 1975), and "Language and Knowledge," *Yale Review* 62 (1973): 290–196; Robert Scholes, *Structuralism in Literature: An Introduction* (New Haven: Yale University Press, 1974); Michael Lane, ed., *Structuralism: A Reader* (London: Jonathan Cape, 1970); Eugenio Donato, "Lévi-Strauss and the Protocols of Distance," *Diacritics* 5 (1975): 2–12; Seymour Chatman, ed., *Approaches to Poetics: Selected Papers from the English Institute* (New York: Columbia University Press, 1972); Roland Barthes, *Writing Degree Zero and Elements of Semiology* (Boston: Beacon Press, 1970); articles by several critics in *The Structuralist Controversy*, ed. Richard Macksey and Eugenio Donato (Baltimore: Johns Hopkins Press, 1970), and in *Modern French Criticism*, ed. John K. Simon (Chicago: University of Chicago Press, 1972); Vernon W. Grass, ed., *European Literary Theory and Practice from Existential Phenomenology to Structuralism* (New York: Delta, 1973); Howard Gardner, *The Quest for Mind: Piaget, Lévi-Strauss, and the Structuralist Movement* (New York: Alfred A. Knopf, 1973); Gerald L. Bruns, *Modern Poetry and the Idea of Language* (New Haven: Yale University Press, 1974). As Bruns suggests in "Rhetoric, Grammar, Language as a Substantial Medium" (pp. 11–41), separating words from things and treating them as self-sustained systems has a long history before Saussure. Bruns himself argues that "poetics . . . must be a structuralism which defines the poem in relation to itself as a system of internal dependencies; but it must also be a phenomenology which defines the poem in relation to its situation . . . its historical existence" (p. 262). My argument is similar. See also Roland Barthes, *Elements of Semiology*, trans. Annette Lavers and Colin Smith (New York: Hill and Wang, 1968), pp. 54–55; Denis Donoghue, *The Sovereign Ghost* (Berkeley: University of California Press, 1976), pp. 78–81.

18. Eugenio Donato, "Of Structuralism and Literature," in *Velocities of Change*, pp. 153–178.

19. Edward Said, *Beginnings: Intention and Method* (New York: Basic Books, 1975), p. 56; Claude Lévi-Strauss, *Structural Anthropology*, vol. I, trans. Claire Jacobson and Brooke Grundfest Schoepf (New York: Basic Books, 1963), p. 24.

20. See, for instance, Antoine-Nicolas de Condorcet's *Sketch for a Historical Picture of Progress* . . . , trans. June Barraclough (London: Weidenfeld and Nicolson, 1955), and August Comte, *System of Politive Polity* (New York: Burt Franklin, 1966), especially vol. III, *Social Dynamics* (originally published in 1876).

21. German is not quite as unique in its departures from the rules as Mark Twain would have us believe, but his view of it reminds us of how ramshackle a grammar may become in the course of time and public handling: "Surely there is not another language that is so slipshod and systemless, and so slippery and elusive to the grasp. One is washed about in it, hither and thither, as in the most helpless way; and when at last he thinks he has captured a rule which offers firm ground to take rest on amid the general rage and turmoil of the ten parts of speech, he turns over the page and reads, 'Let the pupil make careful note of the following *exceptions.*' He runs his eye down and finds that there are more exceptions to the rule than instances of it" ("The Awful German Language," from *A Tramp Abroad* [New York: Heritage, 1966], p. 373). The question for the defender of synchronic linguistics is: How many exceptions can one allow before modifying the rule?

22. Saussure of course does not himself maintain that aloofness and arbitrariness of language holds it immune to change. That very few objects suggest the actual words we attach to them—and no group of objects evokes the arrangement with which we assemble them in grammatical statements—weighs less decisively against the temporality of language systems in his view than is sometimes supposed. He devotes a section of the *Course in General Linguistics*, ed. Charles Bally and Albert Sechehaye, trans. Wade Baskin (London: Peter Owen, 1974), "Diachronic Linguistics," pp. 140–190 to phonetic change, the grammatical consequences thereof, evolution, agglutinative change, and analogy as a creative force in language. As he remarks, "Language never stops interpreting and decomposing its units," and, "The history of each language discloses a motley accumulation of analogical facts," As "continuous reshufflings" of the linguistic deck, these collectively "play an even more important part in the evolution of language than do sound changes" (p. 171). He notices also the diversity of languages, the spreading of linguistic waves, and the prospective and retrospective viewpoints that diachronic linguistics requires. As Warner Berthoff sums up from another perspective: "Linguistics, in its work of describing constitutive structures, has valid reasons for considering language as logically prior to speech and as essentially independent of history. But how can actual language structures have emerged or maintained common functions except through acts of speaking, the purposeful exchanges of relation-confirming statement?" ("The Way We Think Now: Protocols for Deprivation," *NLH* 7 [1976]: 606.)

Structuralist in a different sense is Thomas S. Kuhn's *The Structure of Scientific Revolutions*, which considers the establishment of paradigms in normal science, their alteration in the discovery of anomalies, and the absorption of new paradigms in the rewritten history that stems from discovery. In the course of normal science, the profession of scientists establishes its experimental procedures and its textbooks; it puts forward, simultaneously, a prevailing paradigm and a sense of progress. An anomaly that a given paradigm does not handle well then initiates a debate over the fundamentals of the discipline and eventually leads to a new paradigm. See Thomas S. Kuhn, *The Structure of Scientific Revolutions* (Chicago: University of Chicago Press, 1962), p. 137.

23. For a discussion of pluralism from the perspective of the Chicago critics, see "The Limits of Pluralism," *Critical Inquiry* 3 (1977): 407–448, composed of articles by Wayne C. Booth, M. H. Abrams, and J. Hillis Miller. See also Wayne C. Booth, *Now Don't Try to Reason with Me* (Chicago: University of Chicago Press, 1970), pp. 131–172. The position of both Abrams and Booth is that certain basic facts about a text are indisputable, which limits the scope of pluralism; but beyond that, any of several critical presuppositions may produce valid readings. My emphasis is not so much on the possible validity of different approaches to a text as on the different kinds of continuity and retrievability genres have, and on the conditions of reading as I suggest them at the end of this chapter. Approaches can be judged partly by their suitability to kinds. See also Meyer, *Music, the Arts and Ideas*, p. 180, and again, "The Profile of Pluralism," pp. 172–185; cf. Claudio Guillén, *Literature as System*, pp. 440–441. Hermand and Beck, *Interpretive Synthesis*, p. 205; John P. Anton, ed., *Naturalism and Historical Understanding: Essays in the Philosophy of John Herman Randall, Jr.* (Albany: State University of New York Press, 1967), p. 13. For an interesting variety of pluralism within a theory of orderly social change, see Paul Schrecker, *Work and History: An Essay on the Structure of Civilization* (Princeton: Princeton University Press, 1948; rpt., Gloucester, Mass.: Peter Smith, 1967). As Robert A. Nisbet points out in *Social Change and History: Aspects of the Western Theory of Development* (New York: Oxford University Press, 1969), in attacking the notion of continuous change, what appears to be continuity in some theorists—and one would have to classify Schrecker among them—is really the logical continuity of "instances in a classificatory series." Human behavior does not lack persistent and uniform features, but "the states that humanity successively traverses do not engender one another" (p. 292).

24. Jonathan Swift, *A Tale of a Tub*, in *Gulliver's Travels and Other Writings*, ed. Louis A. Landa (Boston: Houghton Mifflin, 1960), pp. 326–327.

25. George Kubler, *The Shape of Time* (New Haven: Yale University Press, 1962), pp. 69, 70.

26. The linkage between carnival and poetry is ably demonstrated by Josef Pieper's *In Tune with the World: A Theory of Festivity* (New York: Harcourt, Brace, and World, 1965). Pieper cites Plato's comment that the Muses are our festival companions and agrees with Helmut Kuhn in treating both the arts and festivals as events that "stand out of the flow of existence" (p. 39). See also Eric S. Rabkin, "The Fantastic and Literary History," in *The Fantastic in Literature* (Princeton: Princeton University Press, 1956), pp. 151–188. The escape into fantasy is representative of what "every literary world" offers as an alternative to "the contingencies of extra-literary reality" (p. 187).

27. Karl Kroeber makes a distinction similar to Mircea Eliade's between primitive and modern poets in "Poem, Dream, and the Consuming of Culture," *Georgia Review* 32 (1978). He contrasts the ineffectiveness of Keats's dreamer in *The Fall of Hyperion* with the cultural integration of an Ojibwa dream of deer

hunting: "The tribe consists not in listeners or audience merely, but of cultural supporters who can physically aid the poet by giving a social form to the power speaking through him. As the old man sings his dream, the dancers contribute to its recreation by acting like deer: they reproduce his dream for their tribe. The poem thus is means by which psychic energy flows into sociological structure, thence into practical activity, hunting, which makes the participants effective in the natural world, provides them with power." This is quite unlike Keats's frustration over the poet's isolation from constructive social labor, and unlike as well the frequent sense of the modern poet as exhibitionist. Even widely published dreams of modern poets do not become common tribal property; they usually require introduction and critical mediation. Hence, as Kroeber continues: "Keats's poetry is energy-consuming. Response to it demands critical exertion which is absorbed into the poem, becomes subsumed in the strictly literary tradition of which criticism becomes itself a part." The establishing of a vast study industry for poetry is evidence of the alienation of the poem from its public. "It is not easy to find any Western art that doesn't serve as a locus for collecting power to itself, rather than passing it on into socially productive activity. Hence the curious discontinuities in our literary traditions within cultural coherence" (pp. 278–280).

28. Laurence Sterne, *The Life and Opinions of Tristram Shandy* (London: J. M. Dent, 1912), p. 53 (Book I, Chapter XXII).

29. John Crowe Ransom, *The World's Body* (New York: Charles Scribner's Sons, 1938), pp. 233–260. In "Sentimental Exercise," pp. 212–232, Ransom makes a distinction similar to Merleau-Ponty's between use objects and things in themselves, finding the business of poetry to be an aesthetic and cognitive knowledge of the object as an individual and the business of science to be a "predatory" knowledge of universals.

2. Recurrence, Institution, and Literary Kind

1. Joost A. M. Meerloo, "The Time Sense in Psychiatry," in *The Voices of Time*, ed. J. T. Fraser (New York: George Braziller, 1966), pp. 239–240.

2. Raymond Williams, *Culture and Society, 1780–1950* (New York: Columbia University Press, 1960), p. 255.

3. George Kubler, *The Shape of Time* (New Haven: Yale University Press, 1962), p. 98.

4. Cf. Alastair Fowler, "The Selection of Literary Constructs," *NLH 7* (1975): 53. Fowler suggests that "the literary historian's proper study" is "forms in relation to men and their works": "Since literary values are human in origin, they appear most clearly on the scale of normal experience of value: not in phoneme, phrase, local device, or broad genre, but in the integrity of single works and in the stances of their authors . . . Larger entities may have their own unitary force, and be the subject of legitimate histories. But their values ultimately derive from component individual works."

5. See my "Shakespeare's Kingship: Institution and Dramatic Form," in *Essays in Shakespearean Criticism*, ed. James L. Calderwood and Harold E. Toliver (Englewood Cliffs, N.J.: Prentice-Hall, 1970), pp. 58–84; see also Maurice Mer-

leau-Ponty, "Institution in Personal and Public History," in *Themes from the Lectures at the College de France, 1952–1960,* trans. John O'Neill (Evanston, Ill.: Northwestern University Press, 1970), p. 40; Elizabeth W. Bruss, *Autobiographical Acts* (Baltimore: Johns Hopkins University Press, 1976), p. 5. For examples of the shaping influence of habitual experience gradually institutionalized and turned to recurrent literary attitudes, methods, and themes, see Paul Fussell's categories of perception and language in *The Great War and Modern Memory* (New York: Oxford University Press, 1975).

6. See F. Smith Fussner, *The Historical Revolution* (New York: Columbia University Press, 1962), especially pp. 34, 43.

7. See E. D. Hirsch, Jr., "The Historicity of Genres," in *Validity in Interpretation* (New Haven: Yale University Press, 1967), pp. 102–111.

8. See Jerome Hamilton Buckley, *The Triumph of Time: A Study of the Victorian Concepts of Time, History, Progress, and Decadence* (Cambridge, Mass.: Harvard University Press, 1966), pp. 34–52. On the difference between eighteenth- and nineteenth-century evolution, see Michel Foucault, *The Archaeology of Knowledge,* trans. A. M. Sheridan Smith (New York: Harper Torchbooks, 1972), p. 36.

9. See *Leon Trotsky on Literature and Art,* ed. Paul N. Niegel (New York: Pathfinder Press, 1970), p. 18. It should be added, however, that a good many masked reinforcements of class parade under different banners. A brilliant demonstration can be seen in Michel Foucault's *Discipline and Punish,* trans. Alan Sheridan (New York: Pantheon Books, 1977). As Foucault remarks: "Historically, the process by which the bourgeoisie became . . . the politically dominant class was masked by the establishment of an explicit, coded and formally egalitarian juridical framework, made possible by the organization of a parliamentary, representative regime. But the development and generalization of disciplinary mechanisms constituted the other, dark side of these processes" (p. 222).

10. Claudio Guillén argues similarly that literary periods contain a multiplicity of temporal processes and durations running simultaneously, overlapping chronologies, and events of long and short duration. See *Literature as System* (Princeton: Princeton University Press, 1971), p. 464. Cf. Johan Huizinga's description of the antinomy of realistic and nominalistic world views in "The Idea of History," in *The Varieties of History from Voltaire to the Present,* ed. Fritz Stern (New York: Macmillan, 1970).

11. A lengthy chapter of literary history could be devoted to the partial emergence of subterranean movements, whether in veiled allegories and the hieroglyphs of devotees, as in Druid bards like Taliessen, or in rationalized and expounded form, as in Yeats's version of Madame Blatvatsky and the instructions of his later "spirits."

12. See, for instance, Kenneth Burke, *A Grammar of Motives* (Cleveland: World Publishing Company, 1962), published together with *A Rhetoric of Motives.*

13. Northrop Frye, *The Anatomy of Criticism* (Princeton: Princeton University Press, 1957); Paul Hernadi, *Beyond Genre* (Ithaca: Cornell University Press, 1972). See also Ferdinand Brunetière, *L'evolution des genres dans l'histoire de la littérature* (Paris, 1890); Rosalie L. Colie, *The Resources of Kind: Genre-Theory in the Renaissance,* ed. Barbara K. Lewalski (Berkeley: University of California Press);

Irvin Ehrenpreis, The "Types Approach" to Literature (New York: King's Crown Press, 1945); Guillén, Literature as System, pp. 375–419; Fredric Jameson, "Magical Narratives: Romance as Genre," NLH 7 (1975): 135; Michael Riffaterre, "Système d'un genre descriptif," Poétique 3 (1972): 15–30.

14. Frye, Anatomy, pp. 107, 106.

15. Susanne K. Langer, Philosophy in a New Key (Cambridge, Mass.: Harvard University Press, 1942); cf. Geoffrey Hartman, "Adam on the Grass with Balsamum," in Beyond Formalism (New Haven: Yale University Press, 1970), pp. 147–150.

16. Mircea Eliade, Cosmos and History (New York: Harper and Row, 1959), p. 5.

17. See Henri Bergson, Matter and Memory, trans. Nancy M. Paul and W. Scott Palmer (London: George Allen and Unwin, 1911).

18. Literature is not alone among symbol-using activities in mixing discursive and nondiscursive expression, of course. Political systems, religions, and theories of history also tap the latent authority of universals and cyclical recurrence.

19. Northrop Frye, A Study of English Romanticism (New York: Random House, 1968), p. 5.

20. Ernst Cassirer, The Philosophy of Symbolic Forms, vol. 2, Mythical Thought (New Haven: Yale University Press, 1955), pp. 5, 35, 110–111. Cf. Philip Wheelwright, The Burning Fountain (Bloomington: Indiana University Press, 1968), pp. 148–185; Norman H. Holland, The Dynamics of Literary Response (New York: Oxford University Press, 1968), pp. 243–261. As James Jones summarizes, Cassirer's version of myth has six basic attributes: a sympathetic response to the world that dominates logical responses and cause-and-effect relationships; a sense of unbroken continuity and interconnectedness of everything in the world; metamorphosis; time without linear progression; space that is divided not into quandrants and cardinal points but into the sacred and the profane; the absence of death. See his Adam's Dream: Mythic Consciousness in Keats and Yeats (Athens: University of Georgia Press, 1975), pp. 6–7, and Herbert Schneidau, Sacred Discontent: The Bible and Western Tradition (Berkeley: University of California Press, 1976).

21. Kenneth Burke, A Rhetoric of Motives (Cleveland: World Publishing Company, 1962), p. 556.

22. Gerardus van der Leeuw misses that distinction when he writes of the saga, in which myth merely reverts to the temporal: "The saga is a myth, which, during its expansion, has become attached to some specific place or other, or to some sort of historical fact" (Religion in Essence and Manifestation, trans J. E. Turner [New York: Macmillan, 1938], p. 413). Cf. Herbert Weisinger, "The Proper Study of Myth," Centennial Review 12 (1968): 237–267.

23. Francis Bacon, The Advancement of Learning, ed. G. W. Kitchin (London: J. M. Dent, 1915), p. 82.

24. See Terry Eagleton, "History and Myth in Yeats's 'Easter 1916,' " Essays in Criticism 21 (1971): 248–260; Exiles and émigrés (New York: Schocken Books, 1970), concerning Eliot's, Joyce's, and Yeats's uses of myth; and his "Myth and History in Recent Poetry," in Michael Schmidt and Grevel Lindrop, eds., British Poetry Since 1960 (Oxford: Carcanet Press, 1972), pp. 233–219. See also Douglas N. Archibald, "Yeats's Encounters: Observations on Literary Influence and Lit-

erary History," *NLH* 1 (1970): 440–460; Stephen Maloney, "Yeats's Meaningful Words: The Role of 'Easter 1916' in his Poetic Development," *English Record* 22 (1971): 11–18; Cleanth Brooks, *The Hidden God* (New Haven: Yale University Press, 1963), pp. 44–67; Daniel Albright, *The Myth against Myth* (London: Oxford University Press, 1972); Thomas R. Whitaker, *Swan and Shadow: Yeats's Dialogue with History* (Chapel Hill: University of North Carolina Press, 1964); Northrop Frye, "The Top of the Tower: A Study of the Imagery of Yeats," *Southern Review* 5 (1969): 850–871; Helen Vendler, "Sacred and Profane Perfection in Yeats," *Southern Review* 9 (1973): 105–116; Peter Ure, *Towards a Mythology* (London: University Press of Liverpool, 1946). Ethel F. Cornwell, *The 'Still Point'* (New Brunswick, N.J.: Rutgers University Press, 1962), cites Yeats's *Cutting of an Agate* as evidence of Yeats's concept of the still point: "The end for art is the ecstasy awakened by the presence before an ever-changing mind of what is permanent in the world, or by the arousing of that mind itself into the very delicate and fastidious mood habitual with it when it is seeking those permanent and recurring things" (p. 89). Finally, see Robert Langbaum, "The Exteriority of Self in Yeats's Poetry and Thought," *NLH* 7 (1976): 579–597. In *Explorations* (New York: Macmillan, 1962), Yeats recounts Raftery's poem on himself and thinks of how, in reading history, one finds sudden revelations of the future coming not from visible history but from its antiself. The notion comes from Blake's prophetic books where, Yeats writes (1919): "Things must complete themselves before they pass away, and every new logical development of the objective energy intensifies in an exact correspondence a counter-energy, or rather adds to an always deepening unanalyzable longing. That counter-longing, having no visible past, can only become a conscious energy suddenly, in those moments of revelation which are as a flash of lightning" (pp. 258–259).

3. Poetic Recollection and the Phantomized Past

1. Harry Berger, Jr., "Theater, Drama, and the Second World: A Prologue to Shakespeare," *Comparative Drama* 2 (1968): 10.

2. Virgil, *The Eclogues and Georgics*, trans. C. Day Lewis (New York: Doubleday, 1964). For a substantial commentary on the First Eclogue, see Michael C. J. Putnam, *Virgil's Pastoral Art* (Princeton: Princeton University Press, 1970), pp. 20–81. See also John S. Coolidge, "Great Things and Small: The Virgilian Progression," *Comparative Literature* 7 (1965): 1–23.

3. As late as 1804, Edward Davies, in *Celtic Researches* (London, 1804) finds connections between the Christian-mythos-dominated history and nature. More curiously, he links the Celtic alphabet with Druidic tree hieroglyphs. That connection, though probably either Davies' own invention or an error repeated from others, would not have seemed illogical to ancients, who found trees a source not only of bark and leaves for paper but of inscriptions, emblems, and symbols. As Davies speculates concerning the runes of Taliessen, the Druids attached concepts such as spreading, expansion, and unfolding to the leaf and sprig of the oak and thus made hieroglyphics, letters, objects, and significance one and the same thing. Herbert's pun on the "leaves" of scripture in "Heaven" retains a vestige of that notion, as does the divining of destinies in the alchemical metaphors of "Holy Scriptures II." In those whispers that swell

"the Cheek of Fame" in "Upon the Hill and Grove at Bill-borough," Marvell carries the memorial capacity of trees almost to the extreme of Davies' Druid phalanxes of sage trees marching to battle in words and devices.

4. Though romantic recollection separates personal from general history, the two share common patterns: for instance, the growth of civilizations (phylogeny) may be roughly parallel to that of individuals (ontogeny). In both, institutions create barriers between the dream of paradise and its individual fulfillment. Or, as Norman O. Brown remarks in a modern version of that equation, the neuroses of civilizations and individuals may resemble one another. The romantics would agree with him at least in general that "the bondage of all cultures to their cultural heritage is an infringement of freedom," that "mankind is a prisoner of the past." Thus, beginning in a precivilized state of uninhibited dream and erotic freedom, a civilization moves toward controls that are responsible for both its highest achievements and its sickness. Retrieving an earlier state necessitates regression in both cases. Looking forward, the romantic visionary foresees an era that is a kind of regression reversed and transcendentalized. Brown of course is drawing not upon the romantics in this but upon Freud, specifically *Totem and Taboo* and *Moses and Monotheism*. See *Life Against Death: The Psychoanalytical Meaning of History* (New York: Random House, 1959), pp. 11–22.

5. Georges Poulet, *Studies in Human Time* (New York: Harper, 1959), pp. 25, 26, 29.

6. *Peacock's Four Ages of Poetry, Shelley's Defence of Poetry*, ed. H. F. B. Brett-Smith (Oxford: Blackwell, 1967), pp. 4, 16.

7. Ibid., pp. 26, 30. See Royce Campbell, "Shelley's Philosophy of History: A Reconsideration," *Keats-Shelley Journal* 21–22 (1972–73), 43–63; Earl J. Schulze, *Shelley's Theory of Poetry* (The Hague: Mouton, 1966), pp. 191–207.

8. See Frederick Garber, *Wordsworth and the Poetry of Encounter* (Urbana: University of Illinois Press, 1971), p. 28. Cf. Geoffrey Durrant, "Wordsworth and the Poetry of Objects," *Mosaic* 5 (1971): 107–119.

9. William Wordsworth, *The Poetical Works*, ed. Ernest de Selincourt, vol. 2 (London: Oxford University Press, 1952). On Wordsworth's view of the past, see Alan Grob, *The Philosophic Mind: A Study of Wordsorth's Poetry and Thought, 1797–1805* (Columbus: Ohio State University Press, 1973); Barbara Gates, *Wordsworth and Clio: The Poet's Historical Imagination* (Ph.D. diss., Bryn Mawr, 1971); Christopher Salvensen, *The Landscape of Memory* (Lincoln: University of Nebraska Press, 1965).

10. Cited from Hazard Adams, ed., *Critical Theory since Plato* (New York: Harcourt, Brace, Jovanovich, 1971), pp. 441, 437, 441–442.

11. Wordsworth did not settle immediately or exclusively upon personal recollection as a defining stage of poetic reconstructions. Earlier poems tend to offer more extensive residues of the past, like the Druid stones in a ring in the shepherd's haunt of "An Evening Walk." However, even those residues predict the ghostliness that appears later. In the same locality as the Druid stones are shadowy horsemen and the phantom pageants of silent "visionary warriors." Wordsworth is impressed by their splendor and their gorgeous show, which often appear to shepherds as the light dies into a "sullen gleam."

12. For commentary on "Yew-Trees," see Cleanth Brooks and Robert Penn

Warren, *Understanding Poetry*, 3rd ed. (New York: Holt, Rinehart and Winston, 1966), pp. 273-279; Michael Riffaterre, "Interpretation and Descriptive Poetry," *NLH* 4 (1973): 229-257; Geoffrey Hartman, "The Use and Abuse of Structural Analysis: Riffaterre's Interpretation of Wordsworth's 'Yew-Trees,' " *NLH* 7 (1975): 165-190; Gene W. Ruoff, "Wordsworth's 'Yew-Trees' and Romantic Perception," *Modern Language Quarterly* 34 (1973): 146-160. Leslie Brisman, in *Romantic Origins* (Ithaca: Cornell University Press, 1978), in exploring Wordsworth's autogenetic origins, follows up on Hartman's sense of ghostliness in several poems (pp. 276-361.)

13. Mario L. D'Avanzo, " 'Ode on a Grecian Urn' and *The Excursion,*" *Keats-Shelley Journal* 23 (1974): 95-105. See also Geoffrey Hartman, "Wordsworth and Goethe in Literary History," *NLH* 6 (1975): 393-414; James A. W. Heffernan, *Wordsworth's Theory of Poetry* (Ithaca: Cornell University Press, 1969); H. W. Piper, *The Active Universe* (London: Athlone Press, 1962); Georg Roppen and Richard Sommer, *Strangers and Pilgrims* (Olso: Norwegian University Press, 1964), pp. 113-171.

14. See Abbie Findlay Potts, *Wordsworth's Prelude* (Ithaca: Cornell University Press, 1953; rpt., New York: Octagon Books, 1966); Marion Montgomery, *The Reflective Journey* (Athens, Ga.: University of Georgia Press, 1973), and "Emotion Recollected in Tranquility: Wordsworth's Legacy to Eliot, Joyce, and Hemingway," *Southern Review* 6 (1970): 710-721.

15. Wallace Stevens, "The Poem as Icon," in *The Collected Poems* (New York: Alfred A. Knopf, 1954), pp. 526-527.

16. Laurence Lerner, "Olympus' Faded Hierarchy (Antiquity in Keats and Nerval)," in *The Uses of Nostalgia* (New York: Schocken Books, 1972), p. 220. See also Jack Stillinger, *The Hoodwinking of Madeline and Other Essays on Keats's Poems* (Urbana: University of Illinois Press, 1971); Pierre Vitoux, "Keats's Epic Design in Hyperion," *Studies in Romanticism* 14 (1975): 165-183; Brian Wilkie, *Romantic Poets and Epic Tradition* (Madison: University of Wisconsin Press, 1965); Thomas A. Vogler, *Preludes to Vision: The Epic Venture in Blake, Wordsworth, Keats, and Hart Crane* (Berkeley: University of California Press, 1971); James Benzinger, *Images of Eternity* (Carbondale: Southern Illinois Press, 1962); Geoffrey Hartman, *The Fate of Reading and Other Essays* (Chicago: University of Chicago Press, 1975); Bernard Blackstone, *The Consecrated Urn* (London: Longmans, 1962); Herbert Lindenberger, "Keats's 'To Autumn' and our Knowledge of a Poem," *College English* 32 (1970): 123-134; J. Phillip Eggers, "Memory in Mankind: Keats's Historical Imagination," *Publications of the Modern Language Association* 86 (1971): 990-998; Albert S. Gerard, *English Romantic Poetry* (Berkeley: University of California Press, 1968), pp. 215-236; Earl Wasserman, *The Finer Tone* (Baltimore: Johns Hopkins University Press, 1953), pp. 11-62; Jean-Claude Salle, "The Pious Frauds of Art: A Reading of the 'Ode on a Grecian Urn,' " *Studies in Romanticism* 11 (1972): 79-93; Stuart Curran, "The Mental Pinnacle: *Paradise Regained* and the Romantic Four-Book Epic," in Joseph Anthony Wittreich, Jr., ed., *Calm of Mind* (Cleveland: Case-Western Reserve Press, 1971), pp. 133-162; James Land Jones, *Adam's Dream: Mythic Consciousness in Keats and Yeats* (Athens, Ga.: University of Georgia Press, 1975).

17. Cf. Geoffrey Hartman, "Spectral Symbolism and Authorial Self in Keats's 'Hyperion,' " in *The Fate of Reading*, pp. 57-73.

18. See Eggers, "Memory in Mankind," p. 991.

19. W. B. Yeats, *Explorations* (New York: Macmillan, 1962), pp. 148, 151.

20. W. B. Yeats, *Essays and Introductions* (New York: Collier, 1968), p. viii.

21. W. B. Yeats, *On the Boiler* (Dublin: The Cuala Press, 1938), p. 22.

22. W. B. Yeats, *Pages from a Diary Written in Nineteen Hundred and Thirty* (Dublin: The Cuala Press, 1944), p. 9.

23. W. B. Yeats, *A Vision* (New York: Macmillan, 1956), p. 271.

24. Cited from Thomas R. Whitaker, *Swan and Shadow* (Chapel Hill: University of North Carolina Press, 1964), p. 138.

25. W.B. Yeats, *Collected Poems* (New York: Macmillan, 1954), p. 203.

26. See Whitaker, *Swan and Shadow*, p. 230. For discussions of "The Tower" and other Yeats poems that concern the mixture of history and myth, see Bernard Levine, *The Dissolving Image* (Detroit: Wayne State University Press, 1970), pp. 133-156; George Bornstein, ed., "Yeats and the Greater Romantic Lyric," *Romantic and Modern: Revaluations of Literary Tradition* (Pittsburgh: University of Pittsburgh Press, 1977), pp. 91-110; Edward Engelberg, *The Vast Design* (Toronto: University of Toronto Press, 1964), pp. 180-204; Daniel A. Harris, *Yeats: Coole Park and Ballylee* (Baltimore: Johns Hopkins University Press, 1974), pp. 87-113; M. L. Rosenthal, *Sailing into the Unknown: Yeats, Pound, and Eliot* (New York: Oxford University Press, 1978), pp. 26-44, 116-155; Michael Ragussis, *The Subterfuge of Art* (Baltimore: Johns Hopkins University Press, 1978), pp. 85-108. For Ragussis, the tower sequence, especially "Nineteen Hundred and Nineteen," reveals Yeats's understanding of passive mediumship, which prevents the poet from imposing his own will on the materials he draws from the historical cycles.

27. Yeats, *Collected Poems*, p. 455.

28. W. B. Yeats, *The Autobiography* (New York: Macmillan, 1953), p. 87.

29. Vivienne Koch, *W. B. Yeats: The Tragic Phase* (Baltimore: Johns Hopkins Press, 1951), p. 60.

30. T. S. Eliot, *The Sacred Wood* (London: Methuen, 1920), pp. 49, 51.

31. T. S. Eliot, *What is a Classic?* (London: Faber and Faber, 1945), pp. 24, 29.

32. T. S. Eliot, *The Classics and the Man of Letters* (London: Oxford University Press, 1942), p. 8.

33. Christopher Caudwell, *Romance and Realism: A Study in English Bourgeois Literature* (Princeton: Princeton University Press, 1970), pp. 127-128.

34. T. S. Eliot, "East Coker," *The Complete Poems and Plays, 1909-1950* (New York: Harcourt, Brace, 1958). See Grover Smith, *T. S. Eliot's Poetry and Plays* (Chicago: University of Chicago Press, 1950), p. 259; F. O. Matthiessen, *The Achievement of T. S. Eliot* (New York: Oxford University Press, 1959), pp. 177-197; Harry Blamires, *Word Unheard* (London: Methuen, 1969); Hugh Kenner, *The Invisible Poet* (London: Methuen, 1960), pp. 247-276; C. A. Patrides,"The Renascence of the Renaissance: T. S. Eliot and the Pattern of Time," *Michigan Quarterly Review* 12 (1973): 172-196; P. G. Ellis, "The Development of T. S. Eliot's Historical Sense," *Review of English Studies* 23 (1972): 291-301; Staffan Bergsten, *Time and Eternity: A Study in the Structure and Symbolism of T. S. Eliot's Four Quartets* (Stockholm: Svenska Bokforlaget, 1960). Floyd C. Watkins, *The Flesh and the Word: Eliot, Hemingway, Faulkner* (Nashville: Vanderbilt University Press, 1971); John F. Lynen, "Selfhood and the Reality of Time: T. S. Eliot,"

in *The Design of the Present* (New Haven: Yale University Press, 1969), pp. 341–441.

35. Ernest Hemingway, *The Sun Also Rises* (New York: Charles Scribner's Sons, 1924), p. 91.

36. Ernest Hemingway, *A Farewell to Arms* (New York: Charles Scribner's Sons, 1929), p. 3.

37. Hugh Kenner, *Home-Made World* (New York: Knopf, 1974), pp. 140–141.

38. Ernest Hemingway, "In Another Country," in *Men Without Women* (New York: Charles Scribner's Sons, 1927), p. 58.

39. Georges Poulet, "Timelessness and Romanticism," *Journal of the History of Ideas* 15 (1954): 3, 13.

40. Stevens, *Collected Poems*, p. 534.

41. See Wallace Stevens, *Opus Posthumous* (New York: Alfred A. Knopf, 1957), p. 117.

4. Ancestral Gloom and Glory

1. Susanne K. Langer finds all literature equivalent to memory: "The primary illusion created by poesis is a history entirely 'experienced'; and in literature proper (as distinct from drama, film, or pictured story) this virtual history is in the mode typified by memory. Its form is the closed, completed form that in actuality only memories have. Literature need not be made out of the author's memories . . . nor does it necessarily present events explicitly *as* somebody's memories . . . , but the *mode* in which events appear is the mode of completed experience, i.e., of the past" (*Feeling and Form* [New York: Scribner's Sons, 1953], p. 264).

2. John S. Coolidge, "Great Things and Small: The Virgilian Progression," *Comparative Literature* 7 (1965): 1–23.

3. Wallace Stevens, *The Collected Poems* (New York: Alfred A. Knopf, 1954), p. 70.

4. See Michael Fixler, *Milton and the Kingdoms of God* (London: Faber and Faber, 1964), p. 109; cf. Frank Kermode, *The Classic* (New York: Viking Press, 1975), p. 66.

5. Edwin Arlington Robinson, *Collected Poems* (New York: Macmillan, 1965), p. 297.

6. Alfred Lord Tennyson, *Morte d'Arthur*, in *The Poems and Plays* (New York: Random House, 1938), pp. 132–138, ll. 320–323. Concerning Tennyson's view of history and the sort of revival the *Idylls* make, see Georg Roppen, *Evolution and Poetic Belief* (Folcroft, Pa.: Folcroft Press, 1956); Lionel Stevenson, *Darwin among the Poets* (New York: Russell and Russell, 1963); Clyde de L. Ryals, *From the Great Deep: Essays on Idylls of the King* (Athens: Ohio University Press, 1967); John D. Rosenberg, *The Fall of Camelot* (Cambridge, Mass.: Harvard University Press, 1973); William A. Madden, "The Victorian Sense of the Past," *Clio* 4 (1975): 399–408; J. Phillip Eggers, *King Arthur's Laureate* (New York: New York University Press, 1971); Henry Kozicki, "Philosophy of History in Tennyson's Poetry to the 1842 *Poems*," *ELH: Journal of English Literary History* 42 (1975): 88–106. Gerald L. Bruns argues that history is a constitutive part of Victorian thought, which derives meanings from the world of process, event, sequence,

and development. See "The Formal Nature of Victorian Thinking," *PMLA* 90 (1975): 904–919. See also Peter Allan Dale, *The Victorian Critic and the Idea of History* (Cambridge, Mass.: Harvard University Press, 1977).

7. See Robert Huntington Fletcher, *The Arthurian Material in the Chronicles* (New York: Burt Franklin, 1966), expanded second edition with a bibliography and critical essay for 1905–1965 by Roger Sherman Loomis; Kenneth Hurlstone Jackson, "The Arthur of History," in R. S. Loomis, *Arthurian Literature in the Middle Ages: A Collaborative History* (London: Oxford University Press, 1959), pp. 1–11; Arthur C. L. Brown, *The Origin of the Grail Legend* (Cambridge, Mass.: Harvard University Press, 1943); Vida D. Scudder, *Le Morte Darthur of Sir Thomas Malory* (1917; rpt., New York: Haskell House, 1965).

8. Elizabeth T. Pochoda, *Arthurian Propaganda: Le Morte Darthur as an Historical Ideal of Life* (Chapel Hill: University of North Carolina Press, 1971).

9. *The Works of Sir Thomas Malory*, ed. Eugene Vinaver (London: Oxford University Press, 1954), p. 635. I have modernized the spelling.

10. Stephen A. Barney, *Allegories of History, Allegories of Love* (Hamden, Conn.: Archon Books, 1979), p. 183. See also Harry Berger, Jr., "The Spenserian Dynamics," *Studies in English Literature* 8 (1968): 1–18, and "The Prospects of Imagination: Spenser and the Limits of Poetry," *SEL* 1 (1961): 93–110.

11. Michael Murrin, "The Rhetoric of Fairyland," in *The Rhetoric of Renaissance Poetry from Wyatt to Milton*, Thomas O. Sloan and Raymond B. Waddington, eds. (Berkeley: University of California Press, 1974), p. 83. See also Michael Murrin, *The Veil of Allegory* (Chicago: University of Chicago Press, 1969).

12. Northrop Frye, "The Structure of Imagery in *The Faerie Queene*," *University of Toronto Quarterly* 30 (1961): 109–127, also in A. C. Hamilton, ed., *Essential Articles for the Study of Edmund Spenser* (Hamden, Conn.: Archon Books, 1972). See also Frye's *Fables of Identity* (New York: Harcourt, Brace and World, 1963); John Erskine Hankins, *Source and Meaning in Spenser's Allegory* (London: Oxford University Press, 1971); Mark Rose, *Heroic Love* (Cambridge, Mass.: Harvard University Press, 1968).

13. As Kermode writes, "The historical allegory is not the flickering limited affair it is sometimes said to be" but is sustained and interlinked in a significant interplay of "apocalyptic-sibylline prophecy and history." These two realms—the mental landscape of ideas and the historical realm of real nations—need not always be in conflict, of course. Fairyland has no real difficulty in accommodating historical material of a certain kind. The history of ideas, for instance (though perhaps not what we ordinarily mean by history), is quite compatible with it: Kermode lists specific elements of Christian dogma and practice as defined in the church fathers, in John Foxe, the Thirty-Nine Articles, and the Book of Common Prayer. Courtesy books too can be adjusted to fictive treatment and the general intellectual map of the work. Although proper names and specific historical occurrences are a different matter, Spenser insists that the common aim of all such elements is to glorify the gentle deeds of knights and ladies, to blazon them amongst a "learned throng." He can draw his illustrations from widely scattered times and places so long as they fit under captions provided by the ethical and rhetorical scheme for the benefit of that well-educated audience. *The Faerie Queene* is in this respect a mixed store of legend, myth, history, philosophy, dogma, and contemporary reference joined together

by an extensive system of analogies. See Frank Kermode, in Hamilton, ed., *Essential Articles*, pp. 123–150, and in Kermode, *Shakespeare, Spenser, Donne* (London: Routledge and Kegan Paul, 1971). See also Isabel Rathborne, *The Meaning of Spenser's Fairyland* (New York: Columbia University Press, 1947; rpt., New York: Russell and Russell, 1965), and Carrie Anna Harper, *The Sources of the British Chronicle History in Spenser's Faerie Queene* (1910; rpt., New York: Haskell House, 1964).

14. See James Nohrnberg, *The Analogy of the Faerie Queene* (Princeton: Princeton University Press, 1976), p. 44.

15. If we ask if Spenser's faculty psychology is clarified by its contexts and its sources, we must be dubious about an answer. Perhaps closest to his anatomy of intelligence is the Florentine variant of Platonist imagination in Pico's *On the Imagination*. Pico too grants fantasy a rich harvest from the five exterior senses, and from what these provide, the mind constructs imagistic likenesses "in imitation of incorporeal and spiritual nature." But in Pico, unlike Spenser, the soul then employs the imaginative faculty for conceiving likenesses among sensible objects and places them before the intellect. Intermediary as it is, we may make either an upward transformation toward the celestial or a downward transformation into brutishness. See Pico, *On the Imagination*, trans. Harry Caplan (New Haven: Yale University Press, 1930; rpt., Westport, Conn.: Greenwood Press, 1971). See Donald M. Friedman, "Wyatt and the Ambiguities of Fancy," *Journal of English and Germanic Philology* 67 (1968): 32–48; Murray W. Bundy, *The Theory of Imagination in Classical and Medieval Thought* (Urbana: University of Illinois Press, 1927); Isabel G. MacCaffrey, *Spenser's Allegory: The Anatomy of Imagination* (Princeton: Princeton University Press, 1976), especially pp. 13–17.

16. See Edwin Greenlaw, *Studies in Spenser's Historical Allegory* (Baltimore: Johns Hopkins University Press, 1932; rpt., New York: Octagon Books, 1967), p. 196, and Charles Bowie Millican, *Spenser and the Table Round* (1932; rpt., New York: Octagon Books, 1967). Michael O'Connell in *Mirror and Veil:The Historical Dimension of Spenser's Faerie Queene* (Chapel Hill: University of North Carolina Press, 1977) explores Spenser's Roman as opposed to his English models. He is undoubtedly correct to find Spenser's historical dimension nearer Virgil's than is usually granted (see "The Method of the Poet Historical," pp. 16–37). Virgil is nationalistic while Tasso and Ariosto, for instance, are international, cosmopolitan, and episodic. But it is also true, as O'Connell demonstrates in Book I of *The Faerie Queene*, that Spenser replaces the Roman Empire with a Christianized nation seeking to fulfill the paradigm of glory perfected in New Jerusalem. Unlike Augustus, his sovereign is patterned after a celestial archetype and defined within a vaster history; her nation is gathered up into both a systematic moral philosophy and mythology and is made one phase in the overall Eden-to-doomsday chronology. (The next stage in the revision of epic is Milton's further reply that all previous epics of national history and amorous adventure are in error: we must return to the source in Eden and the Creator and prepare for end things, seeing meanwhile the vanity of empire.) See also Millar MacLure's exceptional essay, "Spenser and the Ruins of Time," in *A Theatre for Spenserians*, ed. Judith M. Kennedy and James A. Reither (Toronto: University of Toronto Press, 1973), pp. 3–18.

17. See Thomas P. Roche, Jr., *The Kindly Flame* (Princeton: Princeton University Press, 1964); Catherine Rodgers, *Time in the Narrative of the Faerie Queene* (Salzburg: Institut für Englishe Sprache und Literature, 1973).

18. Joanne Craig, "The Image of Mortality: Myth and History in *The Faerie Queene*," *ELH* (1972): 520-544; cf. Michael O' Connell "History and the Poet's Golden World: The Epic Catalogues in *The Faerie Queene*," *English Literary Renaissance* 4 (1974): 241-267; Harry Berger, Jr., "The Structure of Merlin's Chronicle in *The Faerie Queene* III (iii)," *SEL* 9 (1969): 39-51; Angus Fletcher, "Prophecy and History in *The Faerie Queene*," in *The Prophetic Moment* (Chicago: Chicago University Press, 1971), pp. 37-45.

19. Sir Philip Sidney, *An Apology for Poetry*, ed. Geoffrey Shepherd (London: Thomas Nelson, 1965), pp. 5, 111.

20. Frye, "The Structure of Imagery," in Hamilton, *Essential Articles*, p. 154.

21. See, for instance, Susan C. Fox, "Eterne in Mutability: Spenser's Darkening Vision," in *Eterne in Mutability*, ed. Kenneth John Atchity (Hamden, Conn.: The Shoe String Press, 1972), pp. 20-41.

22. On the Mutability Cantos, see Harry Berger, Jr., "The Mutability Cantos: Archaism and Evolution in Retrospect," modified from *Yale Review* 58 (1969): 214-231, in Berger, ed., *Spenser, A Collection of Critical Essays* (Englewood Cliffs, N. J.: Prentice-Hall, 1968), pp. 136-176; MacCaffrey, *Spenser's Allegory*, pp. 43-433; Nohrnberg, *Analogy of the Faerie Queene*, pp. 739-757; John Lawlor, ed., *Patterns of Love and Courtesy* (Evanston, Ill.: Northwestern University Press, 1966), especially P. C. Bayley, "Order, Grace and Courtesy in Spenser's World," pp. 178-202.

23. James Joyce, *Portrait of the Artist as a Young Man* (New York: Random House, 1928), p. 250.

5. *Milton's Siege of Contraries: Universal Waste and Redemption*

1. Hugh M. Richmond, *The Christian Revolutionary: John Milton* (Berkeley: University of California Press, 1974), p. 174; cf. Arnold Stein, "Justifying Milton's Ways," *Sewanee Review* 84 (1976): 699. See also William G. Riggs, *The Christian Poet in Paradise Lost* (Berkeley: University of California Press, 1972), pp. 133-134.

2. Charles Williams, *Selected Writings* (London: Oxford University Press, 1961), p. 23.

3. William Kerrigan, *The Prophetic Milton* (Charlottesville: University of Virginia Press, 1976). On Christian historiography see C. A. Patrides, *Milton and the Christian Tradition* (London: Oxford University Press, 1966), and *The Phoenix and the Ladder* (Berkeley: University of California Press, 1964); J. H. Plumb, *The Death of the Past* (Boston: Houghton Mifflin, 1970); Peter Burke, *The Renaissance Sense of the Past* (London: Edward Arnold, 1969).

4. As I have argued in "The Splinter Coalition," in *New Essays on Paradise Lost*, ed. Thomas Kranidas (Berkeley: University of California Press, 1969), pp. 34-57.

5. See, for instance, Adam's morning orison, especially as read by Joseph Summers, *The Muses' Method* (London: Chatto and Windus, 1962), pp. 75-81.

6. See Irene Samuel, "Milton and the Ancients on the Writing of History," *Milton Studies* 2 (1970): 131–48. Cf. Patrick Cullen's remarks concerning Milton's genres in *Infernal Triad* (Princeton: Princeton University Press, 1974), p. 182; Harold Bloom, *Map of Misreading* (New York: Oxford University Press, 1975), pp. 125–143.

7. Arnold Stein, *Heroic Knowledge* (Minneapolis: University of Minnesota Press, 1957), p. 6; cf. Burton Weber, *Wedges and Wings* (Carbondale: Southern Illinois University Press, 1975), p. 1.

8. Leo Spitzer, "Understanding Milton," *Hopkins Review* 4 (1951): 17–25. Cf. Marilyn L. Williamson, "A Reading of Milton's Twenty-Third Sonnet," *Milton Studies* 4 (1972): 141–149; E. A. J. Honigmann, ed., *Milton's Sonnets* (London: Macmillan, and New York: St. Martin's, 1966).

9. George Kubler, *The Shape of Time* (New Haven: Yale University Press, 1962), p. 20.

10. On Milton's landscape in Eden, see John R. Knott, Jr., "Symbolic Landscape in Paradise Lost," *Milton Studies* 2 (1970): 37–58; Arnold Stein, *Answerable Style* (Minneapolis: University of Minnesota Press, 1953), pp. 52–74; Harry Levin, *The Myth of the Golden Age in the Renaissance* (New York: Oxford University Press, 1969); A. Bartlett Giamatti, *The Earthly Paradise and the Renaissance Epic* (Princeton: Princeton University Press, 1966), pp. 295–351; Roland Muschat Frye, *Milton's Imagery and the Visual Arts: Iconographic Tradition in the Epic Poems* (Princeton: Princeton University Press, 1978), pp. 219–255.

6. Questers in an Icy Elysée: Moderns without Ancestry

1. M. H. Abrams, *Natural Supernaturalism: Tradition and Revolution in Romantic Literature* (New York: W. W. Norton, 1971), especially pp. 141–198.

2. See Herbert N. Schneidau, "Style and Sacrament in Modernist Writing," *Georgia Review* 21 (1977): 427–453. What is true of Joyce and Pound in the "technique of radical immanence" holds also for others: the signatures of the visible world are not those of the old "polysemous technique" but a collapsing of levels of significance into "concrete specific occurrences" (p. 440).

3. Harry Berger, Jr., "Outline of a General Theory of Culture Change," *Clio* 2 (1972): 49–64.

4. Cf. James Rother, "Modernism and the Nonsense Style," *Contemporary Literature* 15 (1974): 187–202. See also J. W. Saunders, *The Profession of English Letters* (London: Routledge and Kegan Paul, 1964), pp. 31–67.

5. Wallace Stevens, *Opus Posthumous* (New York: Alfred A. Knopf, 1957), p. 117. Other Stevens quotations are taken from *The Collected Poems* (New York: Alfred A. Knopf, 1954).

6. Wallace Stevens, *The Necessary Angel* (New York: Random House, 1951), p. 4.

7. Merle E. Brown, *Wallace Stevens: The Poem as Act* (Detroit: Wayne State University Press, 1970), p. 166.

8. George Kubler, *The Shape of Time* (New Haven: Yale University Press, 1962), p. 72.

9. Cited from Tony Tanner, *City of Words: American Fiction, 1950–1970*

(London: Jonathan Cape, 1971), p. 152, taken from the ending of Lévi-Strauss's *Tristes tropiques*.

10. William Carlos Williams, *Spring and All*, in *Imaginations* (New York: New Directions, 1970), pp. 89, 93.

11. Richard T. LaPiere, in *Social Change* (New York: McGraw-Hill, 1965), p. 39, remarks that because the natural tendency of societies is to stabilize and rigidify once they have reached a certain maturity, change "is the work of socially deviant individuals acting in asocial ways," more like "tumors" than normally growing tissue.

12. William Carlos Williams, *In the American Grain* (New York: New Directions, 1956), pp. 188–190. See also William Carlos Williams, *Selected Essays* (New York: Random House, 1954), p. 68. Williams' view of poetic realism is related to his feeling that there should be no ideas but in things and that the local takes precedence over the universal. See *The Selected Letters*, ed. John C. Thirlwall (New York: McDowell, Obolensky, 1957), pp. 146, 224–225; Anthony Libby, " 'Claritas': William Carlos Williams' Epiphanies," *Criticism* 14 (1972): 22–31; Thomas R. Whitaker, *William Carlos Williams* (New York: Twayne Publishers, 1968); J. Hillis Miller, ed., *William Carlos Williams: A Collection of Critical Essays* (Englewood Cliffs, N.J.: Prentice-Hall, 1966); Roy Harvey Pearce, *The Continuity of American Poetry* (Princeton: Princeton University Press, 1961), pp. 335–348; J. Hillis Miller, "Deconstructing the Deconstructers," *Diacritics* 5 (1975): 24–31, and "Williams' *Spring and All* and the Progress of Poetry," *Daedalus* 99 (1970): 405–434; Hugh Kenner, "The Experience of the Eye: Marianne Moore's Tradition," in *Modern American Poetry*, ed. Jerome Mazzaro (New York: David McKay, 1970), pp. 204–221; Karl Shapiro, *In Defense of Ignorance* (New York: Random House, 1952), pp. 143–170; James K. Guimond, "William Carlos Williams and the Past: Some Clarifications," *Journal of Modern Literature* 1 (1971): 493–502; Charles Olsen, *Selected Writings*, ed. Robert Creeley (New York: New Directions, 1966), pp. 56, 61.

13. William Carlos Williams, *Paterson* (New York: New Directions, 1963), p. 169.

14. Wallace Stevens, *Opus Posthumous*, pp. 255, 256.

15. Cf. Lewis Mumford, *The Culture of Cities* (New York: Harcourt, Brace, Jovanovich, 1938), pp. 447–448.

16. David Dillon, "The Image and the Object: An Interview with Richard Wilbur," *Southwest Review* 58 (1973): 241. On Wilbur's view of objects, see A. K. Weatherhead, "Richard Wilbur: Poetry of Things," *ELH* 35 (1968): 606–617; John P. Farrell, "The Beautiful Changes in Richard Wilbur's Poetry," *Contemporary Literature* 12 (1971): 74–87; Charles F. Duffy, " 'Intricate Neural Grace': The Esthetic of Richard Wilbur." *Concerning Poetry* 4 (1971): 41–50. See also Michael Cooke's review of *The Mind-Reader* in *Georgia Review* 31 (1977): 719–724.

17. W. B. Yeats, *Collected Poems* (New York: Macmillan, 1940), p. 322.

18. Quotations from Wilbur's poetry are taken from *The Poems of Richard Wilbur* (New York: Harcourt, Brace and World, 1963); *Walking to Sleep: New Poems and Translations* (New York: Harcourt, Brace, Jovanovich, 1969); and *The Mind-Reader* (New York: Harcourt, Brace, Jovanovich, 1976).

19. William Carlos Williams, *Selected Essays* (New York: Random House, 1954), p. 68.

20. "Interview with Richard Wilbur," ed. Willard Pate, *South Carolina Review* 3 (1970): 5, 11.

21. For the potential invisible and symbolic interior of Marianne Moore's surfaces, however, see Kenneth Burke, "Motives and Motifs in the Poetry of Marianne Moore," *A Grammar of Motives* (Cleveland: World Publishing Co., 1962), pp. 485-502.

7. Ceres and the Librarians of Babel

1. Eugenio Donato, in an essay unpublished at the time of this writing entitled "The Museum's Furnace: Notes toward a Contextual Reading of *Bouvard et Pécuchet.*" Cf. Hugh Kenner, *The Stoic Comedians* (London: W. H. Allen, 1964), pp. 5-29.

2. John Donne, *The Sermons,* vol. 3, Evelyn M. Simpson and George R. Potter, eds. (Berkeley: University of California Press, 1962), pp. 109-110.

3. Wilbur Sanders, *John Donne's Poetry* (Cambridge: Cambridge University Press, 1971), p. 7.

4. Frank Kermode, *The Classic: Literary Images of Permance and Change* (New York: Viking Press, 1975), p. 117.

5. Jan Brandt Corstius, "Literary History and the Study of Literature," *NLH* 2 (1970): 67. Cf. F. E. Sparshott, "Notes on the Articulation of Time," *NLH* 1 (1970): 311-334; Fred Chappell, "Six Propositions about Literature and History," *NLH* 1 (1970): 513-522.

6. F. W. Bateson, "Literary History: Non-Subject *Par Excellence,*" *NLH* 2 (1970): 115-122.

7. Jeffrey L. Sammons, "The Threat of Literary Sociology and What to Do about It," in Joseph P. Strelka, ed., *Literary Criticism and Sociology.* (University Park: Pennsylvania State University Press, 1973), pp. 30-40. Cf. Robert Escarpit, *The Book Revolution* (Paris: George G. Harrap and UNESCO, 1966), and "The Sociology of Literature," *International Encyclopedia of the Social Sciences* 9 (1968): 417-425.

8. Michel Foucault, *The Archaeology of Knowledge,* trans. A. M. Sheridan Smith (New York: Random House, 1972). See also Hayden V. White, "Foucault Decoded: Notes from Underground," *History and Theory* 12 (1973): 23-54; Dorothy Leland, "On Reading and Writing the World: Foucault's History of Thought," *Clio* 4 (1975): 225-243.

9. Georges Poulet, "Phenomenology of Reading," *NLH* 1 (1969): 53-68.

10. Hayden White, "Literary History: The Point of It all," *NLH* 2 (1970): 173-185.

11. See Peter Burke, *The Renaissance Sense of the Past* (London: Edward Arnold, 1969); C. A. Patrides, *The Phoenix and the Ladder* (Berkeley: University of California Press, 1964); and *Milton and the Christian Tradition* (London: Oxford University Press, 1966), pp. 220-284; Nancy S. Struever, *The Language of History in the Renaissance* (Princeton: Princeton University Press, 1970).

12. René Wellek, *A History of Modern Criticism, 1750-1950* (New Haven: Yale University Press, 1955), and *The Rise of English Literary History* (Chapel Hill: University of North Carolina Press, 1941), p. 14. See also Friedrich Meineke, *His-*

toricism, trans. J. E. Anderson (London: Routledge and Kegan Paul, 1972); Harold Fromm, "Sparrows and Scholars: Literary Criticism and the Sanctification of Data," *Georgia Review* 33 (1979): 255–279.

13. John Chalker, *The English Georgic* (Baltimore: Johns Hopkins University Press, 1969).

14. Adam Ferguson, *An Essay on the History of Civil Society* (1767; rpt., Edinburgh: University Press of Edinburgh, 1966). Ferguson is sometimes given credit for predicting the rise of sociological study, but his chapter on the development of literature (pp. 171–179) does not get very far toward a theory of literary origins in what he calls "rude societies."

15. See William Wordsworth, "Preface to the Lyrical Ballads," in Hazard Adams, *Critical Theory since Plato* (New York: Harcourt, Brace, Jovanovich, 1971), pp. 434, 439.

16. William Hazlitt, *Lectures on the English Poets* (London: Taylor and Hessey, 1818).

17. Percy Bysshe Shelley, "A Defense of Poetry," ed. H. F. B. Brett-Smith (Oxford: Blackwell, 1967), p. 27.

18. Cited from *Green Hills of Africa,* in Carlos Baker, *Ernest Hemingway: A Life Story* (New York: Charles Scribner's Sons, 1969), p. 277.

19. Ernest Hemingway, *Green Hills of Africa* (New York: Charles Scribner's Sons, 1953), p. 71.

20. Earl Wasserman, " 'Adonais': Progressive Revelation as a Poetic Mode," *ELH* 4 (1954): 274–326.

Index